THE
SOCIOLOGY
OF LAW

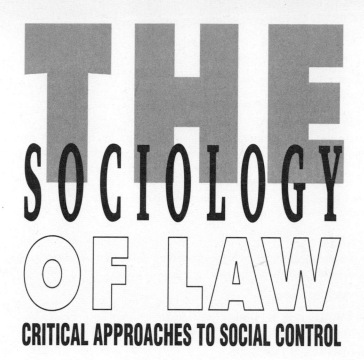

THE SOCIOLOGY OF LAW

CRITICAL APPROACHES TO SOCIAL CONTROL

Brian Burtch

Simon Fraser University

Harcourt Brace Jovanovich Canada Inc.

Toronto   Montreal   Orlando   Fort Worth
San Diego   Philadelphia   London   Sydney   Tokyo

Canadian Cataloguing in Publication Data
　　Burtch, Brian E., 1949–
　　　　The sociology of law

　　Includes bibliographical references and index.
　　ISBN 0–7747–3152–4

　　1. Sociological jurisprudence.　　I. Title

　　K370.B87　　1992　　340'.115　　C91–094481–4

Editorial Director: *Heather McWhinney*
Developmental Editor: *Lorraine Doherty*
Director of Publishing Services: *Steve Lau*
Editorial Manager: *Liz Radojkovic*
Editorial Co-ordinator: *Semareh Al-Hillal*
Production Manager: *Sue-Ann Becker*
Production Assistant: *Sandra Miller*
Copy Editor: *James Leahy*
Cover and Interior Design: *Dave Peters*
Typesetting and Assembly: *Louisa Schulz*
Printing and Binding: *Webcom Limited*

Cover design adapted from an original idea by Greg Holoboff, The Centre for Distance Education, Simon Fraser University.

∞　This book was printed in Canada on acid-free paper.

　2　3　4　5　　　96

For Carol Hird, Gary Brown, and Bruce Arnold

PREFACE

several years ago, I was asked to teach the sociology of law as an under-graduate lecture course at Simon Fraser University. The course consisted of a weekly lecture, supplemented with smaller tutorial sessions with students. Teaching the sociology of law in this way, and later at the graduate level, has been among the more enjoyable of my teaching responsibilities. An appreciation of the origins of law, and how modern laws function, is essential to the study of social sciences and jurisprudence. Beyond this, such courses serve to introduce students to ways of critically reassessing their assumptions of law and also of social relations generally.

As I developed lectures and talked with students in the smaller setting of tutorials, it became important to me to convey some of the key contributions made by classical thinkers and also to use specific, contemporary themes to breathe life into the central issues tied in with the sociology of law. These issues include the growth of feminism and feminist jurisprudence; the struggles for human rights and an end to some of the more blatant forms of discrimination; national and international forces that contributed to systems of injustice (or movement toward justice); changes in the nature of the family, as well as family law and divorce law; and the politics of the criminal sanction.

This book seeks to present an amalgam of theory and contemporary research in the general area of law, social control, and social change. The sociological study of lawmaking and legal processes has its roots in classical social thought. Attention is also drawn to *contemporary* social science research and theorizing in many areas such as the state, social class, gender, and social inequality.

The first chapter covers various ways in which law is defined and the different meanings attached to the concept of law. Law is seen as emblematic of profoundly different, and often antagonistic, ways of interpreting the world. This idea is followed through with an analysis of conservative, liberal, and radical versions of law and social order.

Chapter Two reviews some aspects of the European-based, classical writings of Durkheim, Weber, and Marx. The work of any of these classical thinkers, let alone the three of them together, should be pursued in far more detail. Selected references are provided at the end of this chapter for students who wish to pursue this subject in greater detail.

Chapter Three gives particular emphasis to Canadian issues and research, including the historical origins of law in Canada (and in England, for purposes of comparison). Chapter Four introduces issues of gender, including feminist-based research on law and society, and selected literature on the sexual stratification in the legal profession and the judiciary.

Chapter Five covers a specific case—the wrongful conviction of Donald Marshall, Jr.—with respect to criminal justice and Native people. This is followed, in Chapter Six, by a wider discussion of discrimination in law, using a variety of studies of racial discrimination in society, legal aspects of racial discrimination, and current efforts to reverse long-established patterns of racial imbalance.

Chapter Seven provides a critical look at the legal profession and the judiciary. Chapter Eight discusses issues in the use of the criminal sanction in Canada. Chapter Nine brings forward conflicting interpretations of the role of the law in reproduction, specifically in such areas as separation and divorce (child custody, maintenance, and the formal equality of both spouses before the law), abortion, and midwifery. Finally, Chapter Ten reviews a number of key themes, especially the implications of reforming legal structures, and the role of law in facilitating (or resisting) social change.

My motivation for writing this book is to provide a Canadian-based text that is accessible to an upper-level undergraduate audience and, where applicable, to graduate students in the social sciences and law. To date, while there are a number of edited collections that bring forward a Canadian context in law and social control, there is no text that integrates Canadian examples with more general theoretical work specifically on the sociology of law.

This book is written with Camus's observation in mind: "Those who write clearly have readers; those who write obscurely have commentators" (cited in Asimov and Asimov 1987, 17; see Chapter One for full bibliographical reference). One problem that students have voiced about some of their texts is the excessive use of jargon; another is the assumption that students are already familiar with reams of previous articles and books that have been written on the subject. Such texts can be offputting for undergraduate students in coming to terms with a subject such as law and social control, and, as such, are probably better suited to the graduate or faculty level. This text is clearly a selective work, given the broad, complex issues that it introduces. I expect that it may be used in conjunction with other collections and texts, depending on the needs and outlook of the instructor and students.

Brian Burtch
December 1991

ACKNOWLEDGEMENTS

One of the joys of developing this book has been the ongoing support of colleagues and friends. I wish first of all to express my thanks to colleagues and staff in the School of Criminology. The Centre for Distance Education at Simon Fraser University was very helpful in fostering a distance education course in the sociology of law, and preparing the study guide that was the nucleus for this book. Sharon Rynders and Liz Straker were especially helpful in fine-tuning the final stages of production of this work. A special note of thanks to Brian Phillips and Jack Corse, reference librarians at S.F.U. for assisting with an eleventh-hour request, and for their general support of the School. Colin Campbell and Kerri Reid collected some of the research materials, and Margaret Sharon and Ellen Sangster provided much-needed help with computing resources. I am also very grateful to Richard Ericson, Mary Morton, Simon Verdun-Jones, and Bob Ratner for their encouragement over the years. Many other colleagues deserve an acknowledgement, including Bruce Arnold, Melody Hessing, and Steve Mainprize.

From the inital contact with Heather McWhinney to the ongoing contributions of Sandra Peltier and Lorraine Doherty, I have been fortunate to have the patient support of the HBJ staff. Special thanks to James Leahy for his fresh eye as the copy editor, and to Semareh Al-Hillal for her guidance through the editorial process. I would also like to thank my colleagues who reviewed this text: Tullio Caputo, Elizabeth Comack, and Ron Hinch. Thanks also to Mimi Ajzenstadt, Joan Brockman, Bob Menzies, John Lowman, Karlene Faith, John Gillis, Judith Osborne, Lee Saxell, Patricia Ratel, and Monty Orr for their assistance. Carol Hird has been very supportive throughout the writing of this book. Special thanks to my parents for their support. And my daughter, Leora, always leads by example as she continues on with her own writing.

Publisher's Note to Students and Instructors

This textbook is a key component of your course. If you are the instructor of this course, you undoubtedly considered a number of texts carefully before choosing this as the one that will work best for your students and you. The authors and publishers of this book spent considerable time and money to ensure its high quality, and we appreciate your recognition of this effort and accomplishment. Please note the copyright statement.

If you are a student, we are confident that this text will help you to meet the objectives of your course. It will also become a valuable addition to your personal library.

Since we want to hear what you think about this book, please be sure to send us the stamped reply card at the end of the text. Your input will help us to continue to publish high-quality books for your courses.

CONTENTS

CHAPTER ONE

Introduction to Sociological Theory and the Sociology of Law

At the present as well as at any other time, the centre of gravity of legal development lies not in legislation, nor in juristic science, nor in judicial decision, but in society itself.

(Eugen Ehrlich, *Fundamental Principles of the Sociology of Law*)

INTRODUCTION

In this chapter, we introduce several sociological perspectives on law. These perspectives cover a range of possible approaches to understanding law as power, and underscore the differences among sociologists and others with respect to theories of law and social order. The discipline of sociology is remarkably diverse in terms of its theoretical outlook and methodological approaches. At its barest definition, sociology is a scientific discipline that studies human behaviour. It rests on a growing "body of interrelated scientific positions, or generalizations, that explain social behaviour" (Theodorson and Theodorson 1979, 401). Sociologists also seek to predict and provide empirical verification for human behaviour. In practice, however, many sociologists routinely lament the gulf between theoretical statements and empirical proof of these statements (Menzies 1982, 1–2).

SOCIOLOGICAL PERSPECTIVES ON LAW

The sociology of law is a central tradition within classical and contemporary sociology. Sociologists who study law endeavour to place specific legal cases, laws, regulations, and the general administration of justice into a social context. To this end, sociologists have used materials from other disciplines—history, anthropology, political science, economics, among others—to better explain patterns of legal control within this broader, social context. Much of this work is of a *scholarly* nature and is meant to increase our general knowledge of the social underpinnings and influences on legal process, and how legal process influences social values and behaviour. Other work in this field may be of a more *applied* nature, in that the researcher seeks to evaluate outcomes of particular legal strategies, for example, or to provide practical suggestions with respect to legal policy. The former approach may be referred to as the sociology *of* law; the latter as sociology *in* law. These are two broad approaches to understanding law, and there is of course considerable overlap possible between theorizing about law, and providing practical, applied information on the law. The incorporation of theory and practice is critical for many scholars and practitioners, whether they are seeking liberal reform of unjust laws and policies or more fundamental transformation of these measures, along such diverse lines as conservatism or more radical approaches to society and law.

The difference between scholarly and applied work is only one of the distinctions evident in sociological studies of law. There has been a longstanding, conventional distinction between theories of law that assume a general consensus of values and norms within given societies (consensus, or structural-functional, approaches) and those theories that assume substantial disagreements and conflicts over the nature of law and society. The consensus-conflict debate is, for our purposes, exhausted and oversimplified. New theories of justice and social control challenge the more stock versions of both consensus and conflict theory. Nevertheless, some discussion of the two perspectives is important, as even the modern theories retain some elements of conflict and consensus.

There are many variations within the social-consensus perspective. An American jurist, Roscoe Pound, regarded law as an institution that serves to maintain "social cohesion" through its management of competing interests and claims (Cotterrell 1984, 76–77). This process serves to contain potentially destructive conflicts and to preserve a sense of order as societies change (Cotterrell 1984, 76–77). The assumption of a shared consensus, and the view of the state (including law) as a catalyst, ensuring orderly change in the public interest, has drawn criticism for overlooking persistent inequalities and exclusion in lawmaking and law enforcement. That said, proponents of consensual theories argue that the law, for all its faults, is central and indispensable in ensuring some measure of regularity in social life, political life, and economic transactions.

In recent years, the study of sociological factors in law has been challenged by critical theorists, most notably as a result of a resurgence of interest in Marxist-derived theories of law (referred to as neo-Marxist theories) and a strong interest in decentralized, less formal strategies of social justice. These Marxist-based theories seek to explain social inequality and legal equality with reference to economic factors and the creation of social classes. Feminist scholarship, particularly feminist jurisprudence, has also challenged conventional assumptions about the nature of law, especially its claims of equality of women and men before the law, and about the representation of all citizens within the social contract. These critical theorists have generally emphasized the importance of placing legal and social control in historical context, as a process that cannot be reduced to abstract principles or limited ideologies in support of existing authority relations. These critical studies of law and social control underscore the power of certain ideologies—for example, "white, patriarchial prescriptions" (Backhouse 1991, 7)—used to define patterns of dominance and subordination within societies. There has also been substantial criticism of legal positivism, which is a tendency to treat jurisprudence as an exact science, a rational process that consists of identifiable data and rules (Cotterrell 1984, 10). Such an approach to law is questionable, since "it assumes a certainty and clarity in rules that is by no means apparent..." (Cotterrell 1984, 11).

The postmodern movement is suspicious of modern beliefs in scientific rationality and the grand political ideologies of liberalism and Marxism. Baum (1990) refers to dynamic "new associative patterns" appearing in contemporary societies. Attention is drawn to the complex affiliations and cross-affiliations of people in social movements such as the ecology movement, the peace movement, and the women's movement. Baum (1990) adds that postmodernists emphasize "solidarity, community, conviviality, and spirituality," but not in the more doctrinaire forms of traditional political ideologies. Hunt (1991, 80) notes that at a very general level, postmodernism stands as a "critique of the rationalism of Enlightenment thought," and has often been directed at various forms of socialism and Marxism. Hunt (1991) is critical of some strands of postmodernism, as well as its tendency toward a fragmented approach to politics, and its end-point (as Hunt sees it) of pessimism.

Along with a renewed interest in critical theories of law and social control, there has been a movement by conservative lobbyists to influence various aspects of law, including reforms to family law, efforts to restrict or outlaw access to therapeutic abortions, more severe penalties for juvenile and adult offenders, and restrictions on freedom of expression and speech, to name a few. The more conservative emphasis on increased powers of state surveillance and arrest, cutbacks in the welfare state (together with a free-market ideology), and various punitive dispositions underscores the extent to which the legitimacy of law in modern, complex societies is contested. The conservative nature of many forms of modern law, however, is increasingly under attack from emerging social movements, which challenge dominant ideologies and practices that exclude a variety of citizens from greater participation in law and social opportunities in general (Melucci 1988; Young 1990).

A central theme in this book is the disparity between the *formal equality* promised under the doctrine of rule of law, and the *substantive inequality* that exists within the social order. Ehrlich (1975, 10) wrote that "rules of human conduct" that supposedly governed legal decision-making could vary considerably from rules that judges actually employed in deciding particular legal issues. For

Ehrlich (1975, 497), the "living law" reflected that substantial portion of law that groups or individuals adhered to, distinct from the technical rules of conduct set out in law. The living law[1]—law as it is actually practised—has been assessed by a number of theorists as falling far short of idealized formal law. This critical approach raises the central issue of the extent to which formal legal structures operate on behalf of specific interests while excluding or dominating other groups seeking legal protection or redress.

It is important to keep in mind that there is no single, uncontested definition of or approach to the sociological study of law. Milovanovic (1988) places the sociology of law in a general framework, in which descriptions of case law and legal processes, and the logic of legal principles are explored through the social sciences. The origins of law and the factors that influence the making and application of laws are of central importance. The concepts of *social order* and *social conflict* are crucial, inasmuch as there is great disagreement over the extent to which law actually reflects a widely shared moral consensus or is, conversely, the site of profound conflicts and differing interests. The related concept of "public interest" or "public opinion" has also been criticized. Diverse opinions and interpretations about law and morality have led many to discuss such broad conceptions of the public as glorified artifacts; rather, there are many "publics" within a given constituency (see Cotterrell, 1984, 149).

Milovanovic (1988) identifies two broad approaches to the study of law: jurisprudence and the sociology of law. The first, *jurisprudence*, begins with definitions of law and legal rules as set out by the state and proceeds on the assumption that legal decision-making is rational and that legal processes are legitimate, and indeed essential to social order. Certain conflicts are thus subject to the abstract application of legal principles to "factual situations" (Milovanovic 1988, 4), keeping in mind the doctrine of *stare decisis* (whereby current legal cases are decided with reference to pre-existing decisions, or precedents). The logic underlying decisions in legal cases, while intricate and considered (ideally), is seen as relatively unproblematic as far as the value of legal decisions is concerned.

The second approach identified by Milovanovic is the *sociology of law*. Rather than beginning with legal definitions as codified by the state, or a description of various legal decisions and principles, the sociology of law centres on the social aspects of legal control. The interests served by law, and the dimensions of coercion and domination through law, are important questions in this approach. The sociology of law is more closely linked with social science methodology and theory than with professional legal training or legal practice. These two approaches are not wholly distinct—there is overlap in theory, research, and practice—and Hunt (1980) has written of a movement away from jurisprudence as such, toward a "sociological movement" in the study of law. Jurisprudence is nonetheless more closely associated with the logic of law and the interpretation of legal decisions, while the sociology of law serves to explore central themes of social order, social conflict, and power relations expressed through law.

DEFINITIONS OF LAW

There are many definitions of law. These range from fairly straightforward definitions of the limits and scope of law, and the roles played by legislators, administrators, and pressure groups in forming and changing law, to more critical interpretations of legal powers. The dominant ideology in support of Western legal systems places the rule of law and the establishment of official legal services—be they prosecutorial services, defence lawyering, or the less dramatic but pervasive forms of contract and other economic exchanges—as hallmarks of freedom, widely supported by the public at large. For others, however, this equation of modern law with increased freedoms is a chimera. They see law as a powerful means of maintaining social order, including the preservation and widening of social and legal inequalities (Ericson 1983). Again, this variation in how law is conceptualized and defined indicates the competing approaches to sociological theory and the ongoing work within the sociology of law.

Following his extensive review of different conceptualizations of law, Cotterrell (1984, 46) concludes that state law must be the main focus for the study of law in contemporary Western societies. He defines state law as "that category of social rules for which the processes and institutions of creation, interpretation and enforcement are most visible, formal and elaborate." He adds that law thus refers to doctrines and social rules as they are interpreted and enforced by state agencies, within a politically organized society. Max Weber has established a classic definition of law as a more organized system of sanctions used to ensure compliance or "avenge violation" (Milovanovic 1988, 41).

Not all reactions to deviant conduct are greeted with legal sanctions. The vast majority may be tolerated or treated, not as violations of law as such, but as infractions of a social norm. Hoebel defines a *social norm* as follows:

> A social norm is legal if its neglect or infraction is regularly met, in threat or in fact, by the application of physical force by an individual or group possessing the socially recognized privilege of so acting (cited in Milovanovic 1988, 5).

We could add that a social norm may remain legal, even if its neglect or infraction is not regularly met with physical force or the threat of such force. Legality is not necessarily dependent on such regularity; however, recurring threats or sanctions would likely reinforce the power of specific social norms. Timasheff (1974, 23–24) believed that law fulfilled the social function of "imposing norms of conduct or patterns of social behavior on the individual will."

The issue of what is socially recognized is also significant. Not all legal powers are demonstrably based in public consensus, and some may clearly be unpopular. Certain forms of illegal behaviour may even attract public sympathy and support: the mythical figures of Robin Hood or Jean Valjean (in Victor Hugo's *Les Misérables*) are just two of the literary examples of people fighting against social and legal injustice. There are many contemporary situations in which people resist perceived injustice by challenging the law. Civil disobedience and "direct action" justify the use of force or violence as a political strategy against forms of injustice. In 1990, the well-publicized release of Nelson Mandela ended 26 years of political imprisonment for a man who fought against South Africa's policy of apartheid. In Canada, Native people have increasingly relied on acts of civil disobedience to protest government insensitivity to their plight.

In considering this motif of conflicting definitions and perspectives on the social context of law, we should bear in mind that there have been significant breaks from conventional approaches to law. Smart (1989, 4) challenges conventional definitions of law when she writes that law is inherently contradictory, with "conflicting principles" and contradictory effects wherever law is applied. Thus, while law *claims* a fundamental unity in theory and practice, this supposed unity is continually being challenged. Smart (1989, 4–5) favours alternative views on law and warns of law's considerable power of defining and redefining social life. Law can be used, for example, to discount or limit such alternative approaches as feminist jurisprudence (see Chapter Four). The issue is thus not only how we define law, but how we sustain the integrity of alternative approaches in the face of legal powers that seek to co-opt and undermine these social movements.

PURPOSES AND FUNCTIONS OF LAW

The majestic equality of the law ... forbids rich and poor alike to sleep under bridges, to beg in the streets, and to steal bread.

(Anatole France, quoted in Cotterrell 1984, 124)

Law can be seen as a leavening force in modern political life, easing conflicts or short-circuiting possible conflicts through an elaborate process of public education, surveillance, arrest, mediation, and so forth. There is considerable disagreement, however, over the functions that law serves. Much of this disagreement centres on the relationship between legal ordering and social power. Law can be seen as a dynamic force that relies on a wide range of resources, used in complex ways to ensure the survival of political power despite conflicts within a given political or social order. Turk (1982, 14–15) has developed a conflict-based perspective that translates five facets of power into forms of resource control.[2] These facets of power involve control of

1. the use of *direct physical violence*, exercised by such repressive agencies as the police, militia, and military

2. various forms of *economic power*

3. decision-making with reference to *political power*

4. *ideological power*, in the context of controlling access to specific beliefs and knowledge

5. *diversionary power*, which Turk (1982, 14–15) describes as "control of human attention and living time."

Critical theorists, especially those developing a Marxist-based approach to law, identify three central functions of law in capitalist societies: the repressive function, the facilitative function, and the ideological function. The *repressive* function of law is arguably the most visible and dramatic. This function rests on the coercive powers of the state, as assured by law. This coercive function may vary considerably within or between specific legal regimes: some regimes may rely more heavily on direct uses of force, via the police and military troops, while others may use other incentives and strategies to promote compliance with the law. Powers of arrest, incarceration, and detention are a few examples of the use of direct force by the state. The use of "deadly force"— killing civilians—is an extreme example of the repressive powers of the state (see Chappell and Graham 1985). In Canada, police shootings of aboriginal people and people of colour have generated protests in Winnipeg, Toronto, and Montreal in recent years (McMahon and Ericson 1987, 38–39; Yerbury and Griffiths 1991). The killing of Indian leader J.J. Harper in Winnipeg in March 1988 prompted charges of racist policing policies, and the formation of an inquiry into aboriginal justice in Manitoba (Yerbury and Griffiths 1991, 331).

Some argue that the repressive powers of modern states are used against large segments of the population, and even entire societies. The term *state terrorism* has been coined to describe illegal acts by government officials and others employed by them (such as mercenaries). McMurtry (1988) argues that many modern states use terrorist actions to subjugate "resistant populations" in such countries as El Salvador, Nicaragua, and Chile. State officals backing such tactics ironically disguise them as counter-terrorist actions, justifying their own violence in the interest of "security and defence" (McMurtry 1988). Repressive powers are vital to state rule, but must be accompanied over time by the other two functions: the facilitative function and the ideological function of law.

The *facilitative* function of law represents "the degree to which law aids in assuring predictability and certainty in behavioral expectations" (Milovanovic

1988, 9). The contract-like structure of law thus seeks to provide greater stability and regularity in modern, complex societies. Milovanovic's (1988) discussion outlines how this facilitative function has been interpreted in different ways: for example, Max Weber provided a more favourable outlook on the value of legal rationality as a feature of capitalist development, while Karl Marx provided a powerful critique of capitalism and emphasized the need to replace bourgeois legality with a socialist order that was not dependent on the artifices of state control, including its legal apparatus.

The *ideological* function in law pertains to belief systems, specifically, the way in which legal ideology helps promote domination, legitimation, and hegemony. Sumner (1979, 4–5) emphasizes that the concept of hegemony is vital for a discussion of Marxist and other radical approaches to the social superstructure. Hegemony—a central concept in Marxist theory—has been defined in myriad ways. One definition of hegemony draws attention to its role in generating mistaken, or "falsely conscious," beliefs or misrepresenting actual forms of domination and power in given societies (Sumner 1979, 4–5). Milovanovic (1988, 12) defines hegemony as "the active participation by subjects in the mechanism of their own oppression." This element of consent and compliance in oppression is embodied in the Gramscian approach to hegemony. Antonio Gramsci envisioned hegemony as rooted in historically specific blocs consisting of various allies and coalitions. "This bloc represents a basis of consent for a certain social order, in which the hegemony of a dominant class is created and re-created in a web of institutions, social relations, and ideas" (Sassoon 1983, 201). Hegemony is a means whereby the state and its agents can justify social and legal inequality. This kind of social order assumes that individuals are responsible for their own fate, that there are ample economic and social opportunities within the social structure, or that encroachment on specific civil liberties is tolerable or even desirable.

Turk (1982, 29) believes that established ideological hegemony is the strongest base for political authority. The more a given political agency can secure a base of consensus for its operations, and thus secure its legitimacy, the more likely it is that such agencies can further consolidate control over resources. He implies that there is a synergistic effect, as ideological hegemony may assist in expanding other forms of power, such as economic decision-making and deployment of military resources (Turk 1982, 29–30). Finally, Turk appreciates ideological hegemony as a force that not only enables political authorities to deepen their legitimacy, but may also deflect attention away from entrenched, structural inequalities in societies. He notes:

> Whatever teaches people that order is always better than disorder, that consensus is always preferable to conflict, that governance is the prerogative of some and obedience the duty of others . . . helps to deaden concern about inequalities in the distribution of life chances, and about the institutions that maintain those inequalities (Turk 1982, 29).

Hegemonic power is seen as a dominant, but not exclusive, power within modern societies. It predominates, but does not monopolize, social thought or action in specific societies. Hegemony can thus be faced with opposing, or counterhegemonic, values surrounding law and the social order. One instance of this phenomenon is the midwifery movement in Canada, or more generally, the continuing efforts within the women's movement to remove sexist legislation and practices. Patriarchy, as a hegemonic tradition, is thus challenged by various interest groups and coalitions.

THEORIES OF LAW AND SOCIAL ORDER

This section provides a preview of the more extended discussions of law and social control in the succeeding chapters. Discussions of modern legal structures are inescapably linked to ancient debates concerning morality, authority, property, and the issue of whether (or to what extent) legal regulation of human behaviour is necessary. History and politics thus become central to a more complete understanding of modern legal structures and their functions.

For our purposes, we can group sociological theories of law into a few general categories. First, there is a tradition that views law as a unifying force, settling disputes and conflicts through its formal processes. In this consensual model, law serves a general consensus of opinion about proper conduct in society. In criminal law, a system of punishments is ostensibly made in the general interest to deal with crimes that offend public safety and the public interest in social order. Likewise, complex systems of civil law are built, replacing earlier structures that were based on social customs. The interlocking nature of modern social institutions such as the family, work, education, economy, and so forth is seen as requiring regulatory structures to co-ordinate social needs. In this respect, government powers, including various forms of law, lend coherence to a social system that would otherwise not be viable. This structural-functionalist perspective is, however, largely in disfavour among contemporary sociologists. Some theorists point to the *reification* of society—how society is artificially presented as a real structure that is essentially orderly and constantly adjusting to new social conditions. They often identify embedded social conflicts that undermine the ideal notion of a general consensus of values and opinions. Moreover, many point to the limits of law in ensuring public safety or serving the general interest.

Disenchantment with consensually rooted theories of law and society has generated several competing theories, which constitute the conflict perspective. Despite platitudes from governments surrounding the rule of law and democratic structures, some conflict theorists outline persistent controversies, such as the failure of federal and provincial governments to resolve Native land claims in British Columbia and other jurisdictions within Canada (Tennant 1990) or such racially-motivated legislation as the use of internment policies for Japanese-Canadians during World War II (Adachi 1976). For conflict theorists, the legal apparatus does not automatically or naturally operate in the interests of a shared morality. In their view, law may ameliorate or resolve certain conflicts, but the overwhelming influence of powerful political and economic interests may steer lawmakers and legal authorities to serve the interests of particular groups. The views of conflict theorists are often associated with the early twentieth century writings of Max Weber, specifically his argument that social conflicts can not be reduced to economic or class conflicts, but are many-headed and permeate the social structures of modern stratified societies. There is a considerable body of literature documenting social stratification in Western countries. For example, it has been noted that the top 1 percent (wealthiest) of families in Britain owned between 28 and 33 percent of the nation's wealth in 1988. The corresponding figures were approximately 20 percent in the United States, and roughly 10 percent in Canada (Hunter 1981, 66).

Critical Legal Studies

A number of sociologists have consolidated critical theories of law, using specific studies of how law serves particular interests in conflict situations. The critical legal studies (CLS) perspective exemplifies this tradition of scholarship, which is set against more idealized, liberal notions of law and social order. As such, it allows for a greater role for insurgency in the interest of social justice (Brickey and Comack 1989), and recognizes diverse streams of critical thought, such as feminism, Marxism, socialism, and radical decentralization of decision-making.

The critical legal studies perspective first emerged in the late 1970s, highlighting what Kelman (1987, 1) identifies as the sterility of existing legal socialization and legal education. Kelman (1987, 1) sees CLS as bridging the wide gap between "actual social life" and the artificial, stratified atmosphere of law schools. Opposed to mainstream liberal doctrines of law, CLS theorists address the *contradictions* of liberalism, including the gap between respect for individual decisions and beliefs (subjectivity, individual rights) and the ostensibly objective, factually-based sphere of legal reasoning. Kelman (1987, 4–6) adds that liberalism actually takes on a "right-wing" character, ironically becoming quite illiberal, and resisting progressive innovations in the nature of legal services, for example, activist courts.

Critical legal studies help provide a structure for applying a variety of critical theoretical perspectives on law and social control. These studies challenge the hegemonic, or dominant, status of particular legal ideologies. CLS poses a challenge to structural-functionalist perspectives of the social order, including the premise that laws reflect and adapt to evolving social needs (Kelman 1987, 242). The CLS perspective also outlines regressive developments in contemporary law and legal structures. Kelman (1987, 243) mentions the erosion of community ties that occurs as societies undergo modernization. This process promotes a culture based, in part, on opportunism and isolationism rather than collectivism. Laws may thus serve to obstruct efforts to forge alternative social structures, for example, those designed to resolve neighbourhood conflicts. The modern edifice of law can be seen as a blight, disguised as a blessing. CLS theorists demystify this negative side of formal legal structures and, as noted above, the "privileged" discourse of liberal progression and general social harmony. CLS theorists thus challenge utopian portraits of modern law that misrepresent legal relations as rooted in fairness, and serving a supposed public interest. The critical legal studies perspective draws our attention to law as politics, and rather than adhering to a false assumption of wide social consensus, seeks to empower embattled groups by demystifying legal ideology and developing strategies to counter legal dominance. Tomasic (1985, 17–24) regards the critical legal studies movement as a diverse and dynamic enterprise. The work within this CLS tradition warrants considerable attention, and Tomasic (1985, 18) cautions that it is premature to dismiss Marxist-influenced theories of law and society, given the valuable work by critical legal scholars.

As outlined above, the concept of social consensus has guided some sociologists' theories of law and society. The concept of the *social contract* is worth exploring, as it endures in various forms in several modern legal ideologies. Formulated by Hobbes, Locke, and Rousseau, among others, the general premise of social contract theory is that agreement among citizens forms the legitimate basis for stable government. The legitimacy of government thus properly rests on a wide consensus among citizens on the desirability or inevitability of the rule of law and the necessity of preserving the modern state. Social contract theory presents a world view in which citizens voluntarily relinquish some freedoms in order that the general interest is secured. Barker (1970, xii–xiii) outlines two cardinal ideas guiding social contract doctrine. First, there is a "contract of government" in which the rulers (government) and the subjects (citizenry) agree to the terms of lawful government; and second, there is a contract established to preserve the society itself.

In his treatise *The Social Contract*, first published in France in 1762, the philosopher Jean-Jacques Rousseau presented a strong argument against the automatic legitimacy of any government. He argued that "no man is under any obligation to obey any but the legitimate powers of the State" (cited in Barker 1970, 173). He added that states based on the adage "might is right"—that is, that the most powerful members could rightfully subordinate weaker members—were undesirable. Agreement was thus the sole legitimate foundation for political authority. As such, in Rousseau's formulation, if the state departs markedly from its obligation to govern fairly—to represent public not sectarian interests—it may lose its legitimate support and be removed from office. Rousseau emphasized that in eighteenth century societies, people were not free in general terms, but were often enslaved.

History required that people surrender certain freedoms to allow "the whole strength of the community" to be used as a protector of each citizen's property and freedoms (Rousseau, cited in Barker 1970, 180). Rousseau was not an apologist for unfettered state powers; indeed, *The Social Contract* can be seen as a critique of ways in which private property is treated like a fetish, with an acquisitive spirit leading to sumptuous wealth for a few, and starvation or subsistence living for many others. In this respect, Rousseau argued that each individual must restrict his or her claims to property that is rightfully his or hers, and not make claims on property that rightfully belongs to the community (Barker 1970, 186). Rousseau's critique of the distribution of property, and other forms of wealth, was accompanied by his recognition of the potential for tyranny in government and law. He thus argued for a "code of laws" authored by the people. While Rousseau did not resolve this paradox of substantial state authority, justice, and public authorship of proper laws, he argued forcefully against unjust laws that would promote the suffering of "just men" (Barker 1970, 201–3). Rousseau was wary of placing too much power with the people, as evidenced by his concerns over the "blind multitude" or the "vulgar herd," his terms for those citizens who were not enlightened about their true interests (see Barker 1970, 204 & 207).

Rousseau's *The Social Contract* was influential in re-establishing a political foundation for governments and was a major influence in the social thought that preceded the American Revolution of 1776. Not all commentators are uncritical of Rousseau's approach, however. Many critics of social contract theory have pointed to groups that have been excluded from legal protection or denied other benefits associated with the ideal of the social contract. Some criticize Rousseau for passages that support the subordination of women to men, for example, in family relations. Eisenstein (1981) is critical of the explicit patriarchial values expressed in Rousseau's treatise, including his assumption that fathers or husbands were the natural rulers within families and marriage, while wives were responsible for the nurturance and stabilization of families and households. Eisenstein thus underlines that the social contract was not, in effect, a reflection of all citizens, but rather of a society that was essentially ruled by men. Fine (1984) criticizes Rousseau's failure to make a clean break with the doctrine of private property. While Rousseau is critical of the negative aspects of private property, he does not present clear alternatives to propertied arrangements. Beyond this, Fine (1984) describes social contract theory as a fiction, as imaginary.

Caputo (1988, 3) is correct when he states that students should be encouraged to articulate contradictions they perceive, or experience quite directly, in their own lives. Caputo implies that many students are aware of sexism and racism in law, and otherwise unjust situations, and that critical thinking can be engendered by having students place theoretical issues of law and power in a more concrete context. One question that I pose to students is whether they believe they are part of a social contract. Many respond that they support the overall political structure of democracy, that injustices are gradually being removed, and that, taken as a whole, life is improving in many ways. A general belief—taken from classical social contract theory—is that we have to forfeit some actions in order for the society to operate more fairly and efficiently. The example of rules of the road is frequently offered: if drivers didn't obey red lights, stop signs, and speed limits, then life would become more hazardous for drivers and pedestrians alike. Beyond this example, however, social issues become very problematic as students seek to apply the premise of the social contract to their own lives. Specifically, do women feel they are protected by a social contract? Most female students indicate that they are uncomfortable walking alone at night. Some say that they will not travel for groceries after dark, unless the store is a secure place, or if they have an escort for protection. On the other hand, all students understand that men enjoy much greater freedom of movement than women.[3] It is significant, too, that some Canadian researchers report that attacks on women are often reported in the media as isolated events, not as part of the wider oppression of women (Voumvakis and Ericson 1984).

Other students express concerns over lack of protection for their own interests. Contemporary environmental policies and laws are seen by some as too lax, with little regulation of ongoing pollution and relatively ineffective fines for the polluting companies. Still other students see little influence of affirmative action programs on creating more access to employment for groups that have traditionally been excluded or subordinated in the work force (people of colour, the disabled, women). One can also point to groups that have been denied access to the social contract. In Canada, for example, Native people were denied the vote until 1960.

For less visible minorities, legal or social discrimination can also have profound effects. The contemporary gay liberation movement, in conjunction with general efforts to realize civil rights for male and female homosexuals, can be set against a legacy of legal repression against homosexuals. Weinberg and Williams (1975, 380–97) interpreted many anti-homosexual laws as a symbol of the social rejection of homosexuals. Such laws and rejection serve to "unjustly limit" employment opportunies, for example, by excluding known homosexuals from military service in the United States, and giving dishonourable discharges for those people whose sexual orientation was discovered once in military service (Weinberg and Williams 1975, 397).

There are some signs that social tolerance of homosexuals has increased in recent years, underscoring the dynamic quality of social movements and public attitudes. Weinberg and Williams reviewed the responses of over 3000 American adults from a survey undertaken in 1970. It found that two-thirds of respondents would bar homosexuals from medical practice and government service; and many opposed homosexuals working as judges, schoolteachers, or in the ministry (Weinberg and Williams 1975, 34–35). Almost a decade later, a

Canadian-based survey was interpreted as showing that public attitudes toward homosexuals were liberalizing, with nearly half the sample of 2000 Canadians stating that it was "very easy" or "fairly easy" to accept that many people are homosexual (*Weekend* Poll, 1979). I ask students to consider whether this liberalizing trend is often translated into practice, and if lesbians and gay men can be considered to be firmly established in the social contract. Students give examples of various forms of discrimination that still exist, including social censure (taunting, for example), the predominance of what is known as "heterosexual hegemony" (so as to exclude or marginalize non-heterosexual displays of affection and sexuality), and abrogation of rights to medical treatment and other services (see Dixon 1990).

This exercise of analyzing one's place inside or outside the social contract brings us closer to an understanding of the politics of law. Unlike the idealized view of jurisprudence as a neutral force that acts in an impartial and logical manner, sociological studies of law are based on a clearer emphasis on the impact of economic pressures and political interests in the formulation of specific laws.

SUMMARY

Sociological perspectives on law centre on the importance of legal structures in resisting or producing social change. Under the general definition of sociology of law, however, there are many perspectives in understanding law and social control. For the sake of simplicity, these perspectives can initially be divided into two broad theoretical approaches. The first approach in sociological theory highlights a strong social consensus underlying legal powers and political authority in general. Law is portrayed as indispensable, legitimate (for the most part), and a neutral means of restoring social equilibrium. The second broad approach places much greater emphasis on the law as an index of social, political, and economic conflicts. Law is seen as directly connected with a variety of social contradictions and social conflicts (MacLean 1986). Law in practice is not what it is presented as in ideological terms; it is a form of power that serves specific interests above the general interest and blends repressive, facilitative, and ideological functions in ways that actually disadvantage a wide range of citizens (visible minorities, women, homosexuals, to name only a few).

This book provides a review of these sociological perspectives, with special emphasis on critical social theory, including feminist jurisprudence and theories that derive from Marxist principles of political economy. It is worth noting, however, that, while the discussions to follow are based on such critical literature, none of us speaks *ex cathedra* on these issues. In particular, the debate over whether legal structures can ever serve the purposes of justice remains very much an open question in these times. The examples that follow provide a point of departure for reconsidering the place of law in its wider social context.

STUDY QUESTIONS

❑ While the law is ostensibly designed to protect individuals and protect certain liberties, the application of law—the "living law"—may undermine individual freedoms in Western societies. Discuss briefly.

❑ Elaborate on the three functions of law: repressive, facilitative, and ideological. Briefly give two contemporary examples of your own choosing to illustrate how these three functions of law may influence legal processes. Indicate how these legal functions might be used to repress social action, to effect reforms, or to legitimate the powers of law.

❑ Review the elements of social contract theory. What criticisms have been made of the premise that a social contract (or covenant) is possible, or desirable, within a democratic political framework? To what extent do you believe you are part of a social contract? To what extent are you excluded from this contract?

NOTES

1. Cotterrell (1984, 29) defines the *living law* as "rules that are actually followed in social life," and that serve to deactivate disputes that might be dealt with by state authorities.

2. Turk (1982, 13) is sensitive to the importance of control of resources. Given that "material resources" are important to virtually all human ventures, the control and distribution of these resources can be decisive in the very survival of, or the relative power to be exercised by, individuals or particular groups.

3. Shari Ulrich's song, "I'm Not the One," captures the fearfulness of women who have experienced sexual assault or the threat of it: "I'm not the one/ who dealt the hand in that dirty deal to you/ I'm not the one who broke your heart/ and didn't love you . . . I used to find peace in the darkness/ and wander as free men do/ now there's no place to hide/ from the haunting ghost of you/ I live in a world full of danger now/ we both live with what you've done/ they say time heals all/ but that time will never come . . . " From the recording, *Talk Around Town* (1982), MCA Records.

REFERENCES

Adachi, K. (1976) *The Enemy That Never Was*. Toronto: McClelland and Stewart.
Asimov, J., and I. Asimov (1987) *How to Enjoy Writing: A Book of Aid and Comfort*. New York: Walker and Company.
Backhouse, Constance (1991) *Petticoats and Prejudice: Women and Law in Nineteenth-Century Canada*. Toronto: The Women's Press.
Barker, E. (1970) *Social Contract: Essays by Locke, Hume, and Rousseau*. London: Oxford University Press.
Baum, G. (1990) "The Postmodern Age." *The Canadian Forum* 69 (789): 5–7.
Brickey, S., and E. Comack (1989) "The Role of Law in Social Transformation: Is a Jurisprudence of Insurgency Possible?" *Canadian Journal of Law and Society* 2: 97–119.

Caputo, T. (1988) "Teaching Critical Criminology." *Canadian Critical Criminology* 1 (3): 1–5.

Chappell, D., and L. Graham (1985) *Police Use of Deadly Force: Canadian Perspectives.* Toronto: Centre of Criminology.

Cotterrell, R. (1984) *The Sociology of Law: An Introduction.* London: Butterworths.

Dixon, J. (1990) *Catastrophic Rights: Experimental Drugs and AIDS.* Vancouver: New Star Books.

Ehrlich, E. (1975) *Fundamental Principles of the Sociology of Law.* Translated by W. Moll. New York: Arno Press. First published in 1913.

Eisenstein, Z. (1981) *The Radical Future of Liberal Feminism.* New York: Longman.

Ericson, R. (1983) "The Constitution of Legal Inequality." John Porter Memorial Address. Ottawa: Carleton University Press.

Fine, B. (1984) *Democracy and the Rule of Law: Liberal Ideals and Marxist Critiques.* London: Pluto Press.

Hunt, A. (1980) *The Sociological Movement in Law.* London: Macmillan.

Hunt, A. (1991) "Postmodernism and Critical Criminology." In *New Directions in Critical Criminology,* edited by B. MacLean and D. Milovanovic, 79–85. Vancouver: The Collective Press.

Hunter, A. (1981) *Class Tells: On Social Inequality in Canada.* Toronto: Butterworths.

Kelman, M. (1987) *A Guide to Critical Legal Studies.* Cambridge: Harvard University Press.

MacLean, B. (1986) "Some Limitations of Traditional Inquiry." In *The Political Economy of Crime: Readings for a Critical Criminology,* edited by B. MacLean, 1–20. Toronto: Prentice-Hall.

McMahon, M., and R. Ericson (1987) "Reforming the Police and Policing Reform." In *State Control: Criminal Justice Politics in Canada,* edited by R.S. Ratner and J.L. McMullan, 38–68. Vancouver: University of British Columbia Press.

McMurtry, J. (1988) "States of Terror." *The Canadian Forum* 67 (776/777): 6–8.

Melucci, A. (1988) *Nomads of the North: Social Movements and Individual Needs in Contemporary Society.* Edited by J. Keane and P. Mier. Philadelphia: Temple University Press.

Menzies, K. (1982) *Sociological Theory in Use.* London: Routledge and Kegan Paul.

Milovanovic, D. (1988) *A Primer in the Sociology of Law.* New York: Harrow and Heston.

Sassoon, A. (1983) "Hegemony." In *A Dictionary of Marxist Thought,* edited by T. Bottomore, L. Harris, V. Kiernan, and R. Miliband, 201–203. Cambridge: Harvard University Press.

Smart, C. (1989) *Feminism and the Power of Law.* London: Routledge and Kegan Paul.

Sumner, C. (1979) *Reading Ideologies: An Investigation into the Marxist Theory of Ideology and Law.* London: Academic Press.

Tennant, P. (1990) *Aboriginal Peoples and Politics: The Indian Land Question in British Columbia, 1849–1989.* Vancouver: University of British Columbia Press.

Theodorson, G., and A. Theodorson (1979) *A Modern Dictionary of Sociology.* New York: Barnes and Noble.

Timasheff, N. (1974) *An Introduction to the Sociology of Law.* Westport, Connecticut: Greenwood Press.

Tomasic, R. (1985) *The Sociology of Law.* London: Sage Publications.

Turk, A. (1982) *Political Criminality: The Defiance and Defence of Authority.* Beverly Hills: Sage Publications.

Voumvakis, S., and R. Ericson (1984) *News Accounts of Attacks against Women: A Comparison of Three Toronto Newspapers*. Toronto: Centre of Criminology.

Weekend Poll (1979) "Homosexuals." *Weekend Magazine* (August 18): 3.

Weinberg, M., and C. Williams (1975) *Male Homosexuals: Their Problems and Adaptations*. Markham, Ontario: Penguin.

Yerbury, C., and C. Griffiths (1991) "Minorities, Crime, and the Law." In *Canadian Criminology: Perspectives on Crime and Criminality*, edited by M. Jackson and C. Griffiths, 315–46. Toronto: Harcourt Brace Jovanovich.

Young, I. (1990) *Justice and the Politics of Difference*. Princeton: Princeton University Press.

CHAPTER TWO

The Classical Theorists: Durkheim, Weber, and Marx

INTRODUCTION

Our understanding of modern legal systems is rooted in the classical work of three European scholars of the late nineteenth century. The continuing debates over the nature of legal domination and social justice stand, in large measure, as refinements of such classical approaches. This chapter provides an overview of the writings of Emile Durkheim, Max Weber, and Karl Marx. The three writers share an interest in explaining the relationships among law, economy, society, and politics. There are substantial differences among the three, not the least of which are their theoretical perspectives on politics and the social order.

The French sociologist Emile Durkheim is widely considered as an "order theorist" (Horton 1966), who is ideologically committed to preserving the general contours of the social system. As discussed below, however, Durkheim was not merely an apologist for the status quo in late nineteenth and early twentieth century politics. He is rightly regarded as one of the key thinkers in sociology, whose work covers such diverse issues as sociological method (*The Rules of Sociological Method*), social cohesion, economics, and the sociological significance of particular legal systems (*The Division of Labour in Society* and *Suicide*).

In contrast, the German scholar Max Weber developed a comprehensive theoretical approach that accentuated a multiplicity of social conflicts in modern societies. A proponent of rationalized capitalist economic systems, Weber argued against several elements of Marxist-based doctrines of economic materialism and class conflict. He provided a complex approach to such issues as religion, economics, quantitative and qualitative methodology in the social sciences, the ubiquitousness of social conflicts, variations in legal systems and kinds of domination, and the centralization of bureaucratic administration in government and other spheres.

Karl Marx was a revolutionary nineteenth century thinker who is credited with reformulating the nature of principles of political economy, drawing attention to the exploitation that he believed was inherent in capitalist economic systems. Marx promoted controversial and influential theories on the origins of capitalism—its tremendous disparities of wealth and political power—and predicted the replacement of capitalism with socialism, and eventually communism. Marx was forced to leave Germany, and did much of his greatest work as a private scholar in London. His approach to law, while secondary to his overarching interest in political economy and the revolutionary transformation of capitalist-based economies and societies, remains very influential in current studies of the politics of law and state control.

This chapter offers a selective review of the outlooks of Durkheim, Weber, and Marx on law and society. Particular attention is given to the various ways in which these writers conceptualized law, not only as a system of control, but as a vehicle for social stability or social change. The three writers also differed on the purposes of law and the extent to which legal regulation is desirable or even necessary.

EMILE DURKHEIM (1858–1917)

Biography

Emile Durkheim was born and raised in the Jewish community of France's Alsace-Lorraine district. Durkheim's father was a chief rabbi, and his mother operated an embroidery shop as a cottage industry. The family, according to Lukes (1977, 39) was far from wealthy. Durkheim was a superlative student, completing his school studies easily and proceeding to advanced studies at the École Normale Supérieure in Paris (Lukes 1977, 41–42). Durkheim was appointed to the Faculty of Letters at the University of Bordeaux in 1887, and to the Sorbonne in Paris in 1902. Durkheim's accomplishments included four major studies covering such topics as work, religion, the phenomenon of suicide (and how suicide was best explained by sociological factors), and his *Rules of Sociological Method*. His work attracted considerable acclaim as well as sharp criticism. Durkheim was a prolific writer, producing literally hundreds of essays and other publications between 1885 and 1917 (Lukes 1977, 562–90).

Introduction

Like Weber, Durkheim was concerned with religious influences in social life and studied various religious systems around the world. Milovanovic (1988, 22–23) observes that, although Durkheim was influenced by an eminent psychologist (Wilhelm Wundt), he was opposed to psychological explanations of social behaviour and favoured a scientific approach in which collective life largely defined and determined individual conduct. Durkheim's famous assertion that individual life is born of collective life, not vice versa, underscores this emphasis on social factors. It would be misleading, however, to suggest that Durkheim was concerned only with the larger structures of society and their functioning. As noted below, he was also concerned with issues of justice and supported the protection of human rights at national and international levels. The question of how societies survived, the regulatory purposes of various kinds of laws and customs, and the differing forms of *social* solidarity were of direct interest to Durkheim.

It is important to appreciate that Durkheim believed in the *scientific* approach to social life. To this end, he utilized the available statistics on various aspects of society, and insisted on the importance of logic in investigating sociological phenomena. He opposed the more speculative approaches of metaphysics, preferring an empirically-based science of society. Durkheim believed that measurement and statistical analysis were essential to the scientific development of sociology. Critics of Durkheim have argued that psychological approaches to law, and to social behaviour in general, can also build on rigorous scientific methodologies.

Durkheim was regarded as a proponent of "conservative democracy," who had faith in the scientific redirection of industry and in the development of intellectual and moral thought among the public. In addition, Durkheim advocated greater justice in economic relations (see Lukes 1977, 320). Lacking the intense commitment to socialism espoused by Marx and Engels, Durkheim nevertheless adopted a scientific outlook that was "strongly reformist and revisionist" (Lukes 1977, 323).

Politically, Durkheim discounted the notion that intellectuals should be above politics. Rather, he believed they could serve to advise and enlighten politicians with respect to social policy. Lukes (1977, 330–32) interprets Durkheim's approach to politics as largely reserved: while Durkheim felt that academics had an obligation to speak out on significant social issues, he generally believed that academics were ill-suited to statecraft. Nevertheless, he became deeply involved in some of the political issues of his day, including the First World War[1] and the Dreyfus scandal.

Durkheim, along with the French novelist Emile Zola, played a major part in the turmoil surrounding the conviction for treason of the French captain Alfred Dreyfus. Dreyfus was incarcerated on Devil's Island in 1884 and, despite substantial protests against his conviction, was not exonerated until 1906. The Dreyfus affair, which is covered in greater detail at the beginning of Chapter Six, is widely regarded as an outrageous example of scapegoating and official corruption. The overtones of anti-Semitism and government abuses make the Dreyfus affair far more than a case of malicious and wrongful prosecution.

Durkheim saw the Dreyfus affair as a scandal that consisted of "gross illegalities." He also regarded the affair as an opportunity for the public to participate in a wider movement to forge a higher moral consciousness and renewed involvement in the affairs of France (Lukes 1977, 333). Reproached by many quarters of French society, and braving considerable expressions of anti-Semitic sentiment, Durkheim joined other *Dreyfusards* (intellectuals, artists, and others mobilized against the corruption of the Dreyfus affair) in seeking to reverse Dreyfus's conviction. In his participation in this movement, Durkheim emerged from his customary role of detached intellectual. He provided direct replies against the anti-Dreyfusard historian Ferdinand Brunetière. In his rebuttal of Brunetière, Durkheim defended the *Dreyfusards'* decision to prize "logic" over the official opposition of the authorities. He was unbending in this insistence upon putting "reason above authority" and holding that individual rights ought not to be ignored (see Lukes 1977, 338).

Durkheim's efforts in the Dreyfus case underscore his interest in social justice and his awareness of the ways in which minorities could be used for political purposes. Pearce (1989, 72) notes that Durkheim was critical of the gap between formal constitutional protections in France and the ease with which Jews could be scapegoated. Indeed, the cohesion of many Jewish communities was set against a backdrop of "this need of resisting a general hostility, the very impossibility of all communication with the rest of the population" (Durkheim, cited in Pearce 1989, 71).

Pearce (1989) offers a fresh look at Durkheim's writings, suggesting that the almost "universal consensus" that Durkheim is a political conservative and positivist thinker is too simplistic. Pearce argues instead that Durkheim's work reveals some elements of socialism and can also serve as a corrective to some of the more extreme or overstated versions of Marxism (Pearce 1989, xiii–xiv). Overlaps appear between Durkheim's politics and those of more critical works in the Marxist and neo-Marxist traditions. Pearce (1989, 183) remarks that Durkheim was concerned about the power that could be exercised by the state. Accordingly, Durkheim believed that the state would not necessarily adhere to checks on its power or measures to ensure that the state and its officials were subject to the rule of law. Durkheim was not, however, wholly opposed to state powers, suggesting instead that with the proper development of the state, greater liberty could be realized (Pearce 1989, 187). This vision of an orderly and just society can be derived from Durkheim's contributions to the sociology of law. As Pearce (1989, 193) puts it: "For Durkheim, the rationality of the human subject is produced and sustained by society. Society . . . provides individuals with the capacity to follow its rules and the ability to engage in meaningful and orderly social interaction."

Law and Social Cohesion

There are many dimensions to the general concept of society: social, economic, and political dimensions, for example. For Durkheim, society represented a "moral phenomenon" inasmuch as the individual was inescapably bound and influenced by a moral milieu (Cotterrell 1984, 79). In its ideal form, society stood as a crystallization of widely shared social values.[2] These shared values were not completely established, especially in more complex, modernized societies. Thus, law served as an index of particular kinds of social solidarity, and as a key regulatory device in more complex societies, it served to reinforce important social values.

The concept of social solidarity is fundamental to Durkheim's thought. Durkheim postulated that two kinds of social solidarity characterized social development: mechanical and organic solidarity. First, *mechanical solidarity* was evident in earlier, "simpler" societies in which the division of labour was rudimentary. In keeping with Durkheim's argument that collective life determined individual life, the *collective conscience* (or "conscience collective") was seen as an external force, independent of individual will, that acted as a "social fact."[3] Durkheim saw religion as the origin of the modern collective conscience. In earlier times, religion served an important function of giving coherence to structures and providing a general form of social stability. Nonetheless, the initially cohesive character of religious regulation became, in Durkheim's view, more divisive than unifying in modern societies (Lukes 1977, 518). Lukes notes that Durkheim believed that social institutions, rather than religious institutions, could be most useful in producing "social cohesion" in modernizing societies (Lukes 1977, 518).

In societies where mechanical solidarity was established, individual differentiation in terms of personality was very limited. Cotterrell (1984, 78) notes that in conditions of mechanical solidarity, religion and law often work together and are not easily differentiated. They serve to uphold common values and to offer mechanisms to react to or regulate deviation from social values. Under the force of the collective conscience, individual identity as we know it becomes subordinated to the moral milieu. The collective conscience, according to Durkheim (1966, 96), acted as a source of "general vitality" for the sake of the society as a whole.

Durkheim regarded mechanical solidarity as a means of social integration, but an integration that was characterized by vengeance and often harsh punishments against those who offended the collective conscience. Indeed, for Durkheim (1966, 70), crime was defined as those acts that generated punitive reactions. These crimes, with very few exceptions, were "universally disapproved of" by members of a given society (Durkheim 1966, 70). Durkheim (1966, 87–89) did not discount the repressive sanctions that he thought characterized these earlier societies; rather, while he viewed them as a crude means of social survival and as insufficient for modern societies, he admitted that they served their societies in their need for moral expressions of outrage or disapproval.

In more complex societies, according to Durkheim, mechanical solidarity evolved into *organic solidarity*. Organic solidarity corresponded to a more complex, *inter*dependent division of labour, as well as a weakening of the collective conscience. Organic solidarity is thus associated with the onset of a more co-operative society, in which restitutive law and co-operative law might be used synonymously (see Lukes 1977, 155). The increased division of labour reflected massive social changes, including increased population density in cities and developments in communication and transportation (Milovanovic 1988, 26). Specialized knowledge and specific occupational groups were essential to these more complex societies, where people were increasingly reliant on others.

Criminal law, and other forms of legal regulation, could serve to bolster social cohesion in these new, more variegated societies. Durkheim realized, however, that this regulation by law, and by other normative systems, was not always successful. Industrial conflicts as well as conflicts in social life could lead to severe tensions and breakdowns in the moral order. Durkheim conceptualized such breakdowns as *anomie*, in which social integration did not have adequate regulatory mechanisms (see Cotterrell 1984, 79).

In conditions of organic solidarity, as societies became more populous and complex, punishment became less the property of a group and was administered in a less "haphazard" manner under the aegis of state tribunals (Durkheim 1966, 87). The modern character of punishment served the methodical purpose of "social defence." It emerged as a form of moral denunciation; however, it took on the character of "a passionate reaction of graduated intensity that society exercises through the medium of a body acting upon those of its members who have violated certain rules of conduct" (Durkheim 1966, 96).

The transition from mechanical solidarity to organic solidarity—from repressive law to restitutive law—and the emergence of many new forms of social regulation are vital aspects of Durkheim's theorizing. It is important, however, to bear in mind that the transition from mechanical to organic solidarity did not represent a complete break in norms. Giddens (1971, 77) outlines the nature of this transition:

> The progression of organic solidarity is necessarily dependent upon the declining significance of the *conscience collective*. But commonly held beliefs and sentiments do not disappear altogether in complex societies; nor is it the case that the formation of contractual relations becomes amoral and simply the result of each individual following "his best interest." . . . a society in which each individual solely pursues his own interest would disintegrate within a short space of time. . . . "There is nothing less constant than interest. Today, it unites me to you; tomorrow, it will make me your enemy."

The increasing social density of these new societies and the erosion of a "common morality" (Milovanovic 1988, 26) meant that an ethos of individualism began to eclipse the collective life. As the collective conscience weakened, law became transformed.

The transformation of law was envisioned as a movement away from repressive, harsher sanctions toward restitutive sanctions. *Repressive law* is exemplified by penal law, which inflicts suffering and punishment on rule breakers. Modern forms of repressive law include the systematization of criminal law and its various agencies of punishment, including incarceration. Giddens (1971, 74) defines crime as "an act which violates sentiments which are 'universally approved of' by the members of society." Crime thus involves actions that transgress these universally shared and understood beliefs. For Durkheim, the collective conscience appears as an external, *reified* (or enlarged) force, whose integrity depends on collective reactions against a variety of rule infractions. In simpler societies, the collective conscience is conventionally established through religious systems, which bring coherence to expected behaviours and penalties for violations of these expected behaviours (Giddens 1971, 75).

Restitutive law is a second type of law, one that Durkheim associated with more complex societies. In contrast to criminal law, restitutive forms of law appear in civil law, commercial law, and a variety of procedural laws (Milovanovic 1988, 27). Restitutive law was vested within the framework of the modern, centralized state. As these modernizing societies developed, there was less emphasis on the religious system as a regulatory mechanism. In this secular modern state, legal processes were not as informed by the standard meanings and the sense of shame associated with offences against the collective conscience. Weakening of traditional restrictions thus freed individuals from the ever-present constraints of local life. Ideally, these disappearing forms of constraint would be eclipsed by other, more secular, forms of regulation. Giddens (1971, 74) observes that restitutive sanctions serve not so much to punish wrongdoers as to restore relationships:

> If one man claims damages from another, the object of the legal process is to recompense the claimant, if his claim is upheld, for some sort of loss which he has incurred as an individual. There is little or no social disgrace attaching to the individual who loses a case of this sort. This is typical of most areas of civil, commercial and constitutional law.

Durkheim subdivides restitutive law into *negative relations* (the relations of individuals and things, including property and tort law) and *positive relations* (which are less conflictual and emphasize co-operation between individuals). At this point we should mention the premise that occupational moralities developed alongside restitutive laws (Milovanovic 1988, 27). Certainly, a variety of professional bodies (i.e., the medical, nursing, and legal disciplines) have outlined guidelines for practice and research, and have the power to "discipline" their members by suspension, probation, or barring them from practice. Be critical, however, of the assumption that there exists a "common ideological outlook" within these professional bodies (Milovanovic 1988, 77). As we will discuss in Chapter Nine, there are some schisms and disagreements evident among the memberships of professional bodies such as the medical profession, particularly in addressing such controversial issues as the midwifery movement or the abortion debate.

It is important to note that some researchers have challenged Durkheim's premise that simpler societies were essentially "repressive" in their methods of resolving disputes. On the basis of anthropological studies, Clarke (1976) contends that Durkheim erred in his theory of a repressive-restitutive dichotomy. These studies provided evidence that less complex societies were not necessarily as reliant on repressive sanctions as Durkheim had envisioned. It is also noteworthy that, as Western societies have evolved, many societies still rely on extensive systems of criminal justice, including penal systems. Thus, one can argue that, while there has been a tendency to institutionalize "restitutive" mechanisms in modern law, the repressive function of penal law is still quite evident. In fact, studies show that, in the early 1980s, the United States saw a dramatic increase in the number of people admitted to federal and state prisons (Lowman and Menzies 1986, 101). Keep in mind, however, that there have also been cycles of contraction of prison populations (Lowman and Menzies 1986, 101), and that some industrialized countries such as Japan and the Netherlands have very low rates of imprisonment (Rutherford 1986).

Social Consensus and Social Development

A key feature of Durkheim's theory of social development is the premise that social inequality will be reduced as societies move toward greater division of labour. However, Durkheim allowed for exceptions to this theory of normal social development. Milovanovic (1988, 29–30) refers to "pathological" forms of social development noted by Durkheim. One pathological form emerges in the form of anomie. The concept of anomie is pertinent to an understanding of Durkheim's approach to social pathology. Anomie is said to reflect a state of normlessness, in which previous rules and regulations are in flux, and social life becomes more ambiguous. Taken to its extreme form, anomie would threaten social life as such, as social relations fall into disequilibrium. Anomie is contrasted with Durkheim's assumption that ordinarily societies will develop in such a way that all elements of society adjust to social change. We might conceptualize this as a dynamic process, but one that takes place within a generally stable framework.

Critics of Durkheim argue that he is not attentive to the *divisive* results of social stratification, social inequality, and economic exploitation. This critical view rests on a less optimistic view of social solidarity and the myriad regulations of modern social life. For some critics, then, deviations from orderly social development might reflect deeper, structural aspects of economic and political arrangements. Durkheim also foresaw that a second abnormal form could emerge if the division of labour was forced (Milovanovic 1988, 29).

Class conflicts could become more extensive and threaten social harmony if contractual relations between individuals came to rest on coercion, rather than a more natural relation between the person's position in the economy and the demands and rewards associated with that position. Clearly, such a *forced division of labour* undermined Durkheim's preference for an orderly, meritocratic division of labour.[4]

Durkheim generally favoured the introduction of the *contract* as a partial replacement for status (Milovanovic 1988, 30). In earlier societies, contracts appeared primarily as *real*, or *solemn*, contracts. Divine authority became the guarantor to the contractual undertaking, which consisted of words, sometimes combined with specific rituals or rites. In modern societies, the demands and complexities of trade and commerce rendered these earlier forms of contract obsolete. Thus, the *consensual contract* emerged as the standard form of contractual relations. Durkheim observed, however, that the promissory aspects of the earlier contracts remained with the newer forms of contractual obligations (see Milovanovic 1988, 32). Indeed, it is clear that Durkheim believed that the older norms and expectations were often incorporated into evolving societies (Giddens 1971).

Durkheim's epistemological emphasis on objectivity reappeared in his formulation of *contracts of equity* (Milovanovic 1988, 32). According to Durkheim, contracts freely entered into are not necessarily equitable contracts; that is, some contractual arrangements may be accompanied by extortion, and this would vitiate the apparent fairness of the agreed-upon contract.

Durkheim's approach to social development has been linked with his general support for political liberalism. Lukes (1977, 338–40) criticizes some of Durkheim's critics for misreading Durkheim and incorrectly caricaturing him as politically conservative and essentially hostile to an ethos of individualism. Lukes (1977, 338–40) believes that a more careful reading confirms Durkheim's insistence on the importance of the collective conscience in modernizing societies. Furthermore, for all the elements of structural constraint in his writing, Durkheim was opposed to oversimplified, mechanistic analyses that set individuals within a largely predetermined system of "production and exchange." Certainly, in one of his major works—*Suicide*, published in 1897—Durkheim allowed for the ways in which a society might engulf individuals and produce suffering; nevertheless, for Durkheim, the emerging societies offered opportunities for new thought and expressions. These emerging societies required "a system of different and specialized functions united by definite relations" (Lukes 1977, 153) and a more variegated economic and social structure that rested on bonds of organic solidarity.

Durkheim favoured individualism, but not its manifestations of egoism and narrow self-interest. Durkheim wrote of individualism as a means of establishing a "sympathy for all that is human, a wider pity for all sufferings, for all human miseries, a more ardent desire to combat and alleviate them, a greater thirst for justice" (Lukes 1977, 340–41). To this end, Durkheim was not only committed to peace over war, and to the efforts of the *Dreyfusards*, but also served as a member of the *Ligue des Droits de l'Homme* (League of Human Rights) in France.

Durkheim's contributions to the sociology of law included the formulation of the repressive and restitutive character of law as it evolved in civil society and under the aegis of various agencies, including the modern state. While actively critical of some aspects of state tyranny—as evidenced in the Dreyfus affair—he viewed the centralized state body as indispensable in modernizing societies. His scientific approach was useful in combatting much of the speculation and dogmatism associated with some forms of metaphysics. His broad-based approach to religion, economics, social relations, politics, statistical methods, and ethics provided much of the groundwork for what stands as modern sociology.

MAX WEBER (1864–1920)

Biography

Max Weber was born in Erfurt, Germany, in 1864. He studied law and economics in university, and taught law at the University of Berlin, and later at the University of Freiburg. His doctoral dissertation concerned trading companies in medieval times, and his subsequent work included a study of Roman agrarian history (Parkin 1982, 13). His brilliant career was not without difficulties; in 1898 he suffered a nervous breakdown, which lasted for several years, during which time he neither wrote nor taught (Parkin 1982, 14). Weber was a prolific writer, and his legacy of works is still debated, including the "encyclopedic," two-volume work, *Economy and Society* (1921). Parkin (1982, 14) notes that Weber's scholarly output is "unsurpassed," and reflects a comprehensive grasp of such complex areas as law, the social sciences, history, and religion. Weber was renowned as a conflict theorist. His theoretical approach is critical of Marx's emphasis on the importance of materialist, economic forces on social development.

Capitalism and Law

For many readers, the development of capitalist economic systems appears natural, perhaps almost as a "given." But for Weber, the reasons underlying the rise of capitalism were the subject of intense scholarly interest. The institution of law was a considerable force behind the rise of capitalism. Weber defined law as follows:

> An order will be called *law* if it is externally guaranteed by the probability that coercion (physical or psychological), to bring about conformity or avenge viola-

tion, will be applied by a *staff* of people holding themselves specially ready for that purpose (cited in Milovanovic 1988, 41; italics in original).

For Weber, the legal order was a reciprocal part of the wider social order. Weber's holistic approach to law and society was based on the complex influences among law, religious institutions, society, and forms of domination (Käsler 1988, 144). The extent to which people conformed with legal order—perhaps through fear of repressive forms of law or through a belief in the correctness of legal order—was a central concern for Weber.

Weber was strongly opposed to simplistic models of law. He viewed economic factors as important, but not singular, influences on legal development. According to Weber, law is best understood within a *matrix* of forces; therefore, a scientific, multicausal approach to legal order is essential if one is to truly understand the complex evolution and purposes of specific legal systems (see Milovanovic 1988, 42). This approach posed a challenge to the more materialistically oriented and deterministic forces postulated by Marx. The capitalistic economic system rested on *calculation* and *stability* (Milovanovic 1988, 42), and was not simply a means of exploitation and profit maximization.

Kronman (1983) devotes a chapter of his book on Weber to the topic of law and capitalism. For Weber, the capitalist system of production stood as "the most fateful force" in his time (Kronman 1983, 118). Rather than establish a simple relationship between these forces of capitalism and the growth of formal legal rationality, Weber envisioned the two as "reciprocal" forces (Kronman 1983, 118). Although the two conditions could not be reduced to a simple relationship, Weber attributed great importance to the role of formally rational structures of law and administration in promoting economic calculability (Kronman 1983, 120).

Weber had a keen eye for exceptions to general rules; as such, his theoretical work used historical instances and cross-cultural studies which served to identify patterns of social and economic life that could be qualified by specific variations and influences within particular legal, social, and economic systems. Weber's general approach to the links between the promotion of capitalist transactions and the systematization of formally rational legal structures is a case in point. Weber noted that the English common law was, for the most part, formally irrational. Nevertheless, predictable "market transactions" were fostered in England, despite the lack of university-based, formal legal training (Kronman 1983, 120). Weber noted that English lawyers were oriented to commercial life in their training, and this fact facilitated a reshaping of laws favourable to business interests (Kronman 1983, 121). Thus, apprenticing in law served as a practical training, akin to learning a craft. This, in turn, corresponded with concrete legal training, which was largely congruent with the practical needs of business clients (Kronman 1983, 121).

For Weber, the causal relationships among law, economy, and society were complex. Historically, the absence of a systematized legal order—for instance, classical forms of early Roman law—served to impede the rationalistic process that was essential to modernized economic life. Kronman (1983, 126) adds:

> In the absence of a law of agency or corporations or legal recognition of the principle of free negotiability, commerce can be rationalized only to a limited degree. According to Weber, without these particular legal devices, a stable and continuous system of capitalist production is inconceivable.

For Weber, bureaucratic structures were essential, given the nature of developing capitalist economies. Weber noted that the increasing complexity of bureaucratic operations generated a need for greater precision, reliability, and efficiency in bureaucratic procedures. This combination of needs was imposed on modernizing bureaucratic systems of administration (Runciman 1980, 350). Weber's ideal of a fully rationalized administrative and legal structure was tied with the increasing division of labour and ever-specialized work tasks being undertaken in complex economies. Weber believed that bureaucratization allowed labour to be designed along "purely objective criteria"; for example, "individual parts of the work may be allotted to functionaries who have had specialist training and will continually improve their skills by practical experience" (Runciman 1980, 351).

Bureaucratization was linked with society-wide demands for a "stable and absolute peace for order and protection" (Runciman 1980, 239). Weber traced the growth of modern police forces to earlier structures of kinship, in which an individual's kin would be expected to resolve disputes or avenge injuries. Bureaucratization also stemmed from the growing range of "social policy" activities required of the state (under pressure from certain interest groups) or undertaken by the state. For Weber, such motivations were "economically determined in the highest degree" (Runciman 1980, 239).

Weber was clearly aware of some of the excesses of early capitalism. These excesses included difficult situations for workers and the development of factories where workers faced "bondage to the machine and a common work discipline" (Runciman 1980, 252). Weber disagreed with Marx's prediction of increasing emmiseration of workers[5] and intensified class conflict between workers and the bourgeoisie. Instead, he argued that, with a tendency to "cartelization" (rather than cutthroat competition) by capitalist entrepreneurs and greater stability with respect to banking and credit, many of these predicted "crises" had not materialized (Runciman 1980, 259). Weber also foresaw a continued increase in the number of employees whose interests were aligned more with capitalist and government sectors than with a manual, labouring class. He noted a "rapid increase" in the number of office workers—an increase that exceeded any increase in proletarian workers (Runciman 1980, 258). In addition, Weber envisioned a generation of myriad "interest groups" whose competing interests would prevent them from forming a clear, workable alliance against the bourgeois economic system.

Forms of Law and Legal Thought

Weber formulated two key dimensions of law: formality and rationality. *Formality* referred to "the employment of criteria, standards, and logic" (Milovanovic 1988, 43) in the legal system. Ideally, in *formal* legal systems, legal rules and procedures would be confined within the legal system and not be influenced by external factors. Conversely, *substantive* legal systems would be swayed or directed by political or ideological criteria. Weber believed that no legal system was entirely formal or substantive; rather, a system could be positioned on a continuum between the two pure forms of formal and substantive systems.

The second dimension, *rationality*, is a key concept to the subject of justice. Rationality refers to the use of criteria such that decisions that are made apply to all like cases (see Milovanovic 1988, 44). When similar legal cases are dealt with differently, the process would become "irrational": similar cases would receive dissimilar decisions, and the predictability of legal decisions would be weakened. The purest form of law—formally rational law—is attained only when five criteria are established: application, derivation, "gapless" character of legal propositions, legal irrelevance of that which is not rendered in legal terms, and the all-inclusive legal ordering of social conduct via the legal system (Milovanovic 1988, 46–47). This ideal type of law overcomes elements of ambiguity in rule-making and rule-application, and safeguards the importance of logic and neutrality in deciding particular cases.

Weber added that laws become fully rational when legal rules are applied fairly to equally situated persons, and when legal rules are clearly stated and administered without preferential treatment.

Domination and Law

In Weber's approach, *domination* refers to the probability that a particular group of people will obey certain commands (Milovanovic 1988, 47). Weber formulated three fundamental kinds of domination, which he presented as "ideal types," or pure forms, of domination.[6] These were traditional domination, charismatic domination, and legal domination.

Traditional domination is summarized as a custom or habit that is determined by longstanding obedience to particular rules. Weber used the example of kadi justice in Islam, in which established conventions of sacred tradition governed decisions. Although kadi-based justice was commonly associated with more charismatic forms of justice (discussed below), Weber indicated that it was in fact regulated by "extremely formalistic" interpretations of sacred traditions (Runciman 1980, 230).

Charismatic domination is linked with *personal* qualities of leadership, not with the highly co-ordinated, impersonal character of rational-legal domination. Weber emphasized that charismatic leaders are restricted by "the mission and power" of their characters, not by external regulations. The properties of "submission" to and "faith" in the power of charismatic rules preclude recourse to objective standards of dispute resolution. For Weber, the actions of charismatic rulers had an absolute quality, against which citizens had no means to appeal to other authorities or safeguards. It was an "intensely personal" form of leadership, with a quality of divine authority vested in the bearer of charismatic authority (Runciman 1980, 230). Charismatic domination posed a challenge to the traditional patriarchal structure of societies. The traditional elements of obedience, reverence of traditional obligations, and "bonds of personal loyalty" were often challenged by what Weber saw as the "revolutionary role" of charismatic authority (Runciman 1980, 233).

The essential character of charismatic domination is unstable.[7] Weber pointed out that the tremendous devotion and enthusiasm typical of the initial stages of a charismatic movement rarely maintain their original force. Instead, the original impetus is compromised and overtaken by "the conditions of everyday life":

> The charismatically ruled . . . usually become tax-paying "subjects," contributing members of the church, sect, party or club, soldiers conscripted, drilled and disciplined according to the rules and regulations, or law-abiding "citizens" (Runciman 1980, 237).

The unstable quality of charismatic domination is reflected in legal decisions. In its pure form, charismatic justice is entirely free of rules and the weight of tradition, and remains tied to the subjective powers of the ruler, or the "bearer" of charisma. "Trial by ordeal" is one example of charismatic justice that remains largely free of regular rules (Runciman 1980, 230–31).

Legal domination, in contrast, rests not on the weight of custom or on the personal qualities of a leader, but on the belief that existing laws and regulations are constructed rationally and fairly, and administered impersonally (see Milovanovic 1988, 47). Certainly, Weber was well aware of the limitations of the new rational order being ushered in together with intensified capitalist relations of production.[8] There is, however, an emancipatory quality that can be read into much of Weber's writing. Weber was clearly aware of the profound impact of class structures, including the gap between legal rights and the inability of many individuals to exercise such rights. The ideal type of rational-legal domination could be undermined if inordinately powerful economic interests capitalized on legal resources. For example, Weber was conscious of the limits of the legal dictum that "everyone 'without respect of person' may establish a business corporation"; he felt that "the propertied classes as such obtain a kind of factual 'autonomy,' since they alone are able to utilize or take advantage of these powers" (cited in Käsler 1988, 147). Weber went further, arguing that the reciprocal relationship between law and the economic order of capitalism rested on economic (material) power. Weber wrote that "economic interests are among the strongest factors influencing the creation of law: inasmuch as the authority underlying the legal order relied largely upon 'constellations of material interests'" (Lachmann 1970, 131–32).

Among the criticisms of Weber's theoretical approach, it has been suggested that Weber's view of capitalism appears largely static over time. Binnie (1988, 35) thus notes that, for Weber, capitalism appears to be "an unchanging concept in relation to law." She adds (1988, 35) that he paid insufficient attention to capitalism with respect to *political forms*, concentrating instead on its relationship to economic factors. Binnie (1988) observes that Weber's approach is largely bereft of the ideological aspects of law under capitalism, and is thus too narrow to appreciate the implications of these largely noneconomic features of capitalist relations and corresponding forms of law. Lachmann (1970, 131–33) notes Weber's emphasis on the "plasticity" of social institutions and relationships—a source of the flux and, to some extent, unpredictability of politics, economics, culture, and society. Lachmann points out, however, that Weber's dislike of overgeneralization led him to limit his appreciation of "wider problems" within the larger institutional structures.

KARL MARX (1818–1883)

Biography

Karl Marx was born in Trier, Germany, in 1818. His father, Heinrich Marx, was a practising notary and lawyer. At age twelve, Karl Marx enrolled in the Friedrich-Wilhelm-Gymnasium, a first-class school with a liberal direction. Marx graduated in 1835. In 1836 he was engaged to Jenny Westphalen, and they were married, despite family opposition, in 1843. Marx entered the University of Bonn in 1835, studying jurisprudence. In 1836, however, Marx transferred to the University of Berlin, where he studied history, philosophy, and law. Marx completed his dissertation in 1841, but did not obtain a university appointment (partly due to his reputation as a young Hegelian critic). For a short period of time, he edited a newspaper, but was forced to resign. In 1843, he and his wife began "what was virtually a lifelong exile from Germany" (Kamenka 1988, xvi). Marx worked in Paris, producing the *Economic and Philosophical Manuscripts of 1844*, a critique of modern society.

Marx was, however, expelled from France at the instigation of the Prussian government. He visited London briefly, then settled in Brussels, where he and Engels wrote the famous polemic, *The Communist Manifesto*, published in 1848. Marx was expelled from Brussels shortly thereafter, following a suspicion that he was supplying arms to revolutionaries. Marx returned to Paris briefly and then travelled to Cologne (where he was tried for and acquitted of sedition). From 1849 on, he lived most of his life in London, often in dire poverty. His great work, *Das Kapital*, was never finished, although the first volume appeared in 1867. By 1873, Marx was suffering severe health problems and, while he read extensively, he "was incapable of further serious creative work" (Kamenka 1988, xxii). His wife died of liver cancer in 1881; Marx died in London in 1883.[9]

Introduction

The writings of Karl Marx have had a profound influence on intellectual thought and political practice. In the early 1980s, Karl Marx was the most widely cited political philosopher discussed in social science references. His critique of capitalism and its institutions has influenced social, economic, and political policies throughout the world. Kamenka (1988, xxxviii) describes Marx as "the greatest of the socialist ideologists," while Tucker (1972, vii) comments that "no other intellectual influence has so powerfully shaped the mind of modern left-wing radicalism in most parts of the world." Marxist-based principles remain very much alive, influencing, for example, the development of a critically based criminology (Taylor, Walton, and Young 1973), and the attempts to combine feminist and Marxist analyses of oppression in capitalist societies.

A central concern of our discussion is how Marx (and his successors) viewed law and the state. An important dimension of Marxist approaches to law is the difference between law as it appears and law as it is; that is, the extent to which law under capitalism reflects the specific interests of a dominant class rather than the general interests of all citizens. For Marx, the power of law was essentially oriented toward bourgeois interests. The phrase *bourgeois legality* reflects this partisan quality of law. It is also important to note that Marx saw law as a mystifying force that deliberately misrepresented its true nature. As we shall see, Marx's approach to law under capitalism stands in fairly sharp contrast to those of Durkheim and Weber.

Studies of Law and Political Economy

It is well-established that, for Marx, the study of law was, at most, a secondary interest. References to law in Marx's writings are sporadic and not developed in a comprehensive way; rather, his emphasis was on understanding the *material* forces in history, especially how differing class formations and modes of production influence social and political life.

A complete understanding of the historical development of capitalism required a focus on the material elements of history, along with an appreciation of law and justice. Wood (1980, 3–4) contends that Marx did not explicitly view capitalism as unjust, despite Marx's clear outline of the reality of exploitation of workers, and the misappropriation by the few of the wealth produced by the labouring classes. Rather, Marx rejected the valorization of justice and the assumption that the best possible society could be realized through state-mediated justice (Wood 1980, 5). Wood (1980, 14) assesses Marx's neglect of juridical ideals as deliberate, and not as an oversight:

> Because Marx regarded juridical institutions as playing only a supporting role in social life, he attached considerably less importance to juridical conceptions as measures of social rationality than most previous social thinkers were inclined to do.

The genius of capitalism is that patterns of inequality can be excused, denied, or justified in large part through its ideology of private property and individual acquisition. Marx objected to capitalism as a system not because it was inherently unjust, but, as Wood (1980, 37) contends, because "it is a form of *concealed dominion* over the worker" (italics added). A Marxist-based critique of bourgeois law emphasizes the importance of this concealment of economic power and legal advantage as they are actually exercised in capitalist societies.

Although Marx did not provide a systematic basis for the sociology of law, his critique of the rule of law is a major contribution to an understanding of the nature of class rule in industrial societies. Collins (1987, 1) states that the rule of law is viewed by Marxists as a "pervasive legitimating ideology" in these societies. As such, the task for Marxists is to demystify the tenets of liberal political philosophy so as to revolutionize existing political, economic, and social institutions. Part of this demystification, for Marx, was to place analysis of the modern state in the context of political economy. In *The German Ideology*, published in 1846, Marx and Engels linked economic production with changing forms of human consciousness. Growing contradictions and conflicts in society led to the development of the modern state, a locus for class-related struggles (see Knuttila 1987, 94–95). The state appeared as an "independent form" in which

> the struggle between democracy, aristocracy, and monarchy, the struggle for the franchise . . . are merely the illusory forms in which the real struggles of the different classes are fought out among one another (from *The German Ideology*, cited in Knuttila 1987, 95).

Given this critical emphasis and the unsystematic nature of Marx's contributions to legal philosophy, we might think it odd that Marx figures so prominently beside the classical writings of Durkheim and Weber or modern contributors to the sociology of law. Nevertheless, Marxism remains a vital area of legal scholarship. As noted earlier, in the early 1980s, the Institute for Scientific Information found that Marx was the most widely cited scholar in the social sciences and humanities. There has also been a renaissance of interest by Marxists in the nature of modern legal systems (Cain and Hunt 1979; Beirne and Quinney 1982; Collins 1987, 1). This renewal of interest is particularly impressive, since Marxism has in many respects been discouraged, even vilified, as a desirable form of Western scholarship. As outlined in this section, there are numerous arguments for and against a Marxist, or Marxist-derived, perspective in understanding law, class, and power.

Of the several neo-Marxist approaches to state, law, and economy (see Ratner, McMullan, and Burtch 1987), instrumental Marxism and structural Marxism stand as two core approaches in critically understanding the nature of domination and social change in capitalist societies.[10] *Instrumental Marxism* begins from the premise that the state (including its legal component) serves the general interests of the ruling class, not the general interests of all citizens. As set out in *The Communist Manifesto*, "The executive of the modern State is but a committee for managing the common affairs of the whole bourgeoisie" (Marx and Engels 1979, 82). This instrumentalist approach means that state officials have *very little autonomy* in setting policies, and that their primary role is to assist the bourgeoisie in accumulating surplus value[11] and consolidating their dominant position over the mass of workers.

Milovanovic (1988, 64) discusses some aspects of Marx's *A Contribution to the Critique of Political Economy*. A key point is that, for Marx, people become involved in relationships that are *independent* of their will. These relationships are determined in large measure by the fundamental economic structure of a particular society. This economic *base* underlies and shapes the *superstructure* of social thought, law, politics, and culture. Marx adds: "It is not the consciousness of people that determines their existence, but their social existence that determines their consciousness" (see Milovanovic 1988, 64). This statement reveals the strength and weakness of Marx's writing. Its strength lies in the boldness of his attack on an uncritical acceptance of social contract theory and the essential validity of law; its weakness appears in his tendency to overstate such points or to write in contradictory ways. Specifically, his statement that consciousness is determined by material forces is contradicted by other passages in which he sees human consciousness and material structures as dialectically interrelated.

Marx's historical perspective is evident in his typology of modes of production: slavery, feudalism, capitalism, and communism (with socialism an interstitial mode of production that precedes true communism). Under capitalism, goods that were previously used for subsistence and for barter become transformed into commodities sold for profit (Milovanovic 1988, 64–65). It is essential to appreciate that for Marx, and others working within the Marxist tradition, law was seen as a dynamic force, altering legislation and legal practices in order to resolve crises and contradictions in particular societies at certain periods of time. This *dialectical* approach is often used to argue against instrumentalist theories of law, and provides an understanding of law as a form of struggle that includes workers (Chambliss 1986, 30 & 49).

Milovanovic (1988, 66–67) brings forward two general strands of Marxist theory. The first strand is portrayed as *superstructure as determined by the (economic) base*. The interests of the more powerful class are realized, in part, through the repressive and ideological functions of law. Hence, police and army forces may be mobilized to extend the interests of capital, through warfare at one extreme and by quelling domestic struggles, such as unionization, at the other extreme. An ideology favourable to social stratification, private property, and the accumulation of wealth may also be seen as essentially favourable to the dominant economic class.

Structural Marxists shift attention to the "internal dynamics" (Milovanovic 1988, 69) of capitalism as a complex formation that not only works toward consolidating the dominance of capitalism but also must address challenges and pressures that would weaken this dominant status. They discount Weber's premise that the legal order attains an autonomous status as it moves toward "formal rationality" (Milovanovic 1988, 69). Structural Marxists claim that the capitalist state achieves only a relative autonomy. In this relative-autonomy approach, then, the state is not conceptualized as an instrument that is alternately concealed, misrepresented, and brandished on behalf of capital. Nor are economic forces presented as the essential determinants of social life, since the state assumes greater autonomy in addressing the diverse (sometimes opposed) interests of various constituencies, including social classes.[12]

Instead of adhering to the base-superstructure distinction, this strand of Marxist theory argues that the economic, political, and ideological spheres interact to produce particular "conjunctures" in a given social formation. Taken to its extreme, it sees human agency—the importance of ideas, consciousness, personal actions—as disappearing from the matrix of factors that affect social life. A less stringent interpretation would allow for the influence of social movements, resistance, and class struggle in reshaping the social formation.

Milovanovic (1988, 68) continues his discussion of *domination*, noting that instrumental Marxists view media, family, and educational institutions as transmitters of values favourable to capital accumulation. Moreover, this ideological work is reinforced by the more repressive powers of law. The result is a mixture of *mystification* (to deliberately perplex or hoax) about law such that the real purpose of law is distorted and legitimated; and *repression*, such that relatively powerless citizens are subject to the threat or application of legal sanctions.

Pashukanis and Marxist Legal Thinking

The Soviet jurist E.B. Pashukanis (1891–1937) remains a key figure in the formulation of Marxist legal thinking. His formidable academic accomplishments— Pashukanis authored approximately 200 works dealing with legal history and legal theory (Beirne and Sharlet 1980, Preface)—are contrasted with his denunciation and eventual execution as "an enemy of the people" (Beirne and Sharlet 1980, 70). Pashukanis believed that, while a measure of social regulation was needed in the *transitional period* between socialism and communism, socialist law was fated to wither away (Beirne and Quinney 1982, 21).

The purge of Pashukanis and others in 1937 signalled a reconsolidation of Soviet jurisprudence as a formal, professional institution. Vyshinsky, the Soviet legal scholar who essentially replaced Pashukanis as a leading force in Soviet jurisprudence, published work that criticized Pashukanis's approach and argued for consolidation of a system of law that reflected the will of the people. Law was thus recast as an authentic representation of the people's will and as a necessary force in the ongoing struggle to establish Soviet socialism. Vyshinsky argued that there was a great need to eliminate previously-dominant classes and to protect the emerging Soviet state from "capitalist encirclement" (Beirne and Sharlet 1980, 33). Far from abolishing the state and its legal structures, Vyshinsky contended that the eventual abolition of the state could not be undertaken post-haste. Instead, law would in the interim have a stabilizing quality, ensuring the orderly development of socialism while protecting against the possible undermining of the Soviet state by outside capitalist forces (Beirne and Sharlet 1980, 33).

Pashukanis was associated with the *commodity exchange* school of law in the 1920s. In this approach, law is not simply a reflection of the interests of a dominant class or classes; instead, law emerges from the development of generalized commodity exchange (Beirne and Sharlet 1980, 20–21). Pashukanis argued that the *legal form* emerged from the economic sphere, specifically from the exchange of *commodities* under capitalism. The production of goods for "direct use" was eclipsed by the manufacture of commodities, which are produced for their "use value" (Milovanovic 1988, 70–71). At its extreme, the commodity-based system and the introduction of currency (money) contribute to a masking of the exploitation of social labour and a concealment of real needs.

Pashukanis claimed that there was a parallel between the commodity form and the legal form. In the legal form, there appears to be an equality between individuals. Each person bears rights, and his or her actions are taken to be freely willed. Nevertheless, the *juridic subject* (Milovanovic 1988, 72) is an idealization of individual freedom: in essence, individuals are still constrained by substantive differences in power, and part of this constraint is secured through legal processes. This approach is significant in that, rather than treating law as a neutral, progressive, and natural development in civilization, it sees law under capitalism as rooted in materialist conditions and oriented to the protection of property relations and class power.

Pashukanis provided a valuable framework for understanding law, including his argument that the *appearanc*e of law was belied by continuing inequalities maintained by the legal apparatus. Just as the commodity form was associated with unequal efforts and rewards (between the bourgeoisie and the proletariat), so also the legal form served to perpetuate inequality. Beirne and Sharlet (1982, 308) note that the logic of the commodity form, and the logic of the legal form "are universal equivalents which in appearance equalize the manifestly unequal: respectively, different commodities and the labour which produced them, and different political citizens and the subjects of rights and obligations."

Criticisms of Marxist and Neo-Marxist Theory

Poor Integration of Theory and Empirical Research.   Critics have commented on the gap between *theorizing* about the state on the one hand and *concrete, empirical analysis* of the nature of state control. Knuttila (1987, 119) concludes that the *instrumentalist* perspective developed by Miliband suffers from an underdeveloped theoretical framework, while Poulantzas's *structuralist* approach lacks empirical analysis. Clearly, then, neo-Marxist theory requires an integration of empiricism and theory before it can fully explore the nature of the state and its legal apparatus. Radical criminology has also been criticized for the weak empirical basis of many of its assertions. Hagan (1985, 224), for example, comments on the imprecise wording used by some Marxist criminologists, including the murky and poorly operationalized concept of the ruling (or governing) class, or their use of the term "interests served under capitalism." Such opaque terminology hinders careful measurement and verification of the claims of Marxist and other radical criminologists.

Durkheim argued that the primacy given by Marx to economic factors had not been verified scientifically, by either Marx or his followers. Durkheim believed that economic factors were important, but that in terms of social development, economic factors were properly regarded as "secondary and derivative" (Lukes 1977, 232).

Biased Analysis of Law and Politics.   Some critics express concern over Marxism's myopic analysis of law and politics in capitalist societies. They argue that neo-Marxist approaches are built on a thoroughgoing critique of capitalism without an appreciation of the progressive or positive aspects of capitalist societies. For example, Collins (1987, 14) makes the point that the Marxist ideological critique of liberal-pluralism and the rule of law is not entirely convincing. Such critiques are directed against existing power arrangements, without formulating a more positive theory of law and power (see Collins 1987, 14). We could add that some critical outlooks ignore beneficial aspects of the rule of law, including provisions that safeguard individual freedoms while inhibiting the actions of the most powerful sectors in society. In addition, Marxist theories that hinge on simplified versions of class conflict are open to the criticism that they are falsely simplistic: they reduce the complexity of social and economic conflict (Collins 1987, 45–47).

Irrelevance of Marxist Theory. Marxist theory has also been dismissed as no longer pertinent to modern political and economic issues, since Marx was writing about an earlier form of capitalism. The Marxist tenets of the decline of the state and escalating class conflict lead some theorists to argue that the Marxist approach is antiquated and irrelevant. Some believe that Marxist doctrinaire thinking, like all forms of dogma, is no longer relevant in a changing world. Consider the following exchange between Bill Moyers (1989, 501) (host of the PBS program "A World of Ideas") and the late Professor Northrop Frye:

> *Frye*: Doctrinaire Marxism will not work anywhere in the world—not because it's Marxism, but because it's doctrinaire. I don't think anything doctrinaire will work anywhere.
>
> *Moyers:* And by "doctrinaire," you mean—?
>
> *Frye*: I mean a simplified deductive pattern that carries out policies from major premises about ideology—
>
> *Moyers*: —instead of from the experience of the real world.
>
> *Frye*: Yes.

A related criticism is that Marxist theories of law have become stale and catechismal, not subject to empirical verification. This criticism has not gone without challenge. Collins (1987, 5), for example, charges that contemporary Marxism is far from dogmatic, and that contemporary Marxist research involves the refinement and replacement of various facets of classical Marxist theories. There has been a dramatic revival of interest in Marx and neo-Marxism in Western scholarship, including attempts to apply Marxist approaches to such major developments as the welfare state (see Gough 1979).

Unclear Framework of Law.   The analysis of the nature of law in neo-Marxist writing is at times not very coherent. Marx did *not* emphasize the study of law in his writing, and Marxists have not yet resolved whether or not law is to be retained under communism. There exist substantial splits on the topic of law among neo-Marxists, centring on such questions as (1) should the legal apparatus as we know it be abolished? (2) should reform be undertaken, since it may simply consolidate the hegemonic powers of the state by giving legitimacy to the law? and (3) should particular elements of law, for example, human rights safeguards, be retained?

Political Repression.   Critics also point to the danger that neo-Marxist practices may be implemented in a manner that destroys popular political expression. Writing in 1918, the German socialist leader Rosa Luxemburg foresaw that, as political life became repressed,

> life in the soviets must become more and more crippled. Without general elections, without unrestricted freedom of the press and assembly, without a free struggle of opinion, life dies out in every public institution, and becomes a mere semblance of life, in which only the bureaucracy remains as the active element (cited in Carnoy 1984, 63).

Critics also have reservations about the actual implementation of political power. For example, although Emile Durkheim respected socialism for its potential in reorganizing the economic system and securing a higher morality, he was leery of the potential for violence and class-divisiveness he saw in late nineteenth century struggles for socialism (see Lukes 1977, 246–47).

Woodcock (1990, 6), in his appreciation of the work of the Canadian poet Gary Geddes, cautions against the repressive aspects of leftist administrations:

> . . . the bottom line of Marxist movements when they have achieved power has often been, as Bakunin prophesied a century and a quarter ago, a tyranny that is even worse than its predecessor because the revolutionaries know from experience the methods of resistance to them that is likely to arise. This happens in Russia, and with the Khmer Rouge, it recurs with depressing regularity in China, and—despite the great liberations of eastern Europe—it continues in North Korea, Cuba, Ethiopia, and Albania, in all of which the process started with revolutionaries as idealistic and engaging as any that Gary Geddes so often celebrates.

Political repression may take other forms. Some argue that the development of Marxist-influenced policies has tended toward nationalism, while repressing possibilities for international solidarity. Karenga (1981, 238–39) illustrates this tendency with the transition from German socialism to German nationalism and the growth of "Russification" in the USSR. Karenga (1981, 239–40) also raises two related points: first, that Marxism suffers from "Eurocentrism"—the tendency to exalt European countries and struggles as "the hope of mankind"; and second, that Marxism tends to reduce struggles for justice and equality to class. Marxism that places the economic base as the primary focus of study and struggle thus must be aware of racism and other factors. Karenga (1981, 240) puts this bluntly: "The Marxist expectation of working class unity across racial and ethnic lines is complicated by the racial ideology, privileges, status and access which the white working class possess and treasure."

Interestingly, the repressive aspects of Soviet life have become something of a media staple in North American culture. From the 1939 film *Ninotchka*, to the more recent film *Moscow on the Hudson*, material deprivation and political repression are presented as a central motif in Soviet life. This equation of "Marxism = political repression and totalitarianism" has been challenged by Marxists. Beirne and Quinney (1982, 2) contend that there is a renewed interest among Marxists in law and social regulation. Moreover, this modern interest is not static, but more open and rigorous. Overturning simplistic stereotypes of Marxism includes moving beyond instrumentalism. Instrumentalism—about which Marx and Engels wrote (as noted earlier) that "The executive of the modern state is but a committee for managing the common affairs of the whole bourgeoisie"—is now widely seen as overstated. More sophisticated theories and approaches have since been mounted within the Marxist tradition. While acknowledging the value of instrumentalism in uncovering the extraordinary influence of powerful economic interests in capitalist societies, Beirne and Quinney (1982, 16–17) note that not all legislation is so influenced by dominant classes.

The point here is that many contemporary Marxists claim to have shifted away from the more doctrinaire, stultifying aspects of political rule or scholarly theorizing. This renewed interest in Marxism thus stems largely from an interpretation of Marx and his more humanistic, emancipatory objective, and less from political regimes ostensibly modelled on his original or revised principles. Svitak (cited in Benn 1980, 38) is quite clear about the humanistic objectives prized by Marx and by contemporary Marxists who object to some of the repression in socialist bloc countries. Svitak, arguing against the stereotype of Marx as the father of fascism, claims that Marx "strove for a wider humanism than that of the bourgeois democracies that he knew, and for wider civil rights, not for the setting up of the dictatorship of one class and one political party" (cited in Benn 1980, 38).

Oppositional and Negative Approach.   Fine (1984, 1–3) advocates the application of Marxist-based principles of political economy and law to modern legal struggles. He expresses concern, however, over the polarization of some legal critiques; specifically, that some doctrinaire Marxists fail to appreciate the contribution of liberal principles and achievements. Fine also decries what amounts to a "sectarian refusal" among some Marxists to forge alliances with liberals. He notes that Marxism may appear to be little more than "a negation of liberalism" (Fine 1984, 1), in which liberal ideals of equality before the law, judicial neutrality, and the like may be dismissed as fraudulent, and propertied relations cast as essentially exploitative under capitalism. Fine clearly recognizes the importance of critiquing the *class* nature of capitalist law, but adds that a monolithic critique of liberalism is unsatisfactory and mistaken.

To summarize, Marx and his followers have insisted on setting any analysis of law in the wider context of economic and political relations. This is true for law under capitalism as well as for socialist legality. The *historical* dimension is crucial to neo-Marxist perspectives on law, especially the view that laws protect such capitalist features as private property, investment, and profit-maximization, while *mystifying* the substantive inequalities through an idealization of law as essentially just and impartial. Worsley (1984, 23–33) provides a thoughtful critique and appreciation of the complexity of Marxist theoretical approaches. Worsley credits Marx with revealing in holistic fashion the moving forces of history, thus challenging the more bourgeois, event-filled approaches to human history. Marx also positioned the ordinary people—the great mass of labourers—as a decisive force in this unfolding history. Worsley suggests, however, that the extension of Marx's thought has been troubled by some more doctrinaire approaches, which involve untenable, "Jesuitical casuistries" [deceptive or false arguments] about capitalist and noncapitalist societies (Worsley 1984, 32). He believes that for Marxism to develop fully, it must grapple with the "relative autonomy" of the social systems it seeks to understand and appreciate the pitfalls of imposing a deterministic framework on these complex societies (Worsley 1984, 26).

SUMMARY

Emile Durkheim, the most famous French sociologist of the late nineteenth and early twentieth centuries, was a proponent of the importance of "the social," that is, the importance of social rules and societal needs in explaining social development. Durkheim's approach thus emphasized *collective* forces as influential on individual conduct and beliefs: "Collective life is not born from individual life, but it is, on the contrary, the second which is born of the first" (cited in Milovanovic 1988, 24).

Durkheim formulated the concept of the "social fact," which is external to the will of individuals and which *constrains* individual action. Societies survive through the development of the *collective conscience*, which represents the sentiments and identities of the social group. Earlier forms of society were held together by *mechanical solidarity* in which individuality was minimized, and legal forms were primarily *repressive* and punitive, akin to penal law.

With the advent of industrialized societies, and the more complex division of labour, social solidarity evolved into *organic solidarity*. This new form of solidarity reflected the greater dependence of individuals on others, as folk customs and bonds became loosened. The collective conscience in these industrialized, specialized societies was weakened, but did not vanish altogether. Indeed, according to Durkheim, organic solidarity represented an even stronger force than mechanical solidarity. It reinforced complementary obligations in these complex societies. *Law* became important as a means of ensuring social solidarity. Ostensibly, law took on a more *restitutive character* in industrialized societies.[13]

Durkheim opposed the system of inheritance of wealth and privilege, as this contradicted the ethos of individualism in modern societies. Inheritance constituted a form of inequality in societies that were of a more meritocratic spirit (Milovanovic 1988, 34).

Overall, legal forces were a part of wider structural constraints that permitted societies to function. Legal rules and customs were seen, ideally, to operate in ways that preserved the overall order of these complex societies.

The metaphor of society-as-organism is evident in much of Durkheim's writing. He wrote of the necessity of establishing regulatory mechanisms to coordinate social functioning: "It is necessary that the way in which organs should co-operate . . . at least in the most frequent circumstances, be predetermined" (cited in Lukes 1977, 155). For these newer societies to survive, however, the bonds of organic solidarity needed to be strong; hence the need for a state regulatory body.

This *structural-functionalist* approach remains influential in contemporary sociological analysis and political ideology. Durkheim's approach highlights the importance of social equilibrium and social order. Nevertheless, as outlined by Caputo et al. (1989), more critical, conflict-oriented interpretations of law have become prominent in recent decades.

Max Weber investigated many themes that Durkheim had addressed. Like Durkheim, Weber placed great importance on the influence of law on social life and argued for comparative (cross-cultural) studies of legal and social phenomena. For Weber, the study of legal systems was something that was to be undertaken in a comprehensive empirical and theoretical manner. Weber's substantial contributions have influenced the development of sociological theory generally and the theoretical framework of the sociology of law in particular. Weber's scholarship encompassed sociology, jurisprudence, philosophy, and economics. The development of capitalism, and its relation to Protestantism and law, was one of his primary concerns. He is widely acknowledged as the first writer to seek to establish a comprehensive sociology of law.

Weber contested Marx's premise that the legal order and the social order were largely determined by economic factors. Law was influential in shaping economic development; moreover, a number of factors interacted in a matrix, to produce a particular legal and political order. Käsler (1988, ix) credits Weber with developing intellectual approaches with great scope and flexibility, unlike Durkheim who "set out a systematic position early in his writings and thereafter persistently maintained and elaborated it."

Weber categorized three "ideal types" of *domination*: (1) *traditional domination*, in which obedience is based on custom or habit; (2) *charismatic domination*, an unstable form of domination based on the personal qualities of a particular leader; and (3) *legal domination*, in which there is a widespread belief that laws are legitimate and properly administered in an efficient, impersonal manner by a legal bureaucracy.

Marx offered a thoroughgoing critique of capitalism and its overall tendency to develop systems of law that were, in the final analysis, more favourable to bourgeois interests than to those of the proletariat. Unlike Durkheim or Weber, Marx envisioned that the growing infrastructure of capitalist-worker relations and the looming powers of the modern state contained irreconcilable contradictions. These contradictions would, he thought, usher in a transition from capitalist domination, to socialism, and finally to communism.

It is in the writings of Marx that such topical concepts as hegemony, mystification, and bourgeois legality were developed, even if they were not directly set in the systematic study of legal systems. Marx envisioned an end to formal legality as we know it, as the antagonistic relationships between worker and owner led to a transformation of society. Law was not only associated with direct expressions of coercion and repression; it also served a key ideological function in (mis)representing legal relations as equal for all and as a source of progress and social betterment. Modern movements such as feminist and civil rights groups often incorporate some aspects of Marxist thought, especially the notion that economic stratification and the undue consolidation of wealth among the few are used to exclude or exploit more marginal groups.

STUDY QUESTIONS

❑   Emile Durkheim and Max Weber addressed legal processes as a means of estab-lishing a general theoretical framework of social development. Review the key points of Durkheim's and Weber's approaches to the evolution of law, social soli-darity, and social conflict. Provide at least *three* criticisms each of Durkheim's and Weber's approaches to law. What do you see as the key strengths or applica-tions of the two authors' perspectives on law, social solidarity, and conflict?

❑   Review the key elements of neo-Marxist approaches to law. Where does law orig-inate from? Whose purposes does law serve? Outline the repressive, facilitative, and ideological functions of law under capitalism.

❑   Contrast instrumental Marxism with structural Marxism, including their theoreti-cal approaches to the autonomy (or lack of autonomy) of the state.

❑   What specific reservations or criticisms do you have regarding a Marxist-based sociology of law? To what extent is this approach useful in understanding the nature of legal control?

NOTES

1. Durkheim was deeply involved in the French efforts to resist the Germans during World War I. Lukes (1977, 548) observes that almost one-third of Durkheim's students were killed in the First World War. Durkheim sought to counter German war propa-ganda and completed an analysis of events leading to the declaration of war in 1914 (Lukes 1977, 548–50).

2. The connection between Durkheim the objective scientist of society and Durkheim the man can be seen in Durkheim's childhood experiences in the Jewish community of Alsace-Lorraine. Durkheim admired the cohesiveness of such groups as religious minorities whose communities afforded them "a feeling of relief that is immeasurably bracing and sustains one against the difficulties of life" (Lukes 1977, 40).

3. The concept of the "social fact" was presented as a force that was external to the con-sciences of individuals and had a general constraining effect throughout a group. This emphasis on social factors acting upon people and constituting "beliefs, tendencies, practices of the group taken collectively" (Lukes 1977, 14) helped to establish a struc-turalist framework of social regulation of individuals and the groups they formed.

4. Giddens (1971, 80) notes that the conditions for organic solidarity require an occupational system based on merit not privilege. The forced division of labour would consist of the "unilateral imposition" of rules by one class against the interests of another. Giddens (1971, 80) adds that, for Durkheim, "these conflicts can be obviated only if the division of labour is co-ordinated with the distribution of talents and capacities, and if the higher occupational positions are not monopolised by a privileged class."

5. Weber based much of his argument on passages from Marx and Engels's *Communist Manifesto*. Weber maintained that the bourgeois class had to provide a minimum standard of living for workers to maintain bourgeois domination. The theory of emmiseration ("increasing misery") of workers as capitalism developed "has nowadays been explicitly and universally abandoned in this form as incorrect by all sections of the Social Democratic movement . . . " (Runciman 1980, 257).

6. The ideal type was used to outline ideal forms of law or other social phenomena. Weber was aware that in reality few societies would fit this ideal conceptualization (see Hunt 1980, 101).

7. Weber wrote that "pure charisma recognises no 'legitimacy' other than that conferred by personal power, which must be constantly re-confirmed" (Runciman 1980, 229).

8. "Relations of production" is used to refer to the ways in which human labour and existing economic and technological resources are organized, producing, in the Marxist tradition, "forces of production" that profoundly influence politics and law, and indeed all aspects of human existence (see MacLean 1986, 9).

9. Biographical sketch of Karl Marx is paraphrased from E. Kamenka, ed. (1988) *The Portable Karl Marx*. Harmondsworth: Penguin.

10. Other neo-Marxist approaches include *capital logic* (in which economic forces become more prominent in determining social formations and law) and *class conflict*, epitomized by the work of the late Italian scholar Antonio Gramsci. For Gramsci, the balance of class conflicts meant that the state had to "win the consent" of the governed, using not only repressive measures but also ideological appeals to gain legitimacy; for example, the use of repressive force (police, militia) and ideological persuasion, in which the state mediates labour-capital relations (see Ratner and McMullan 1989).

11. "Surplus value" refers to the value of work beyond that which the worker is paid for (known as *exchange*). A key point of Marxism is that workers are oppressed under capitalist relations: they must sell their labour power for wages, and these wages do not reflect the actual worth of the labour performed.

12. The criminal justice apparatus in the modern state can be viewed from a relative-autonomy perspective. Different levels of the criminal justice system can be distinguished, with conflicts emerging at the macro level of economy and justice, through intermediate levels, and down to the micro level of interstaff and interagency conflicts (see Ratner, McMullan, and Burtch 1987).

13. As noted earlier, Durkheim's premise that law had become more restitutive in character has not been borne out by anthropological studies of law and custom. Earlier societies were not necessarily as punitive (repressive) as Durkheim assumed (Clarke 1976) and modern industrialized societies have developed an extensive system of jails, prisons, and other punitive institutions that contradict the restitutive spirit envisioned by Durkheim (Culhane 1985; Rutherford 1986).

REFERENCES

Beirne, P., and R. Quinney, eds. (1982) *Marxism and Law*. New York: John Wiley & Sons.

Beirne, P., and R. Sharlet (1980) *Pashukanis: Selected Writings on Marxism and Law*. London: Academic Press.

——— (1982) "Pashukanis and Socialist Legality." In *Marxism and Law*, edited by P. Beirne and R. Quinney, 307–27. New York: John Wiley & Sons.

Benn, T. (1980) *Arguments for Socialism*. Harmondsworth: Penguin.

Binnie, S. (1988) "Some Reflections on the 'New' Legal History in Relation to Weber's Sociology of Law." In *Canadian Perspectives on Law and Society: Issues in Legal History*, edited by W. Pue and B. Wright, 29–42. Ottawa: Carleton University Press.

Cain, M., and A. Hunt, eds. (1979) *Marx and Engels on Law*. London: Academic Press.

Caputo, T., M. Kennedy, C. Reasons, and A. Brannigan, eds. (1989) *Law and Society: A Critical Perspective*. Toronto: Harcourt Brace Jovanovich.

Carnoy, M. (1984) *The State and Political Theory*. New Jersey: Princeton University Press.

Chambliss, W. (1986) "On Lawmaking." In *The Social Basis of Law*, edited by S. Brickey and E. Comack, 27–51. Toronto: Garamond Press.

Clarke, M. (1976) "Durkheim's Sociology of Law." *British Journal of Law and Society* 3 (2): 239–55.

Collins, H. (1987) *Marxism and Law*. Oxford: Oxford University Press.

Cotterrell, R. (1984) *The Sociology of Law: An Introduction*. London: Butterworths.

Culhane, C. (1985) *Still Barred From Prison: Social Injustice in Canada*. Montreal: Black Rose Books.

Durkheim, E. (1966) *The Division of Labour in Society*. Translated by G. Simpson. Toronto: Collier-Macmillan.

Fine, B. (1984) *Democracy and the Rule of Law: Liberal Ideals and Marxist Critiques*. London: Pluto Press.

Giddens, A. (1971) *Capitalism and Modern Social Theory: An Analysis of the Writings of Marx, Durkheim, and Weber*. Cambridge: Cambridge University Press.

Gough, I. (1979) *The Political Economy of the Welfare State*. London: Macmillan.

Hagan, J. (1985) *Modern Criminology: Crime, Criminal Behavior, and Its Control*. New York: McGraw-Hill.

Horton, J. (1966) "Order and Conflict Theories of Society as Competing Ideologies." *American Journal of Sociology* 71: 701–13.

Hunt, A. (1980) *The Sociological Movement in Law*. London: Macmillan.

Kamenka, E., ed. (1988) *The Portable Karl Marx*. Harmondsworth: Penguin.

Karenga, M.R. (1981). "The Problematic Aspects of Pluralism: Ideological and Political Dimensions." In *Pluralism, Racism and Public Policy: The Search for Equality*, edited by E. Clausen and J. Bermingham, 223–46. Boston: G.K. Hall.

Käsler, D. (1988) *Max Weber: An Introduction to His Life and Work*. London: Polity Press.

Knuttila, M. (1987) *State Theories: From Liberalism to the Challenge of Feminism*. Toronto: Garamond Press.

Kronman, A. (1983) *Max Weber*. London: E. Arnold.

Lachmann, L. (1970) *The Legacy of Max Weber*. London: Heinemann.

Lowman, J., and R. Menzies (1986) "Out of the Fiscal Shadow: Carceral Trends in Canada and the United States." *Crime and Social Justice* 26: 95–115.

Lukes, S. (1977). *Emile Durkheim: His Life and Work: A Historical Study*. Harmondsworth: Penguin.

MacLean, B. (1986) "Some Limitations of Traditional Inquiry." In *The Political Economy of Crime: Readings for a Critical Criminology*, edited by B. MacLean, 1–20. Toronto: Prentice-Hall.

Marx, K., and F. Engels (1979) *The Communist Manifesto*. Harmondsworth: Penguin.

Milovanovic, D. (1988) *A Primer in the Sociology of Law*. New York: Harrow and Heston.

Moyers, B. (1989) "Northrop Frye: Canadian Literary Critic." In *A World of Ideas*, edited by B. Flowers, 494–505. New York: Doubleday.

Parkin, F. (1982) *Max Weber*. London: Tavistock.

Pearce, F. (1989) *The Radical Durkheim*. London: Unwin Hyman.

Ratner, R., and J. McMullan (1989) "State Intervention and the Control of Labour in British Columbia: A Capital-Logic Approach." In *Law and Society: A Critical Perspective*, edited by T. Caputo, M. Kennedy, C. Reasons, and A. Brannigan, 232–49. Toronto: Harcourt Brace Jovanovich.

Ratner, R., J. McMullan, and B. Burtch (1987) "The Relative Autonomy of the State and Criminal Justice." In *State Control: Criminal Justice Politics in Canada*, edited by R. Ratner and J. McMullan, 85–125. Vancouver: University of British Columbia Press.

Runciman, W., ed. (1980) *Weber: Selections in Translation*. Translated by E. Matthews. Cambridge: Cambridge University Press.

Rutherford, A. (1986) *Prisons and the Process of Justice*. New York: Oxford University Press.

Taylor, I., P. Walton, and J. Young (1973) *The New Criminology: For a Social Theory of Deviance*. London: Routledge and Kegan Paul.

Tucker, E., ed. (1972) *The Marx-Engels Reader*. New York: W.W. Norton.

Wood, A. (1980). "The Marxian Critique of Justice." In *Marx, Justice, and History*, edited by M. Cohen, T. Nagel, and T. Scanlon, 3–41. Princeton: Princeton University Press.

Woodcock, G. (1990) "Gary Geddes: Political Poet." *The Canadian Forum* 69 (792): 5–9.

Worsley, P. (1984) *The Three Worlds: Culture and World Development*. London: Weidenfeld and Nicolson.

CHAPTER THREE

The Historical Foundations of Law

INTRODUCTION

Understanding the complexities of modern legal processes is a daunting task, and many researchers and teachers continue to contribute to this expanding field of scholarship. But even if it were possible to fully evaluate the workings of modern legal processes—lawmaking, law enforcement, and social change— our understanding of law would be very limited if we did not understand the *origins* of law.

This chapter presents an overview of how law emerges as an institution and whose interests it may have served over time. We will review several works on Canadian labour history as well as certain historical bases for criminal legislation affecting women (laws concerning prostitution, rape, and sexual assault). This chapter also provides historical backdrops to Native land claims and other issues considering aboriginal peoples. To begin with, we will consider the origins of criminal law in England. This discussion assesses key works by Hay (1975) and Beattie (1986). As noted above, we will also outline the historical treatment of prostitutes in Canada as an example of the conflicting values over legal regulation and crime control.

HAY: "PROPERTY, AUTHORITY, AND THE CRIMINAL LAW"

Douglas Hay has written an extensive treatment of the origins of English criminal law and its reliance on a complex repertoire of terror, majesty, and mercy in advancing the interests of a propertied class and a government bent on social order. Hay (1975, 17) begins with a reference to the popular appeal of the death sentence, a severe sanction that was, in Hay's words, "cherished" by eighteenth century rulers in England. Criminal law was thus based on *terror*, in the form of punishments meted out to the "labouring poor." Hay emphasizes that the exercise of law was closely associated with the protection of private property. He cites John Locke's assertion that "government has no other end but the preservation of property" (Hay 1975, 18). This *economic* foundation of criminal law contrasted sharply with the dominant ideology that linked crime with *moral degeneracy* (Hay 1975, 20). The symbolic apparatus of terror and the proliferation of offences that might be sanctioned by death did not result in a great increase in actual executions of criminals (Hay 1975, 22). There were difficulties in implementing this "bloody code." These difficulties included the refusal of juries to convict their peers, and the reluctance of some people to prosecute others, knowing the convicts might face the death penalty.

Hay states that during this period, a number of reforms were made to the English criminal law, partly along the classical lines recommended by the eighteenth century scholar Cesare Beccaria. "Real progress," however, did not occur until the 1820s and 1830s (Hay 1975, 24). Against the obdurate working-class offenders, the diminishing power of terror had to be refashioned into "a much more effective instrument of terror" (Hay 1975, 25). Hay thus interprets law as a dynamic force in which the repressive elements of the legal order are complemented by more sophisticated control measures.[1] In this conception of law, we see the play of symbolism and ideology complementing the state-approved executions. Hay outlines three aspects of English legal ideology: majesty, justice, and mercy.

Majesty refers to the development of criminal law as a "formidable spectacle" (Hay 1975, 27) in the quarter sessions (every three months) and the assizes (twice a year). The costumes and demeanour of the judges and the pomp of the ceremonies created a theatrical aspect in which "the powers of light and darkness" (Hay 1975, 27) were drawn out and ritualized for the greatest impact on the throng. The need for social order, presented as desirable, natural, and progressive, was accompanied by the need for vengeance against the wretched offenders, who were not uncommonly portrayed as a kind of contagion (Hay 1975, 28–29). In this theatre, the judge played the roles of priest, deity, and, sometimes, the mere mortal (see the Chelmsford example from 1754 in Hay 1975, 29). Law became a kind of "secular sermon"—mysterious and imbued with the gravity of divine as well as earthly punishments and justice. The occasional theatres of the quarter sessions and the assizes were assisted by exemplary punishments, as meted out by the special commissions (Hay 1975, 31). These "rituals of justice" were presented as healing processes, which restored moral balance in eighteenth century English society.

Justice, the second aspect of English legal ideology, is established through the veneration of the rule of law. The adherence to "strict procedural rules" and the formalities of assessing cases were facets of a legal structure that claimed to be rooted in the principle of *equality before the law* (Hay 1975, 32–34); the gallows became, symbolically, a great leveller. Hay argues that the law was applied unevenly: some people were convicted on flimsy evidence, while others escaped punishment through legal loopholes. Nevertheless, the doctrine of legal equality and a *universal morality* obscured the fact that the protection of property was the very bedrock of the criminal law: "The trick was to extend the communal sanction to a criminal law that was nine-tenths concerned with upholding a radical division of property" (Hay 1975, 35).

Hay notes that the third aspect—*prerogative of mercy*—was present throughout the administrative structure of eighteenth century England (Hay 1975, 40). Indeed, the discretionary elements of (1) the pardon and (2) the lenient disposition attracted criticism and praise. Hay outlines a legal system that is checked by fear and compassion and in which the hope of mercy—and the granting of merciful dispositions—served in "justifying the legal order" (Hay 1975, 43).

Pleadings of the day placed great emphasis on the *respectability* of the accused, and his or her witnesses and supporters, not simply on their *social class*. Nonetheless, Hay (1975, 45) notes that pardons were often used to favour the more privileged sections of English society, and, in turn, patronage and favours were returned (Hay 1975, 45–48). As Hay notes, the criminal law again fronted its selective, or biased, operations on the principle of its fairness and neutrality:

> [The law] allowed the rulers of England to make the courts a selective instrument
> of class justice, yet simultaneously to proclaim the law's incorruptible impartiali-
> ty, and absolute determinacy. It allowed the class that passed one of the bloodiest
> penal codes in Europe to congratulate itself on its humanity (Hay 1975, 48–49).

At the conclusion of his essay, Hay notes that the apparent *benevolence* of the ruling class, as expressed through law, was not simply altruistic: "It contained within it the ever-present threat of malice" (Hay 1975, 62). The *repressive* powers of the state, then, were aided and leavened by the appeal to its merciful and egalitarian promises, forces that served in general to consolidate the powers of the ruling class.

Hay's interpretation of the nature and implications of criminal law in eighteenth century England has generated criticism. Langbien (1983, 96) contends that Hay's conclusion of a "ruling-class conspiracy" against the working class is "fundamentally mistaken." Langbien (1983, 99) indicates that Hay was preoccupied with larger-scale disturbances such as "food riots" and work-related protests, actions which fit the class-conflict explanation in eighteenth century England. Langbien counters, however, that if criminal behaviour as a whole is examined, one will find far more intra-class offences. Most of the offences studied by Langbien—that is, offences prosecuted at four sessions of the Old Bailey Court, between 1754 and 1756—involved crimes against the person (homicide, assault), theft, burglary, forgery, and the like. He concludes that there is little sense of "romantic crimes"—those committed by the oppressed against the powerful; many crime victims were themselves poor[2] (Langbien 1983, 100).

Langbien (1983) also criticizes Hay's assumption that the death penalty was used to a greater extent in eighteenth century England. Langbien (1983, 96) reports that the death penalty was being used less often for convicted felons. He notes that prosecution of criminals was not largely the prerogative of wealthier persons. In fact, prosecutorial discretion was limited in many ways, including the automatic investigation of suspicious deaths by the coroner's system. In addition, "potential prosecutors" sometimes decided not to prosecute but rather to forgive the offender or simply forgo prosecution for reasons of time and expense. Langbien (1983, 103) therefore challenges the premise that wealthier victims could substantively "manipulate" prosecutorial power in their private interests. Langbien (1983, 104) also mentions the practice in which juries devalued the estimated worth of stolen goods or down-played the seriousness of offences. Building on these and other practices, Langbien (1983, 105) takes strong exception to theories that use available documents to construct an argument for a ruling-class, elitist interpretation of English criminal law in this period:

> I concede, although the actual evidence for it is thin, that elite victims must have been treated with greater courtesy...What I resist is the idea that such practices justify treating the prosecutorial system as having been constructed for the purpose of furthering the class interests of the elite ...The whole of the criminal justice system, especially the prosecutorial system, was primarily designed to protect the people, overwhelmingly non-elite, who suffered from crime.

BEATTIE: *CRIME AND THE COURTS IN ENGLAND, 1660–1800*

Beattie (1986) provides a magnificent account of changes in the application of criminal law in his award-winning book, *Crime and the Courts in England, 1660–1800*. The book is too exhaustive in scope to review in detail. We can, however, summarize Beattie's account to trace some key transformations in the nature of judicial administration and the corresponding institutions concerned with crime and its punishment.

Beattie (1986, 619) traces a shift from the more severe, and quite limited, range of punishments in 1660 (branding, public flogging, or hanging convicted offenders) to the creation of "secondary punishments," including imprisonment or transportation (sending the convicts to penal colonies, such as Australia). Beattie (1986, 619) acknowledges the spirit of humanism that accompanied this transformation of punishments; however, he concludes that their creation "derived as much from a concern for effectiveness in penal matters as for fairness and humanity."

Beattie does not adopt an explicitly Marxist approach in his study of crime and the courts. Nevertheless, he builds his study in conjunction with a number of social-historical studies of English law and punishments. Beattie's assessment of these earlier studies, together with his study of court records in Surrey and Sussex, underscores the importance of class factors in establishing and reforming particular laws. Beattie (1986, 621–22) concludes that criminal law in eighteenth century England served to preserve "the established social and economic and political arrangements of the society" and also to implement certain changes sought by more powerful groups. The influence of the "propertied elite" was maintained by the broadened range of discretionary charges and punishments embedded into criminal law as it evolved (Beattie 1986, 621–22).

Beattie does not restrict his analysis to an instrumentalist reading of elite interests and state powers. Acknowledging the symbolic and material powers served by the edifice of criminal law, Beattie (1986, 622) argues that the ideological power of law had to attract a considerable degree of public approval:

> If the criminal law had served only the interests of the propertied classes it would hardly have attracted the widespread approval that was clearly bestowed upon it ... However constrained in practice access to the courts was for the working population, the law appears to have been widely accepted in society as a means of settling disputes and ameliorating public grievances.

Beattie (1986, 624) dramatizes the difficulty in challenging the use of capital punishment, particularly throughout the seventeenth century; there was little organized ferment against the administration of criminal law. Beattie (1986, 623) found that there were few signs of opposition to such principles as hanging during the century or more following the Restoration. The need for new measures—well beyond the brutal spectacles epitomized by public hangings and mutilations—is traced to the burgeoning developments in the mercantile and commercial spheres of the English economy. New concerns were voiced, calling for the establishment of a disciplinary network of reformatories and workhouses. Again, Beattie (1986, 624–25) interprets this mobilization of concern not as mere philanthropy, but as an imperative for the good of the economy and for those who benefited inordinately from it. Beattie (1986, 624–25) writes that the growth in social concern and the call for new institutions "were all related concerns to the propertied classes of London." He notes that new forms of coercion were necessary to establish sufficient discipline and levels of health for the labouring classes.[3]

CRIMINAL LAW, PROSTITUTION, AND MORAL REFORM

McLaren (1988) examines the origins of early twentieth century laws governing prostitution in Canada, especially streetwalking and keeping a bawdy-house. Focusing on the period between 1900 and 1920, McLaren notes the development of organized reform movements, which espoused a *social gospel* rooted in Protestant evangelism. Seeking the eradication of vice and immorality, such groups as the Women's Christian Temperance Union and the Young Women's Christian Association sought to improve the "moral health and harmony" of Canada, using rescue work, public education, and legal reform (McLaren 1988, 329–30). These groups viewed prostitution in moral terms, with very little attention to the economic forces that might impel women to prostitution. Prostitutes and those thought to be in danger of becoming prostitutes were liable to a strict regimen of labour, frugality, and "moral education" (McLaren 1988, 330). Prostitutes brought before nineteenth century magistrates were often sentenced to jail—and in cases thought to be incorrigible, for quite lengthy terms (McLaren 1988, 334).

While law is credited with a dynamic character, adopting new procedures and principles to deal with changing social conditions, early twentieth century law concerning prostitution was quite contradictory. For example, prostitutes were routinely prosecuted, while their customers were initially immune from prosecution. The double standard re-emerged when prostitutes later faced possible charges of being inmates in a bawdy-house (which was a more serious, indictable offence), while clients "found in" bawdy-houses were liable only to a summary conviction charge (McLaren 1988, 330–31).

Another contradiction was evident in the variety of magistrates' attitudes and decisions concerning prostitution. McLaren (1988, 336–47) identifies three types of magisterial responses to prostitution: toleration, traditionalism, and activism. *Tolerance* was perhaps most evident in frontier areas of Canada. In Fort William, Ontario, Magistrate William Palling suggested in 1880 that prostitutes provided necessary, or understandable, sexual services to transient men; in addition, prostitutes may have served to help more reputable women avoid being accosted by these "rough men" (McLaren 1988, 337).

Magistrates who took a more *traditional* outlook did not espouse complete tolerance of prostitution. Nor were they heavily swayed by the efforts of more zealous reformers to eradicate prostitution. Prostitution was generally seen as inevitable and as a reflection of working-class practices and values that could not be easily transformed. Management of prostitution, especially its more extreme forms of exploitation, was thus sought.

The third kind of response to prostitution took the form of *activism* on the part of women magistrates who sought to attain political, social, and economic rights for women. These magistrates were also sensitive to biases in law enforcement that allowed men who preyed on, or otherwise exploited, girls and women to escape prosecution. When such men were prosecuted, it was not unusual for the case to be dismissed altogether or the man to be given a lenient disposition (McLaren 1988, 344–45). These reform-oriented magistrates, among them Judge Emily Murphy of Edmonton, were also critical of the state's financial interest in prostitution, which was most transparent in the fining of prostitutes and the lack of services to assist in rehabilitating them.

McLaren (1988, 347) concludes that despite the differences concerning the seriousness of prostitution as a social problem and the extent to which the law ought to (or could) remedy the problem, there was a widely-shared belief among the magistrates that prostitution would prevail, partly due to the strong sexual drives of men and what was seen by some as "the inherent looseness of working-class women." Criminal law was used to contain some aspects of prostitution, often without enquiring into the social and economic forces influencing prostitutes. McLaren notes that instead of providing a deep influence on magisterial practices, the social reform movements were often resisted, illustrated by the judicial practice of giving more lenient sentences for prostitutes over time.

Lowman (1989, 32–37) sees a legacy of entrenched contradictions in Canadian efforts to regulate or prohibit prostitution. At various times, police have simply tolerated forms of brothel prostitution, while at other times—in Vancouver from 1903 to 1917, for example—police have shut down brothel operations. Lowman cites the example of the 1976 closure of the Penthouse Cabaret in Vancouver, which resulted in the displacement of prostitution onto the street (Lowman 1989, 32). One of the ironies that emerges from this attempt to eliminate prostitution is that it forces prostitutes out of the closed quarters of brothels into the more public (and more dangerous) form of street solicitation. Lowman (1989, 39) observes that street prostitutes are especially vulnerable to violence. He refers to the deaths of over 20 prostitutes in the Vancouver area over a three-year period in the late 1980s, and the killings of nearly 50 prostitutes in the vicinity of Seattle. The latter killings have been linked with the so-called "Green River Killer" (Lowman 1989, 39).

The visibility of street prostitution has generated calls to abolish prostitution, or at least remove it from residential neighbourhoods. Lowman (1986, 207–8) notes that opposition to street prostitution by neighbourhood groups is not confined to concerns over noise and public safety; it also involves a concern over the "blight" (Lowman 1986, 207) associated with prostitution, and concerns over further deterioration of the neighbourhood. The point remains that attempts to legislate prostitution out of existence have been unsuccessful in Canada. Moreover, the legacy has been that such laws discriminate against women who work as prostitutes, and these laws tend to deflect attention away from the *structural* factors (such as sexual socialization and unemployment) that underlie prostitution (Lowman 1987, 110–11; Lowman 1991, 130).

CANADIAN RAPE LAW: WOMEN AS PROPERTY, WOMEN AS PERSONS

The crime of rape has traditionally been ignored or downplayed as a part of legal history (Backhouse 1983, 200). Despite a growing number of studies it has still not attracted considerable attention as a part of research on criminal law in Canada or the United Kingdom (Clark and Lewis 1977; Smart 1976, 93).

Backhouse (1983) reviewed the development of rape legislation and rape trials in nineteenth century Canada. She noted that as rape law evolved in Canada, it gradually departed from the influential legislative model adopted from England. In 1869, the Canadian Parliament passed the Canadian Counterpart Act, which retained the death penalty for rape even after England had abolished it. The Canadian legislation was considered more severe than English law and practice of the day, especially the provision for capital punishment for those found guilty of statutory rape of a girl under ten years old. Backhouse (1983, 207–8) adds that this relatively harsh legislation had a less stringent requirement of proof for rape cases; specifically, even slight degrees of vaginal penetration would suffice for conviction. Over time, the Canadian Parliament modified some of the harsher elements of the law, replacing the death penalty with life imprisonment (Backhouse 1983, 208). Backhouse's research is valuable not only in pointing out the different ways in which countries frame such criminal laws but also the ways in which women came to be regarded under legal ideologies of the time. Backhouse interprets changes in nineteenth century rape legislation as a reflection of society's changing views of women, as property and as persons. Women were increasingly acknowledged to possess their own integrity. This was the beginning of a break from the ideology of women as property. The latter view was described by Backhouse:

> Historically, the view was that men held property rights in women and that the value of this property was diminished if the woman had sexual relations with someone other than her husband. Ownership implied exclusivity, and sole control over the woman's potential for childbearing (Backhouse 1983, 208).

Over time, it became important for defence counsel in a rape trial to establish that the woman had "resisted" the assault. Women who could not meet this requirement were often seen as contributing to the rape itself. Backhouse (1983, 219) draws a portrait of the kind of woman who might properly resist such attacks. The "ideal" victim would be respectable and domesticated, choosing to "remain safely in the home, surrounded by family responsibilities," not exposing herself to the threat of sexual attack; when confronted she would resist, succumbing only because of the rapist's sheer "physical force."

Clark and Lewis (1977) use a historical framework to assess their research on rape in Metropolitan Toronto in 1970. The authors present a feminist interpretation of how women became viewed as property—of their fathers or husbands—within a general legal framework that was based on the dual notions of (1) the importance of private ownership of property and (2) the natural superiority of men, including their rightful mastery of women (Clark and Lewis 1977, 112). Rape law reflected this historical valuation of women as property. Not all women were treated equally under the law. For some women, deviation from the expected female role left them without effective legal recourse. These "open-territory victims" of rape were seen as devalued in their sexual and reproductive worth and were described variously as promiscuous, welfare-dependent, divorced, and so forth (Clark and Lewis 1977, 123–24). Box (1983, 157–59) remarks on the substantial influence of media accounts of rape—characterizing women as deserving victims, for example—and also comments on the criminal justice system's contributions to distinguishing between "legitimate" and "illegitimate" victims of rape. The rationalizations of the rapist are thus echoed and supported by the mass media and the courts.

Clark and Lewis's (1977) research serves to underscore a critical interpretation of sexual politics, including the pervasiveness of coerced, rather than freely chosen, sexuality. Clark and Lewis's study, together with other commentaries on rape and criminal law, signals a movement away from the perception of rape as an isolated criminal act or as psychological aberration and toward the idea that rape is situated in a social context.[4] This movement pressured reform, and led to the enactment of sexual assault legislation in Canada.

Canadian legislation dealing with the sexual offences of rape, attempted rape, and indecent assault was replaced in 1983 by legislation dealing with various kinds of sexual assault. The movement to sexual assault legislation has attracted some criticism from researchers concerned about the limits of such legal reforms. Gunn and Minch (1986) interviewed victims of sexual assault in Manitoba and followed the process of legal investigations of alleged sexual assaults. The authors found that only a tenth of the original charges led to conviction; the vast majority (approximately 70 percent) of the charges were "filtered out" of the legal system. Gunn and Minch (1986, 133) concluded that women bringing forward allegations of sexual assault face "social and structural" opposition. The legal system, like the social system in general, manifests considerable scepticism and explaining-away of sexual assaults. Even when a conviction was registered, average sentences were only 3.2 years—this for an offence that has a maximum penalty of life imprisonment. The authors added that despite the removal of a spousal immunity approach, spouses convicted of sexual assault tended to receive even more lenient sentences—for example, six months' imprisonment and one year's probation in a 1983 case and three months' imprisonment for a husband convicted in 1987 (Gunn and Minch 1986, 98, 118–19).

This research illustrates the gulf between legal reforms and actual protections for women and underscores the myriad reasons why many victims are discouraged from proceeding with sexual assault charges. Various myths about sexual assault are reinforced by the legal system and the media—for example, that some assaults are provoked, or victim-precipitated, others can be attributed to the victim's conduct or appearance (blaming the victim), or the lack of palpable injuries on the victim as a defence argument that no harm was done

(Gunn and Minch 1986, 17–18). The authors pointed out that there is considerable inertia in moving the legal system and changing public attitudes so as to facilitate successful prosecutions and appropriate sentencing for persons convicted of sexual assault.

Others have also questioned the extent to which the new sexual assault legislation was a victory for Canadian women. Hinch (1988) found that police in Halifax, Nova Scotia might be reluctant to recommend charges for "open territory" victims—women who might be exposed to "potential character assassination" in court if the defence was allowed to explore the victim's previous sexual history (Hinch 1988, 291). Hinch views the law as contradictory in this respect, as it leaves some room for admission of reputational evidence about the complainant. Hinch (1988, 284–85) also found that in some incidents, "sexual assault" was defined in such a way as to hinder potential prosecutions. Such narrow interpretations and the retention of the "honest but mistaken belief" defence (Hinch 1988, 292) underscore some tangible limitations to a legal reform that was widely hailed as a victory for women.

LABOUR LEGISLATION IN CANADA: CRITICAL-HISTORICAL STUDIES

Conflicts over legislation are also evident in the history of labour law. Caputo and his associates (1989) provide an overview of labour-related laws, together with critical studies of labour law at various points in this century. They begin with two accounts of contemporary Luddism[5] to highlight the topic of worker alienation.

Many critical scholars agree that law has played a significant role in the structural conflicts between worker and management. Since World War II, North American labour relations have been described as "business unionism," in which the more revolutionary elements of the labour movement have been discarded, and a more co-operative style of negotiating established. Caputo et al. (1989, 208) indicate that this is a complex process. The law takes on a *repressive* character when it restricts such activities as union formation, picketing, and so on. Most scholars are well aware of the coercive aspects of provincial and federal labour law from earlier in this century (Morton 1980); however, they also draw our attention to ways in which such laws and regulatory agencies seek to soften violence and dissent among the work force. At the same time, labour law provides a level of protection and benefits for many workers. This balancing of interests is not interpreted as a justification of the neutrality associated with liberal-pluralist ideals of law and the state. Rather, critical theorists see this as a dialectical model of law that emphasizes the role of law in resolving specific contradictions in specific situations, leaving the overall economic structure intact (Chambliss 1986).

Caputo et al. (1989, 210) trace the use of law in labour conflict to Industrial England and the efforts by merchants to establish themselves in the production process, as feudalism was being eclipsed and eventually replaced by capitalism. The terrible conditions of eighteenth and nineteenth century industrial capitalism in England are outlined, along with the harsh, disciplinary nature of work in the factories (Caputo et al. 1989, 211). This Dickensian motif of brutality was alleviated over time, as protections for workers became embedded in law—limitations on hours of work and on the use of child labour as well as some safety provisions—despite resistance from such groups as the National Founders Association (Caputo et al. 1989, 211).

Court decisions in the United States and Canada in the early twentieth century were largely favourable to capitalist interests in restricting labour organization and promoting the ideology of free trade and capital accumulation. Thus, it is argued that capitalism and its corresponding labour laws reflected struggles over work and a process of legal development that, in the long run, facilitated capital accumulation and was largely contrary to a socialist approach to control over the work process.

Huxley (1989) provides a detailed account of the nature of collective bargaining, focusing on Canadian labour relations and legal decisions. Huxley's essay is a reprint of an article published a decade earlier. Nevertheless, Huxley's theoretical approach is useful in the general context of the nature of law in mediating social conflicts. He notes that the pattern of strikes in Canada is distinctive, implying that we should be careful about generalizing from one nation to another, or from a specific period of time to another. This caveat is significant if we are to avoid broadbrush generalizations that ignore significant differences in state and law between countries or within smaller jurisdictions (e.g., provinces, states, and the like). The main impact of Canadian labour legislation, according to Huxley, has been (1) to significantly restrict the implementation of the "strike weapon" and (2) to legitimate the ideology of the involvement of the state in resolving or controlling labour conflicts (Huxley 1989, 218).

One problem confronting workers and owners alike has been the disruptive effect of work stoppages due to strikes. Huxley argues against a "strictly economistic" interpretation of these prolonged strikes. Thus, other (noneconomic) factors need to be understood, including the power of ideas and of political organization in the contest between workers and owners (Huxley 1989, 219–20). This labour contest has resulted in the successful institutionalization of industrial conflict, that is, in securing the state's three functions of favouring management's capital accumulation, coercing labour's compliance (such as through back-to-work legislation), and legitimating government involvement in labour issues (Huxley 1989, 220). Notwithstanding legal protections for workers, Canadian labour legislation appears to have promoted lengthy strikes by banning strikes during the life of a collective agreement and by deferring specific negotiations or demands until after the expiration of an existing agreement. Structurally, then, law and management tactics are presented as encouraging strikes in a manner that facilitates capitalist accumulation.

A study by Ratner and McMullan (1989) complements Huxley's (1989) article. Ratner and McMullan focus on the evolution of labour conflicts and legislation in British Columbia, a province with a history of high levels of capital-labour conflict. The authors take a dynamic approach to labour conflict, arguing that the turn-of-the-century policies of state coercion and repression have largely become replaced by a more benign policy of *stabilization* of capital-labour conflicts. Once again, this objective of stabilization does not imply that it is in everyone's interest to acquiesce to labour law procedures.

For Ratner and McMullan (1989), capital-logic theory is rooted in a Marxist approach to class conflict and capital accumulation. The capital-logic approach is distinct from some neo-Marxist approaches that stress *economic factors* (also known as "economism") or *ideological factors* as pivotal in state-labour relations. The logic of capital is "predominant" in capital-logic theory. Ratner, McMullan, and Burtch (1987, 99) note that in capital-logic theory, the "state and law function to secure the conditions for capital accumulation according to the developing 'logic' of capitalist economic relations," and that the balance of class forces is partly influential for state policies. While the ideological power of law is important in distorting or mystifying the exploitative nature of the work process (Ratner, McMullan, and Burtch 1987, 234), the specific forms of *class struggles* and the *appropriation of surplus value* are decisive in creating economic relations and the corresponding form of the state, including its legal apparatus.

Ratner and McMullan's (1989, 237–45) discussion of industrial strikes and state intervention uses specific examples of B.C. labour conflicts as a "test" for the capital-logic theory. The Nanaimo coal strike (1912–1914) is depicted as the most bitter and prolonged strike in B.C. labour history. The authors see this strike as typical of B.C. labour relations prior to 1930, pointing to the extremely dependent nature of the B.C. economy on external markets, the need to establish safeguards for union organization and workers' safety, and the limited repertoire of the state, which could either refuse to become involved in the labour-capital conflict, or use the *coercive* powers of the court, police, and militia against the strikers. The authors conclude that this situation led to division and disorganization among B.C. workers.

Another example—the Blubber Bay lumberworkers' strikes of 1937 and 1938—reflects the protracted and bitter conflicts within the forestry sector. The exacerbation of "already poor health and safety conditions" (Ratner and

McMullan 1989, 240) led to growing antagonism among workers and managers alike. The affiliation of Blubber Bay workers with the International Woodworkers of America (IWA) was also a point of contention during the strikes. In 1937, the province passed the Industrial Conciliation and Arbitration (ICA) Act, which recognized the right of labour to organize and promoted the use of conciliation as a means of resolving labour conflicts. As Ratner and McMullan (1989, 240) note, the state was now acting in a coercive and adjudicative role.

The third example—the B.C. lumberworkers' strikes of 1946 and 1947—is set in the context of the Industrial Conciliation and Arbitration Act of 1947 (Ratner and McMullan 1989, 243–45). While gaining protections for labour against outlawing union shops and checkoff clauses (i.e., membership in the union became compulsory, not optional), the ICA Act meant that unions could be sued, since unions were now accorded legal status. Ratner and McMullan (1989, 244) argue that this Act helped to consolidate the regulatory powers of the B.C. government, and blunted the radical character associated with communist activity within the union movement. Indeed, Morton (1980, 210) notes that by 1950, the Communist influence once prominent within Canadian labour politics had given way, leaving a less radical union stance.

As Ratner and McMullen point out, the legislation could be interpreted as an advance for labour or as a new, more sophisticated means of containing labour. The authors place great emphasis on the latter interpretation (containment). Ratner and McMullan (1989, 247) conclude, however, that there was an increasing *centralization* of state, labour, and capital in the late 1940s. The locus of resolution of capital-labour conflict shifted from the workplace to the courts where the "class bias" of the state was obscured, and the legitimacy of state intervention was entrenched in provincial labour law. Class bias has been identified in other legislative initiatives, including a structural-Marxist interpretation of the development of anti-combines legislation in Canada. Smandych (1985) discounts liberal-pluralist interpretations of this legislation as well as the rather crude instrumentalist approaches. He points to differences *within* the capitalist class over the need for regulation of unfair practices, and the significance of "a threatening confrontation" that is likely between capitalists and workers.

Keep in mind that there have been challenges to these critical outlooks on historical legal measures. For example, critics charge that Marxist-based explanations of labour relations fail to account for relatively high levels of satisfaction reported by citizens in contemporary Western societies. It is best to keep a critical eye on the assumption that labour relations invariably constitute an "unrelenting guerilla war" (Caputo et al. 1989, 207) in the workplace. Clearly, there are elements of subversion and resistance in worker-employer relations but there are alternative approaches as well that stress harmony in the work force in such a way that employees become willing participants in the workplace, even accepting layoffs and firings without extensive protests.

LAW, ECONOMY, AND RACIAL ISSUES

The dynamic quality of law pertaining to the economy is also evident in societies subjected to colonization. Prior to European contact, many societies had not implemented the formal economic systems associated with capitalism. Moreover, relying more on custom than on Western-style use of due process and rule of law, these societies were faced with overwhelming pressures to suit their dispute-resolution processes to the laws of colonial regimes. This section provides a consideration of recent work on economic and legal transformations in some areas of Africa, and foreshadows more contemporary discussion of legal conflicts and racial discrimination brought forward in Chapter Six.

Kennedy (1989) raises several important questions about the nature of law in the context of colonial regimes. Native labour needed to be harnessed in order to exploit the vast natural resources of sub-Saharan Africa. This process of enlisting, or even conscripting, indigenous labour was facilitated by diverse systems of colonial administration (see Kennedy 1989, 30). As with other scholars exploring historical developments on a wide scale, Kennedy's (1989) analysis appreciates the diversity of state structures, rather than oversimplifying the question of particular means of establishing state control and legal orders. Kennedy (1989, 30) adds that one major step in the colonizing process was the creation of *reserves*. These reserves, designated for indigenous Africans, required the movement of Africans away from lands now needed by the colonizers for economic reasons.

Kennedy's essay pays particular attention to the creation of laws that forced Africans to become wage labourers and thus altered their livelihood from subsistence to the more surplus- and profit-oriented requirements of capitalism. Kennedy thus seeks to apply historical and economic factors in analyzing the introduction of *formal, legal systems* to societies that had been primarily based on custom. Social changes are also significant in modifying forms of law and colonial administration. Kennedy (1989, 30) shows that the need for these laws emerged with the depopulation of many African territories. The practice of slavery in the Americas and Europe required the forced emigration of Africans, resulting in a labour shortage in Africa. The laws of the day thus reinforced the rights of property owners and reflected the economic needs of the colonial era: conquest, increased production of commodities, and cheap labour.

The international dimension also emerges in Kennedy's (1989, 31) discussion of rivalry between nation-states. Colonial regimes were required to exploit natural resources in colonized lands. This requirement became even more important in the face of three decades of economic depression in Europe in the late nineteenth century. The costs of war among competing nations were temporarily averted through a form of "détente" (Kennedy 1989, 31–32), with African territories partitioned by agreement of the colonizing nations themselves—Portugal, Belgium, Germany, and France.

Kennedy's approach is valuable, inasmuch as he develops an international framework for analyzing the origins of a variety of laws that reshaped social and economic life throughout the sub-Sahara. His broad approach remains sensitive to *variations* within particular regimes, ranging from the finer details of colonial administration to the larger developments of the repeal of slavery and the granting of nationhood to territories once deemed colonies of various European nation-states.

Kennedy's essay also contributes to Marxist or neo-Marxist theories of economic development. For Kennedy, the political economy of specific territories is a crucial factor in shaping legal systems. These legal systems are, in turn, useful in protecting powerful economic interests. Nevertheless, the safety of capitalist colonial interests is not guaranteed by these legal forms, although Kennedy suggests that, on the whole, these colonial laws have left an indelible mark, establishing capitalist systems throughout Africa.

There are weaknesses in Kennedy's analysis that should be considered. First, Kennedy does not provide substantial detail on the *process of colonization*—the combinations of inducements and force that were brought to bear on Africans. Second, there is little discussion of *human agency* as a force in the colonial and postcolonial periods. What forms of resistance were generated against imperialism and partitioning, for example? Where did uprisings occur, and how did imperialists react? In short, Kennedy fails to take into account the human factor—the actions and beliefs of the Africans who were subjected to colonization. It would also be useful to consider such forces as the anti-slavery movement, including the work of William Wilberforce and his supporters in England. The strength of Kennedy's essay, nevertheless, is his realization that the economic impetus underlying the dramatic social changes in Africa under colonization is linked with legal structures. His essay is also useful for purposes of comparison with similar developments in Western societies. One example of the imposition of legal and economic regimes on aboriginal peoples is the settlement of what we now know as Canada.

Havemann (1989) also brings forward the international dimension in law-making and economic forces. Havemann's outline of Canada's treatment of Native peoples underscores the irony of the Canadian government's official opposition of South African apartheid and its own history of ignoring Native land claims at home.

Havemann (1989, 55) allows for the *contradictory* nature of law in Canada, whereby (1) legal enactments promoted a form of "pacification" of Native peoples, but (2) law also served as "an arena for struggles to define and assert rights for indigenous peoples in the Americas since the sixteenth century." The law that was forced on indigenous peoples served as a kind of legitimation for the developing cultural and economic forms of the European settlers. Havemann asserts that discrimination against indigenous peoples is frequently invisible, and that policing patterns are frequently oriented toward maintaining "social hygiene" or blaming the victims for their poverty (Havemann 1989, 62). This process of placing blame on economically and politically less powerful groups deflects attention away from underlying historical and economic realities. The maintaining of material interests and legal ideologies, and the suppression of indigenous peoples' interests are thus combined.

There is clearly a strong public and scholarly tradition that links discrimination against indigenous peoples to a history of conquest. This discrimination is legitimated by legal processes ranging from land claims, to citizenship issues, to the overrepresentation of Natives in criminal sentencing (Havemann 1989, 68–72). The issue of race discrimination in law is developed in Chapter Six, which considers international studies of criminal justice, civil rights, and the treatment of aboriginal peoples.

SUMMARY

The works discussed in this chapter share a common interest: placing contemporary social conflicts concerning criminal law and other forms of legislation (e.g., labour law) in the context of historically rooted conflicts over the nature of law and society. These works also reinforce the importance of *legitimation* of political and legal authority, buttressed by more *repressive* threats or actions that coerce specific populations. These studies thus touch on a fundamental issue of the politics of law: the use of the criminal sanction against those who, in general, are least able to defend themselves. As Beattie (1986) and others have emphasized, criminal law, historically, has not been deployed primarily to protect people's lives and health. The most commonly used laws were those designed to protect property. As set out in this chapter, current scholarship on the history of the criminal law in England still raises the question of whether English criminal law simply reflected popular concerns over property and safety, or whether it was a hegemonic device designed to serve the interests of a propertied, privileged class.

Lowman (1989) and McLaren (1988) discuss the application of criminal law to sexual offences. Lowman (1989) notes that prostitution has been evident in North America for many years, and that ongoing attempts to curb prostitution have ironically led to "displacement" of prostitutes and a failure to establish a coherent framework for protecting prostitutes from violence and exploitation. Lowman (1989, 45) proposes regulation of prostitution—and the sex trade in general—through administrative law, not the criminal law. Critics of modern legal reform point out that there has been no dramatic improvement in either protecting women from the act of rape itself or in establishing methods of punishment or treatment for rapists, beyond the legal reforms associated with the prosecutorial process.

A number of studies have addressed the repressive elements of labour legis-

lation, especially that designed to address unionization and work stoppages. As
noted earlier in this chapter, most scholars agree that the historical evolution of
labour law could not have been restricted to use of repressive sanctions (e.g.,
police arrests, deployment of the militia, heavy fines for violation of labour
injunctions, and so forth). Rather, the repressive function of law has been offset—but not eliminated—by formal and informal processes of labour negotiation and mediation through the state.

An appreciation of the historical application of laws would be incomplete
without reference to ways in which criminal laws, and other laws regulating
conduct, were developed along racial and class lines. As outlined earlier, this
includes profound transformations in how work was governed, and how property (including entire tracts of land) was defined. Students should be aware that
for centuries, such institutions as slavery were crucial in limiting the legal status of millions of people. At the same time, there emerged a growing sense
among these oppressed people, and within western societies generally, that
such racist practices ought not to be sustained. The anti-slavery movement
mounted in many countries, including England and America, was a direct
effort to abolish slavery and the laws which supported it (see Genovese 1976;
Jordan 1968, Chapter 9). Much of the remainder of this book will address
attempts to reverse legislation and legal practices that discriminate on the basis
of race, gender, and other factors.

STUDY QUESTIONS

❏   How does Hay's account of English criminal law point to elements of mystification and class interest in the exercise of law, and not to the more consensual perspective developed by Durkheim?

❏   Critically evaluate Kennedy's (1989) discussion of the relationship between colonization and capitalist interests. To what extent was law useful in promoting an
ideology of civilization while masking the necessity of exploiting labour and other
resources? Indicate clearly to what extent you agree or disagree with Kennedy's
argument.

❏   Contrast Hay's interpretation of eighteenth century English criminal law with that
of John Langbien. What elements of elitism and popular protection are highlighted, or overlooked, by each author?

❏   Many scholars have drawn our attention to the *repressive* qualities of labour law.
Discuss whether laws are in fact directed in a repressive way against workers or
other groups in work-related disputes. Critically assess the liberal notion that law
can act in a neutral manner and serve the public interest.

❏   What is the value of the "instance study" approach that Ratner and McMullan take
in explaining labour disputes and legal interventions? Critically assess the merits
of Marxist-derived theories of the state in regulating labour-management conflicts.

NOTES

1. See Michel Foucault's *Discipline and Punish: The Birth of the Prison* (1977) for an articulation of how the ethos of discipline developed in France. Foucault's work is a critical and innovative treatise on the dynamics of power.

2. Langbien (1983, 101) is hardly sympathetic to these criminals, whose trials were held at the Old Bailey. He suggests that most were employed and had not committed crimes out of necessity, but from temptation. He adds that it is a distortion of fact to "turn these little crooks into class warriors."

3. Beattie (1986, 624) observes a transformation in the value accorded to labourers in the eighteenth century. Labourers were increasingly recognized for their contributions to the changing industrial and financial ventures in England that made up the "mercantilist state" in this era.

4. Many writers have contested the premise that rapists are essentially pathological. Clark and Lewis (1977, 136) cite research to support their conclusion that rapists are in many respects "average" men. Smart (1976, 105) maintains that, in the context of sexual socialization, rapists are seen as normal: female sexuality is repressed and made passive, whereas the aggressive character of male sexuality is amplified.

5. Luddism was a nineteenth century English movement that protested the introduction of machinery into the workplace, which the Luddites saw as a threat to workers' employment. The term "Luddite" is loosely applied to those protesters who sabotaged some aspect of their workplace. For an account of the Luddite movement, see Thompson (1968). Thompson (1968, 549) observes that, while the Luddites are conventionally depicted as motivated by a "blind opposition to machinery," in fact, they were protesting the introduction of the factory system, the reduction of wages, and other facets of nineteenth century capitalism.

REFERENCES

Backhouse, C. (1983) "Nineteenth-Century Canadian Rape Law, 1800–92." In *Essays in the History of Canadian Law: Volume II*, edited by D. Flaherty, 200–74. Toronto: The Osgoode Society.

Beattie, J. (1986) *Crime and the Courts in England, 1660–1800*. Princeton: Princeton University Press.

Box, S. (1983) *Power, Crime, and Mystification*. London: Tavistock.

Caputo, T., M. Kennedy, C. Reasons, and A. Brannigan, eds. (1989) *Law and Society: A Critical Perspective*. Toronto: Harcourt Brace Jovanovich.

Chambliss, W. (1986) "On Lawmaking." In *The Social Basis of Law: Readings in the Sociology of Law*, edited by S. Brickey and E. Comack, 27–51. Toronto: Garamond Press.

Clark, L., and D. Lewis (1977) *Rape: The Price of Coercive Sexuality*. Toronto: The Women's Press.

Foucault, M. (1977) *Discipline and Punish: The Birth of the Prison*. New York: Pantheon Books.

Genovese, E. (1976) *Roll, Jordan, Roll: The World the Slaves Made*. New York: Vintage Books.

Gunn, R., and C. Minch (1986) *Sexual Assault: The Dilemma of Disclosure, the Question of Conviction.* Winnipeg: University of Manitoba Press.

Havemann, P. (1989) "Law, State, and Canada's Indigenous People: Pacification by Coercion and Consent." In *Law and Society: A Critical Perspective,* edited by T. Caputo, M. Kennedy, C. Reasons, and A. Brannigan, 54–72. Toronto: Harcourt Brace Jovanovich.

Hay, D. (1975) "Property, Authority and the Criminal Law." In *Albion's Fatal Tree: Crime and Society in Eighteenth Century England,* edited by D. Hay, P. Linebaugh, J. Rule, E.P. Thompson and C. Winslow, 17–63. New York: Pantheon Books.

Hinch, R. (1988) "Inconsistencies and Contradictions in Canada's Sexual Assault Law." *Canadian Public Policy* 14 (3): 282–94.

Huxley, C. (1989) "The State, Collective Bargaining, and the Shape of Strikes in Canada." In *Law and Society: A Critical Perspective,* edited by T. Caputo, M. Kennedy, C. Reasons, and A. Brannigan, 218–31. Toronto: Harcourt Brace Jovanovich.

Jordan, W. (1968) *White Over Black: American Attitudes Toward the Negro, 1550–1812.* Chapell Hill: North Carolina University Press.

Kennedy, M. (1989) "Law and Capitalist Development: The Colonization of Sub-Saharan Africa." In *Law and Society: A Critical Perspective,* edited by T. Caputo, M. Kennedy, C. Reasons, and A. Brannigan, 30–35. Toronto: Harcourt Brace Jovanovich.

Langbien, J. (1983) "Albion's Fatal Flaws." *Past and Present* (98): 96–120.

Lowman, J. (1986) "You Can Do It, But Don't Do It Here: Some Comments on Proposals for the Reform of Canadian Prostitution Law." In *Regulating Sex: An Anthology of Commentaries on the Findings and Recommendations of the Badgley and Fraser Reports,* edited by J. Lowman, N. Jackson, T. Palys, and S. Gavigan, 193–213. Burnaby, British Columbia: School of Criminology, Simon Fraser University.

——— (1987) "Taking Young Prostitutes Seriously." *Canadian Review of Sociology and Anthropology,* 24 (1): 99–116.

——— (1989) "Prostitution Law in Canada." *Comparative Law Review* 23 (3): 13–48.

——— (1991) "Prostitution in Canada." In *Canadian Criminology: Perspectives on Crime and Criminality,* edited by M. Jackson and C. Griffiths, 113–34. Toronto: Harcourt Brace Jovanovich.

McLaren, J. (1988) "The Canadian Magistracy and the Anti-White Slavery Campaign, 1900–1920." In *Law & Society: Issues in Legal History,* edited by W. Pue and B. Wright, 329–53. Ottawa: Carleton University Press.

Morton, D., with T. Copp (1980) *Working People: An Illustrated History of Canadian Labour.* Ottawa: Deneau and Greenberg.

Ratner, R., and J. McMullan (1989) "State Intervention and the Control of Labour in British Columbia: A Capital-Logic Approach." In *Law and Society: A Critical Perspective,* edited by T. Caputo, M. Kennedy, C. Reasons, and A. Brannigan, 232–49. Toronto: Harcourt Brace Jovanovich.

Ratner, R., J. McMullan, and B. Burtch (1987) "The Relative Autonomy of the State and Criminal Justice." In *State Control: Criminal Justice Politics in Canada,* edited by R. Ratner and J. McMullan, 85–125. Vancouver: University of British Columbia Press.

Smandych, R. (1985) "Marxism and the Creation of Law: Re-Examining the Origins of Canadian Anti-Combines Legislation 1890–1910." In *The New Criminologies: State, Crime, and Control,* edited by T. Fleming, 87–99. Toronto: Oxford University Press.

Smart, C. (1976) *Women, Crime and Criminology.* London: Routledge and Kegan Paul.

Thompson, E.P. (1968) *The Making of the English Working Class.* Harmondsworth: Penguin.

CHAPTER FOUR

Feminist Theory and Law

And if I hurt my knee
my good leg shows my poor leg
what to do

and if I hurt my arm
my good arm rubs my poor arm
into place

and if I hurt an eye
my good eye sees beyond the other's range
and pulls it onward   upward
into space

The sun's eye warms my heart
but if my good heart breaks
I have no twin
to make it beat again

(Dorothy Livesay, "Look to the End")

INTRODUCTION

This chapter presents a critique of law and social control from feminist perspectives. The contemporary women's movement has influenced legal policy and thinking, as well as political, cultural, and social institutions. There are now substantial efforts to make women's issues and interests more visible within societies that have traditionally limited and discounted these interests. The continuing interest in sociological approaches to law has been accompanied by a dramatic growth in women's studies, including feminist research and theory. If we accept the premise that social life is increasingly regulated by—and accountable to—government in general (Held 1984, 1), including state-administered law, it is clear that women's lives are similarly constrained by law.

This chapter develops themes we have considered previously, including a sceptical approach to the legal order and the ways in which women are limited by the ideological and repressive powers of law. Contradictions in law are especially important in understanding how conflicts surrounding gender are reproduced in legal settings. One theme addressed in this chapter is the extent to which law can serve to further women's interests. Boyd and Sheehy (1989) and other scholars offer insights into the limits of liberal conceptualizations of law and the merits of feminist rethinking.

FEMINISM AND CANADIAN LAW REFORM

Boyd and Sheehy provide an extensive review of theoretical work concerning feminism and law in Canada. They note that the feminist movement in law is not strictly a twentieth century phenomenon. Women's groups have been lobbying for legislative and judicial reform since the late nineteenth century. The feminist perspective, like the Marxist perspective, challenges the dominant *liberal* perspective of law as just and impartial. It is significant, however, that the bulk of scholarship and literature on women and the law in Canada can be traced to a liberal outlook, which accepts basic social institutions and assumes that the law can be made into a "neutral body of rules," such that women can be treated fairly as legal subjects (Boyd and Sheehy 1989, 255).

Feminist scholarship thus tends to draw a bold line at jurisprudential approaches that ignore gender as a factor in society at large or in the legal sphere. Feminist scholarship "takes into account a woman's perspective or interests" (Boyd and Sheehy 1989, 255); thus, any discussion of citizens' rights or powers must take seriously the role of *gender relations* in the exercise of law. These discussions must also consider the differences—biological, social, economic, and political—that often define and influence women's statuses and perspectives. The abstract notion of an individual treated as an equal in social life, before the courts and other legal mechanisms, is seen by feminists as false and misleading. Such abstract ideologies serve to exaggerate the actual gains secured for women and use the artificial measure of formal rights and enactments to assess social reforms.

Although feminism grew out of liberal philosophy, some feminists are critical of the "gender-neutral," liberal emphasis on individual rights. They place greater emphasis on the *limited* achievements of legal reforms and the need to analyze women's roles within society (Boyd and Sheehy 1989, 254). Critics of liberal feminism thus argue that law has long served as an instrument of patriarchy, defining women's place in all social spheres. It is hardly surprising that the task of bending existing laws and institutions away from this patriarchal legacy will require more than amendments and reforms to law.

The 1970 Royal Commission on the Status of Women in Canada documented patterns of *discrimination* against women and recommended liberal solutions to women's inequality. These liberal solutions included eliminating legislation that differentiated on the basis of gender. This meant removing, for example, conventions that barred women from certain occupations or pension arrangements that benefited male but not female workers (Boyd and Sheehy 1989, 256). Liberal feminist approaches centred on the gap between *formal equality* as an ideal and *substantive inequality* as practice. Boyd and Sheehy (1989, 256) note that liberal feminist approaches highlighted discrimination in the socialization of female law students and in women's career patterns within the legal profession generally. Limitations on women's access to abortion was also emphasized, together with a critique of the lack of action on women's equality claims under the Canadian Bill of Rights. A number of researchers have criticized federal and provincial human rights codes for their limited impact in addressing discrimination (Boyd and Sheehy 1989, 257). This situation speaks once more of the gulf between law on the books and the "living law"—law as it is actually applied.

Following the passage of the Charter of Rights and Freedoms in 1982, feminist approaches to law were extended to *result-equality feminism*. That is, the focus shifted away from considering whether or not laws were equally applied to questioning the actual impact of legal processes in a society where relations were not equal between the sexes. Boyd and Sheehy (1989, 257) claim that result-equality feminism provided a "major transformation" in liberal feminist theory. There was greater attention to ensuring that women had input in the drafting of legislation and litigation of issues pertaining to women's equality. Boyd and Sheehy (1989, 257) credit result-equality feminism with creating an awareness of the gender bias that underlies law and social relations. As such, result-equality feminism

> demands an extensive rethinking of the underlying assumptions and content of legal rules, on the theory that equal application of a male-oriented legal system cannot drastically alter women's disadvantaged position.

Not all research has confirmed a lack of progress in the legislation against sex discrimination. Malarkey and Hagan (1989) note that in Ontario the Female Employees Fair Remuneration Act of 1951 appears to have reduced disparities between men and women in certain occupations. The Ontario law was also known as the Equal Pay Act, and stated that "no employer and no person acting on his behalf shall discriminate between his male and female employees by paying a female employee at a rate of pay less than paid to a male employee employed by him for the same work done in the same establishment" (Malarkey and Hagan 1989, 301).

The authors note that, historically, some occupations have blatantly discriminated against women. In 1858, male teachers in Toronto earned approximately twice as much as female teachers, although women teachers greatly outnumbered men: in 1858 there were 6297 female teachers in Toronto, compared with 2200 male teachers. Malarkey and Hagan (1989, 296) add that great disparities in teachers' incomes remained in place "well into the twentieth century." Such gender-based disparities did not go unchallenged. Since the 1950s, trade unions, women teachers' associations, and government officials, among others, sought to have the egalitarian spirit of the Equal Pay Act established concretely.

Malarkey and Hagan (1989) used a time-series regression analysis of male-female incomes up until 1981. They found that the legislation appeared to have a modest effect in narrowing the wage differential in some occupations, while in others, the disparity became greater. The authors conclude that equal pay legislation, for its inconsistency, provides some basis for encouragement, and that more effective legislation is warranted.

It has been said that Marxist and socialist analyses are "often abstract at the expense of context" (Boyd and Sheehy 1989, 259) and masculinist in that they ignore women's perspectives. There are, of course, exceptions, including scholars who incorporate feminism and socialism into their critical analyses. Boyd and Sheehy (1989) cite the work of Shelley Gavigan, a socialist feminist, who acknowledges women's resistance to law and the importance of continuing struggles for women's autonomy. Gavigan appreciates that law has served as a means of securing state dominance, as well as the dominance of the professions. Law is not one-dimensional, however. Gavigan credits law with the ability to react to pressures from women to regulate their own conception and pregnancy (see Gavigan 1986), for example. Other examples include the refusal of the courts to uphold arguments favouring a "male veto" over therapeutic abortion decisions and the establishment of mandatory arrest policies for police called to attend at domestic assaults.

Feminist approaches to law can only be understood in relation to women's position in society. This is a very controversial area. Some people assert that women's position has been dramatically improved with respect to equality; others state that this supposed improvement has been greatly exaggerated, and that, indeed, regressive measures are eroding women's status. Robertson (1990) suggests that there is a cultural taboo on confronting and acknowledging misogyny (the "M" word, as Robertson puts it), including its extreme form—murder of women by men. Stanko (1990, 97) documents "the daily indignities of sexual intimidation" experienced by women in England. For Stanko, a *gestalt* of fear of assault, experience of sexual harassment, and other forms of victimization leads to strategies of avoidance—taking precautions in public areas as well as in more "familiar" surroundings, such as the workplace and the home. Implicit in these accounts of women's experiences of threat and intimidation is a sense that law is not designed to offer adequate protection to women.

Some critics note a tension between the gains of the latest wave of feminism and a contemporary backlash against feminist principles. A range of policies, including greater access to daycare, pay equity, and increased hiring of women in positions in which they are underrepresented, have all been subject to back-lash (see McCormack 1991). Even the most shocking forms of violence against women, including the killing of female engineering students in Montreal, have generated attempts to defuse feminist interpretations of the killings as part of a larger structure of male control (Baril 1990; Lakeman 1990). Demands for the integrity of women's bodies have yet to alter some practices, however. The practice of female sexual circumcision, which includes cutting of the clitoris as well as stitching to close most of the vaginal opening, is one example. In some African and Middle Eastern societies these operations are used to reduce women's sexual desire and decrease the chance that women will be sexually active before marriage. Female circumcision has been interpreted as a custom which inhibits sexual pleasure for women and, as such, represents a form of control and domination over women. It has been estimated that in 1982, 84 million females were circumcised in African countries (Seager and Olson 1986, 3–4). Worldwide, violence against women continues, in such forms as sexual assault, domestic violence, and harassment. The killing of fourteen female students at l'École Polytechnique at l'Université de Montréal in 1989 stands as a reminder that there is no safe place for women. Some commentators have dismissed this incident as an aberration, rather than as an extreme form of everyday violence. The "take back the night movement" demonstrations in recent years mark an effort to reduce violence against women, and also to secure greater freedom of movement for women at all hours of the day and night.

Violence against women takes many forms. It is important to appreciate, however, that much of the literature on women's status and efforts to achieve equality has concentrated on less dramatic and more pervasive forms of social control of women than violent assaults. One example of gender socialization and social control is the power of school curricula to stream female students into studies and into occupations that are considered appropriate for their sex. The formal ideology of equality in schools—in which each student is free to pursue his or her interests and to develop his or her potential after formal schooling—is seen by some writers as an egalitarian fiction.

Beyond the more overt "streaming" of male and female students into courses and programs, there has also been evidence of less perceptible forms of discrimination. These "micro-inequities" (Sandler and Hall, cited in Renzetti and Curran 1989, 97) include gender-laden references (e.g., assuming all physicians are men and all nurses are women), and quite subtle behaviours, such as a teacher's tendency not to call on female students for responses or to interrupt females' responses more frequently than males' (Renzetti and Curran 1989, 97). The influence of social class and gender relations in schooling systems is significant, according to Marxists and feminists. The school is interpreted as a control institution that perpetuates capitalist and patriarchal relations rather than as a truly public resource, tailored to personal needs and aptitudes (Russell 1987, 229).

Another example of discrimination referred to earlier in this chapter is the pattern of disparity between men and women in income and assets. In Canada, the tremendous increase in women working outside of the home in recent decades has not necessarily produced parity in earnings or social power with their male counterparts. A study published by the Canadian Advisory Council on the Status of Women—*Women and Labour Market Poverty* (Gunderson and Muszynski 1990, 66–67)—found that while women constituted only 29.9 percent of the working poor in 1971, they formed nearly half (46.4 percent) of the working poor in 1986. The authors refer to such processes as the "feminization of poverty" (Gunderson and Muszynski 1990, 66–67).

According to a 1981 U.S. study of several occupations, women's earnings average 64.7 percent of their male counterparts' earnings. In some sectors, such as sales, women earned 52 cents for every dollar earned by men (Seager and Olson 1986, section 19). Renzetti and Curran (1989, 195–96) claim that sexist ideologies about women and work still structure hiring practices. In North America, women's role was traditionally restricted to domestic matters, and when women took employment outside the home, it was often seen as "secondary" to men's employment. Renzetti and Curran add that, although it is commonplace for people to view this traditional ideology as obsolete and irrelevant to modern life, a number of U.S. studies point to the persistence of sexist beliefs about women's work, specifically, that women are more likely to leave their jobs to raise children, or that women's physical limitations make them unsuitable for certain jobs (Renzetti and Curran 1989, 196).

In the United States, *affirmative action programs*, designed to force or encourage employers to employ and promote "women and minorities," are ostensibly meant to reduce sex discrimination. Nonetheless, Renzetti and Curran (1989, 200) report that sex segregation in the workplace remains "extensive." They suggest that narrow interpretations of court decisions have often served to reduce the impact of affirmative action doctrine; in some cases, such as flight attendant work, traditionally female jobs have been opened up to men, again on the grounds of sex equality (Renzetti and Curran 1989, 200).[1]

In England, research on the Sex Discrimination Act lends support to the argument that formal enactments do not significantly alter an overall pattern of male domination and privilege. Gregory (1979) outlines several difficulties with this Act, including technical interpretations of complaints under the Act, a focus on individual cases rather than systemic discrimination against women in the work force, and limited penalties for offenders. Women who are discriminated against may decide not to lay a complaint, for reasons of inconvenience, scepticism in the ability of government officials to right such wrongs, and so forth.

Given this context of social change and resistance to changes in the status of women, the role of law is frequently seen as pivotal in weakening or extending women's freedoms. Gregory (1979, 150) concludes that while women and minorities are disadvantaged in terms of "basic bourgeois rights," it is advisable to seek the greatest benefits possible from such legislation as the Sex Discrimination Act. That said, Gregory (1979, 150) notes that this legislation has generally served to mystify discriminatory practices and to "contain" attempts to secure basic rights for disadvantaged groups. Garrett (1987, 97–103) indicates that employment patterns for women altered with industrialization in England. In pre-Industrial England, all family members worked, without the artificial distinction between "domestic" work and waged work, or other forms of labour. With industrialization, labour was generally divided along gender lines, with women excluded from heavy work, skilled trades, the professions, sciences, and the civil service (Garrett 1987, 98). In modern times, approximately two-fifths of women workers are concentrated in a handful of occupations, a pattern that has been documented not only in England, but in several European countries and North America (Garrett 1987, 102).

Boyd and Sheehy (1989, 257–58) warn us of the consequences of abstracting legal principles such that the social context of gender and law is not considered. Specifically, the ongoing push for gender-neutrality in law includes the formal provision for men to claim maintenance (spousal and/or child support) from women in the event of separation. What was previously referred to as "maternity leave" was extended to men, in the more inclusive term "paternity leave." In a sense, these developments could herald new options in childrearing, with men now enabled to spend more effort and time with childrearing. As will be discussed with respect to family law (Chapter Nine), however, there is little evidence that most men are even approximating parity with women in terms of such responsibilities as child care and other forms of domestic work. Many critics have also noted that the tendency for women to assume caretaking functions—for dependent children, elderly parents, and so on—has been compounded by lack of support services, such as daycare facilities (Pascall 1986, 80–87). There have been numerous studies documenting women's contributions in such spheres as household labour (e.g., Luxton 1980). Feminist work thus highlights unrecognized—and often unwaged—work, tying modern examples to a legacy of what constitutes "women's estate" in earlier societies (Mitchell 1973, 103).

To understand feminist theory and law, we must review several studies of women's status before the law. These works bear on such issues as the nature of legal domination for women and possible strategies for changing legal structures. A common point of these studies is the limited progress women have made within Western societies, including rather small gains in the legal sphere and in social policy. We begin with Zillah Eisenstein's historical examination of law. Then follows a look at Carol Smart's discussion of feminist jurisprudence, *Feminism and the Power of Law* (1989). Next we summarize Beatrix Campbell's *Wigan Pier Revisited* (1984). Campbell's work is a brilliant study of poverty and social class in northern England. Her point of departure is George Orwell's classic work *The Road to Wigan Pier* (1937). Campbell re-examines Orwell's approach, placing her work in the context of women's subordination, and their resistance to patriarchy and poverty. Campbell illustrates the limits to a masculine-focused study of poverty, especially given the "feminization of poverty" in today's world. The section on Campbell is followed by brief looks at the work of Elizabeth Comack and Catherine MacKinnon.

EISENSTEIN: *THE RADICAL FUTURE OF LIBERAL FEMINISM*

Eisenstein's approach to the politics of feminism in her somewhat self-explanatory title—*The Radical Future of Liberal Feminism* (1981)—is a landmark work. Eisenstein provides a detailed review of historical writings on state and law, using this backdrop to argue for the necessity of feminist politics that move beyond the gradual approach of liberalism. Eisenstein (1981, 114) defines *liberal individualism* as "the view of the individual pictured as atomized and disconnected from the social relations that actually affect his or her choices and options." As such, liberal individualism is extremely limiting, ignoring political and historical contexts, while celebrating opportunities for individual expression and rights. Eisenstein counters that *structural forces* impede individual expression. These structural forces could include cultural definitions of appropriate roles for women, economic forces that limit women's work, and legal forces that define or constrain women's freedoms. The promise of equality via liberalism cannot be fully met, given these limiting forces. Students interested in Eisenstein's approach may wish to read some of her other writings concerning capitalism, patriarchy, and laws affecting reproductive choice (see Eisenstein 1979, 1988).

Eisenstein provides several insights into the collaboration between the acclaimed English philosopher John Stuart Mill, and Harriet Taylor, his collaborator and spouse. She contends that Mill and Taylor offered a vision of liberation that, ultimately, is available primarily to middle-class men and "an elite of middle-class women" (Eisenstein 1981, 115). This remains a contentious point, for Mill, as a utilitarian, supported public education. It is arguable that his vision of liberty was not as narrowly focused on a small elite as Eisenstein implies.

Mill and Taylor place great emphasis on gifted, educated individuals as leaders in society. For Mill and Taylor, the danger of democracy and socialism is that the masses may become unduly influential in shaping politics despite what is seen as their lack of knowledge (see Eisenstein 1981, 118–19). A system of *plural voting*[2] is favoured over the democratic formula of "one man, one vote." An opposing view was taken by Engels, who believed that the working class was aware of the contradiction between the national interest and the specific interests of the bourgeoisie (Eisenstein 1981, 120). This is a very useful counterpoint, as it brings forward a less optimistic view of the educated classes and a more positive outlook on the capacities of manual workers.[3]

Eisenstein addresses the concepts of *ideology* and *gender* in her discussion of how Victorian married women were defined by their domestic status. Eisenstein (1981, 131) contests the stereotype of Victorian married women as idle, noting that few middle-class households could afford the domestic helpers needed to manage the household and raise children. This relegation to the household was offset, to some extent, by efforts to enfranchise women, a project that became the "major political concern" of Mill and Taylor (Eisenstein 1981, 132). Further to this, Mill and Taylor linked the emancipation of women, including greater freedom within marriage, with economic independence (Eisenstein 1981, 133).

For Mill and Taylor, the supposed weakness of women's constitutions was not in-born, and many arguments to the contrary were ill-founded. Eisenstein (1981, 134) cites excerpts from Mill's writings in which he outlines how "women's nature" is an *artificial construct*, reflecting the "societal needs" affecting women, not their innate abilities or their potential powers. Eisenstein adds that Mill and Taylor nevertheless accepted the patriarchal division of appropriate male and female spheres (Eisenstein 1981, 134–35), for example, the assumption that women are best suited to childrearing, and men for work that requires more "muscular exertion."

Eisenstein (1981, 136) underscores the contradictions between Mill and Taylor's emphasis on individualism and independence of women, on the one hand, and their acceptance of women's proper responsibilities within the household. This linking of women's nature to the domestic sphere undermines the emancipatory message of Mill and Taylor; the exclusion from public life impeded the development of the "exceptional woman":

> There is no way that any single "exceptional" woman can become completely free of the patriarchal structural relations of society. She remains defined in relationship to this structure even when, as an "exception," she tries to defy it. This is the consequence of the *structural reality of power* rather than a reflection of liberal individualist options (Eisenstein 1981, 138; emphasis added).

One concern with Eisenstein's approach is the ease with which she criticizes the limitations of such concepts as "citizen rights" (Eisenstein 1981, 115). Eisenstein is correct in arguing against a "simplistic reading" (Eisenstein 1981, 116) of liberal individualism that divorces the topic of individual rights from the concepts of patriarchy and the structural discrimination against women as a group. What is troubling about Eisenstein's approach is that she seems to diminish these struggles for greater liberties, especially in the context of greater respect for women's rights. Specifically, the writings of Taylor and Mill on utilizing one's faculties, on securing the vote, and the dangers of government censure remain central to political theory and daily practice. Eisenstein also fails to substantiate certain generalizations. For example, she contends (1979, 117) that the middle class is more likely to accept customary practices and ideas uncritically. Eisenstein provides no basis for this portraiture of

Babbitry,[4] but she nevertheless provides an articulate critique of liberal ideology and the effects of capitalism and patriarchy for working-class men, and working-class and middle-class women (Eisenstein 1981, 138).

SMART: *FEMINISM AND THE POWER OF LAW*

Carol Smart's *Feminism and the Power of Law* (1989) provides a careful theoretical discussion of feminist jurisprudence. As a feminist, Smart examines several examples of how the law has been misapplied in such areas as rape (or sexual assault, as it is now defined in Canadian criminal law), child sexual abuse, pornography, and the wider issue of how women's bodies may be subject to the power of law. Smart's research focuses primarily on the United Kingdom but is clearly applicable to feminist jurisprudence in Canada and elsewhere.

Smart's work rests on the belief that women need to promote "a new way of seeing" in such a way as to reconceptualize existing models of literature, law, and social activities (Smart 1989, 1). This process of seeing anew is difficult, especially in the relatively short time span of modern feminism. Nonetheless, Smart (1989, 2) notes that voices that have previously been suppressed are now surfacing, illustrated by the growing contributions to literature and art by women of colour. This point is also made clearly by Chrystos, a Native woman and poet who has written a collection of poems entitled *Not Vanishing* (1988) and a more recent book of poetry, *Dream On* (1991). Her work offers a stark and vivid portrait of American history, including genocide and everyday patterns of discrimination against and assimilation of minorities. Building on her experience of Asian, Native, black, Latin, and white people, Chrystos asserts that, despite the material and spiritual deprivations of her people, "we are not Vanishing Americans."

Smart (1989) supports the development of a new consciousness of gender and race that will effect a change in dominant discourses and definitions. This objective is, however, subject to the power of law. The growing feminist knowledge base, and the feminist critique of law and social control, are often "disqualified" by law. Thus, while some legal reforms may be advantageous to women, feminists should be cautious in resorting to legal solutions. The co-opting power of law is a factor that feminists and others must address. Debates over equality and the utility of law are necessary, but

> they have the overwhelming disadvantage of ceding to law the very power that law may then deploy against women's claims. It is a dilemma that all radical political movements face, namely the problem of challenging a form of power without accepting its terms of reference and hence losing the battle before it has begun (Smart 1989, 5).

Smart sees law and masculine culture as essentially congruent. Smart (1989, 3) adds that the liberal emphasis on rights has ironically become more of a weapon against women than a force that acts in favour of feminism. Smart (1989, 67) notes that some strong battles on the part of the women's movement have not resulted in substantial legal reforms but, rather, in measures that provide only slight improvements in the position of women—a point that is developed by Morton (1988) and others.

For Smart, the task of developing a *feminist jurisprudence* requires a shift away from conventional, liberal law reform—in which women are "added" into existing legal considerations—and toward a fundamental rethinking of legal values and justice principles. The promise of feminist jurisprudence—as a general theory of law, accompanied by practical measures to transform women's status—has not been fully met, according to Smart; feminist jurisprudence has become divided and fragmentary. Moreover, there is disagreement over the value of legal struggles (Smart 1989, 66). Smart (1989, 72) cautions against "grand theorizing." Taking the conventional definition of jurisprudence—in which law is presented as an entity, unified and guided by "basic principles of justice, rights, and equality" (Smart 1989, 69)—she insists that a feminist-based approach can "deconstruct" abstract, overgeneralized theories of law, and thus outline everyday applications of the power of law. Further, Smart (1989, 70–72) is critical of a tendency to present feminist jurisprudence as a superior, scientific theory. In other words, she warns against the tendency to view this approach as "the truth," which, in turn, is validated by its methodologies and epistemology. This approach can become a variant of legal positivism or of the "privileged discourse" that others have used—the very tendency that some feminists decry in legal theory. Smart (1989) appears to argue against such catechismal, dogmatic approaches, allowing instead for a more flexible kind of feminist jurisprudence that respects the value of intellectual comparisons and modifications.

Sexual Offences and Legal Discourse

Smart addresses the ways in which women's sexuality is defined and distorted. Using the examples of rape (in Canada, legally redefined as "sexual assault") and child sexual abuse, Smart offers a powerful critique of cultural representations of women's sexuality. Beyond this, she views the criminal trial for accused rapists not as a corrective for hateful actions against women, but as a forum that reinforces a cultural depiction of women's sexuality as problematic and pathological. Her work thus stands as a direct challenge to the complacent view that women have benefited from what has been dubbed "the sexual revolution," or that reforms in criminal law have been a major contribution toward sexual equality.

Rape, as a legal definition, is a narrow construct for Smart (1989, 26). In fact, this narrow, legalistic definition serves to disqualify other possible discourses that are seen as irrelevant or inferior. Rape law thus acts to disqualify women and their sexuality. Smart (1989, 26–27) notes that in Western societies, the rape trial constitutes a celebration of women's lack of power. The trial also magnifies the ways in which female heterosexuality is constructed as fundamentally different from male heterosexuality.

In Western cultures, sexuality is conventionally presented as "phallocentric," that is, focused on male pleasure. In contrast, other forms of sexuality that challenge this phallocentrism are discounted as "incomprehensible and pathological" (Smart 1989, 28). Smart acknowledges that female pleasure in sexuality is possible; however, the weight of a male-oriented construction of sexuality does not coincide with the realization of women's sexual potential. It follows that, as female sexuality is seen as mysterious, capricious, and unrealized, the solution to sexual problems is paternalistic in character:

> If all women are seen as having the thing that men most need, if they are also seen as grudging with it, or as so out of touch with their "real" sexual feelings that they deny it to themselves and to men, then the problem for men is how to gain control of women's sexuality in spite of women themselves (Smart 1989, 30).

Thus, women become separated, or alienated, from their own sexuality. In a sense, this idea of patriarchal control of women's sexuality can be greatly oversimplified, as sexuality is reduced to a "one-dimensional prudery" that undermines women's potential for sexual satisfaction (Smart 1989, 30).

Smart uses the rape trial to illustrate the ways in which women's experience of sexuality is distorted and disqualified. If women themselves are unable to know their own sexuality, some defence attorneys and other officials could use this premise to argue that women might enjoy "sex" even in its more violent manifestations. Smart thus raises the fundamental question of how sexual misconceptions permeate the workings of law and society. Reviewing some rapists' excuses for their attacks—women led them on, rape was a man's right, and so forth—Smart (1989, 31) states that this rape discourse is not restricted to the rapists, that is, to the minority of men who have been convicted of rape or sexual assault. Instead, this forceful denial of female sexuality permeates male discourse, taking the forms of resentment, frustration, and anger, which are translated into the "material and psychic oppression" of women (Smart 1989, 32).

One of Smart's central points is that law presents an authoritative claim on truth. As such, it is a very powerful mechanism in allowing—or disallowing—conflicting claims about such events as rapes. On the surface, the very existence of rape law would seem to consolidate women's rights to be free of unwanted sex. As Smart (1989, 34) notes, however, there is an obverse side to this view. When the accused in a rape trial is found innocent, this represents "a finding of sexual complicity on the part of the victim. The woman must have lied . . . ." Acquittal thus can be translated into a confirmation of phallocentric values.

The very conduct of the trial undermines the high-flown ideal that women warrant protection from men's advances. Smart (1989, 35–36) provides several examples from judicial utterances in rape trials that underscore how women's testimony can be disregarded or trivialized. Women are liable to be "untruthful and invent stories"; "Women who say no do not always mean no"; "Women who hitch-hike are 'asking for it.'" These quotes are excerpts from judges' statements from 1976 to the early 1980s (Smart 1989, 35). Smart adds that even though some men are convicted of rape and imprisoned, only a very small minority of men who sexually abuse women are tried, let alone convicted. This reality confirms earlier Canadian research that documents the ways in which rape charges are formed and the ways in which coercive sexuality influences the finding of rape charges as founded or unfounded (see Clark and Lewis 1977; Boyle 1991, 100). Once again, there is a substantial gap between legal rhetoric of protection and equality before the law, and the reality of rape as a crime almost invariably directed against women, with a very low rate of conviction for accused rapists.

Smart's critique of rape law raises several fundamental questions. First, it restores a vital link between culture and legal institutions. To the extent that cultures are essentially misogynistic, law will reflect much of this discreditation of women's accounts and actions. Smart's work can also be linked with other work that dramatizes the ways in which women's sexuality is commodified, for example, the way advertising emphasizes youth, beauty, and allure while bypassing women who do not fit this ideal image of beauty.

While Smart's arguments mesh with a feminist critique of women's victimization, there are counterarguments to her views, especially the point that women are in fact controlled by others in their sexual expression and enjoyment. The recent work of Sheila Kitzinger, *Women's Experience of Sex* (1987), breaks new ground in appreciating the diversity of female sexuality. Exploring the sexual and reproductive powers of women, Kitzinger (1987) provides a thoughtful account of heterosexuality, lesbian sexuality, celibacy, birth control, childbirth, and aging and menopause, bringing forth a woman-centred appreciation of intimacy and expressiveness. Kitzinger, like Smart, is fully aware of the power of the dominant culture in oversimplifying and discounting women, in creating objects out of individual subjects. Nevertheless, Kitzinger's work suggests that the influence of the patriarchal culture is far from complete, that resistance to, and understanding of, sexual politics is underway in many societies.

The issue of child sexual abuse is another example of the politics of law. A 1975 police investigation into child abuse at the Mount Cashel orphanage in Newfoundland was suppressed until 1989, when news of beatings and sexual abuse of children was finally brought to light (Harris 1990). Ironically, it is virtually impossible to prosecute those who sexually abuse children, yet it is almost inevitable that children, as part of these proceedings, are damaged (Smart 1989, 51). Describing the response of criminal law in controlling sexual abuse, Smart refers to a mixture of "consternation and complacency" on the part of government officials and social reformers. Legislation in the Victorian era, while providing mechanisms for prosecuting those who violated children, including those who sold girls into prostitution, could also be punitive toward the victims. Greater numbers of girls became subject to monitoring and moral intervention, illustrated by the practice of incarcerating some girls in reformatories or industrial schools. This practice was justified as a protection for girls who might be in "moral danger" (Smart 1989, 51).

The combination of alarm and complacency was also evident in legislation against incest. Some jurists did not believe that such acts were possible; others referred to incest as "mischief," adding that the number of cases must be very small (Smart 1989, 53). In recent times, while legislation and resources—child protection agencies, for example—remain in place, Smart (1989, 55) notes that the criminal law has been "massively under-utilized" to fight child abuse. Protection agencies rely far more on care orders—removing children from their homes—than on applying the criminal law to remove the victimizers, who are almost invariably fathers. Clearly, the limited response of law in addressing child abuse is seen as another example of the superficial treatment of a social problem whose roots lie in male sexual socialization, not in offender pathology alone. Moreover, despite challenges to the therapeutic approach—treatment of abusive fathers and an ideology of family reintegration—traditional family therapy is still used in Britain for many cases of child sexual abuse. The assessment of allegations of abuse through clinical experts and legal discourse combine to silence children's accounts. This tendency to ignore or challenge some statements by children may have been heightened by the much-publicized "Cleveland Crisis" in the late 1980s.[5]

CAMPBELL: *WIGAN PIER REVISITED*

The study of oppressed peoples has been a staple in literature, social criticism, and the social sciences. George Orwell's *The Road to Wigan Pier* (1937) is a classic study of poverty in the north of England during the depression of the 1930s. *The Road to Wigan Pier* described the life of English coal miners to make an incisive critique of the elitist view that disparaged manual labour.

In 1982, an English journalist embarked on a six-month journey to several cities in northern England. Beatrix Campbell retraced the journey taken by Orwell in the 1930s. Campbell's book, *Wigan Pier Revisited* (1984) is a critical reassessment of Orwell's book, in which the roles of men and women are now viewed from a feminist perspective. Campbell (1984) does not lionize the work of the men, as Orwell did, but rather establishes an outlook in which women's interests are limited by men:

> Men and masculinity, in their everyday, individual manifestations, constitute a systematic bloc of resistance to the women of their own community and class. Both individual men and the political movements men have made within the working class are culpable (Campbell 1984, 5–6).

Orwell's study is quite remarkable, especially in his appreciation of manual labour and its contribution to civilization. Campbell's work constitutes an important break with Orwell's outlook, however, inasmuch as she adds to the recent tradition of women's history, examining their specific contributions to work, family, and other spheres (see also Luxton 1980).

Campbell, while sensitive to the plight of the women she met, does not promote a sense of victimization among women, singly or as a group. She refers to women in temporary shelters—meant to offer a "safe house" for women and children who have been abused—as "survivors" (Campbell 1984, 7). The seriousness of the problem is nevertheless clear, inasmuch as there were similar shelters in approximately 100 other English cities at the time of Campbell's research. Even in the physical safety and camaraderie of the shelter, Campbell (1984, 93) remarks that "all of the women in the refuge are poorer than men," with less income, time, clothing and the like. Another status these women have in common is that they have all been battered. Campbell (1984, 95) contends that various forms of violence against women (sexual assault, sexual harassment, domestic assault) are not the result of economic deprivation, but, rather, of a dynamic process rooted in "men's power and women's subordination." One can also point to the inadequacy of the legal response, an issue that comes up in the work of Elizabeth Comack (1988) regarding prosecution of abusive husbands in Canada.

COMACK: "JUSTICE FOR BATTERED WOMEN"

The widespread use of violence against women has generated considerable interest in providing greater protection for women. Comack (1988) reviews two legal decisions concerning wife battering in Manitoba to illustrate the contradictory nature of legal responses, including the usefulness of the battered-wife syndrome argument. Comack discusses two criminal trials— Lavallée and Leach—that were convened in Winnipeg in 1987.

Angélique Lavallée was acquitted on a charge of second-degree murder in the fatal shooting of her common-law husband. It was established that Lavallée had been beaten on many occasions by her husband. She had also been hospitalized several times for treatment of these injuries. A key point in the defence argument was that such a history of abuse may produce battered-wife syndrome, which may be considered in absolving or mitigating punishment (Comack 1988, 9). It is noteworthy that Lavallée's acquittal was appealed by the Crown, which questioned the relevance of the battered-wife syndrome argument with respect to this case.

In the case of Verna Mae Leach, there was also a history of abuse from her common-law husband. Unlike Lavallée, however, she was sentenced to two years' imprisonment for the nonfatal stabbing of her partner. The defence argument was based on self-defence, not on the battered-wife syndrome argument.

Comack (1988) uses these two cases to formulate her argument that the continuing phenomenon of wife assault is linked to *structural conditions* that limit women's choices. Comack does not imply that all women are powerless or that legal decisions are entirely unhelpful to all women who have been abused. Nevertheless, the influence of male bias, and the entrenched misunderstanding of these structural limitations on women, remain central to Comack's critique of the ideology and practice of criminal law. For Comack, the battered-wife syndrome argument is far from a complete legal victory. She foresees interpretations of it that could be used against women, for example, to question a mother's competency to care for her children. Comack (1988, 11) is also critical of the extremely narrow focus associated with the defence; it could, ironically, expand the powers of the psychiatric profession to diagnose and treat women, but without focusing on patterns of inequality between men and women.

Even in jurisdictions that have formally approved resources in support of mandatory arrest policies for alleged domestic assault, police discretion and other factors may interfere with full implementation of such services. Sherman and Cohn (1989, 140–41) found that some officers on the Minneapolis police force reported considerable variations in willingness to use their mandated powers of arrest in such cases. Some officers always arrested suspects on probable cause; others never did.

MACKINNON: *FEMINISM UNMODIFIED*

Catherine MacKinnon (1987, 1) offers a strong appraisal of the movement for women's legal rights. She suggests that the women's movement is approaching a "crossroads" and alludes to a "string of defeats and declines" for women, including lack of effective sex-equality provisions for pay, opposition to women's right to safe abortions, a movement toward men gaining or sharing custody of children after separation, and other developments that leave the ideal of women's equality before law far from realized in the United States. Two positive exceptions that MacKinnon refers to are policies concerning sexual harassment and some initiatives with respect to marital rape and domestic assault.

MacKinnon (1987, 2–3) cautions against women's complicity in a politics of male supremacy. An unmodified feminism would thus be leery of co-optation and the dispensation of small concessions. MacKinnon (1987, 4) notes that, in large measure, what is referred to as feminism in law reflects

> the attempt to get for men what little has been reserved for women or to get for some women some of the plunder that some men have previously divided (unequally) among themselves.

MacKinnon's work directly confronts the fusing of sexuality, control, and collaboration between men and women. She notes that feminists believe women's accounts of sexual use and abuse by men. As such, feminism resists attempts to dismiss or trivialize a range of sexual practices that, in fact, constitute sexual violation. Such an approach goes well beyond technical or legalistic definitions of violence to an appreciation of the net effect of women's feelings of subordination to men and the various practices that can intimidate them and lead to feelings of terror. Women face an arrangement based on terror: "Just to get through another day, women must spend an incredible amount of time, life, and energy cowed, fearful and colonized, trying to figure out how not to be next on the list" (MacKinnon 1987, 7).

One criticism of MacKinnon's approach is that it tends to settle on coercive expressions of sexuality without balancing this with an appreciation of more positive expressions of heterosexuality. In fairness, however, MacKinnon (1987) is dealing with momentous legal questions, and in keeping with the title of her work—*Feminism Unmodified*—MacKinnon (1987, 5) resists any dilution of the seriousness of these issues, drawing our attention to deep-seated expressions of misogyny in society and even in "liberal legalism."

MacKinnon (1987) continues to emphasize the importance of exploring power and acting against coercion in other sections of her book. For example, she notes that the concept of sexual harassment as a "law of injuries" is a relatively new invention. It is traced to feminism's insistence that women's experience of coercive sexuality be taken seriously. For MacKinnon, laws against sexual harassment represent a practical strategy for stopping the exploitation of women. It is "a demand that state authority stand behind women's refusal of sexual access in certain situations that previously were a masculine prerogative" (MacKinnon 1987, 104). MacKinnon (1987, 105) concludes that, relative to other legislation concerning sex discrimination, the law against sexual harassment works "surprisingly well" for women. Nevertheless, she notes that most victims still do not file complaints against harassers. Women who are especially abused—"viciously violated"—are often ashamed to report the violation (MacKinnon 1987, 114). Those most victimized may be rendered silent, enduring their victimization for fear of public disclosure and further invasion of privacy. MacKinnon (1987, 116) concludes that legislation against sexual harassment can make a difference if a legal initiative is established from "women's real experience of violation." Legal doctrine and male metaphysics—the tendency by some men to theorize, to abstract issues from their social contexts—clearly predominate, but this does not eliminate the importance of feminist-oriented legal initiatives. As MacKinnon (1987, 116) allows, "law is not everything in this respect, but it is not nothing either."

SUMMARY

The women's movement has uprooted many myths concerning the supposed nature of the sexes and the institutions that promote and benefit from discriminatory practices against women. The sphere of law has attracted considerable attention, in part because much of women's oppression and control is vested in law, and also because many feminists—and others supportive of women's struggles—believe that the law can provide leverage against entrenched patterns of sexism.

It is important to note that much of the work within feminist jurisprudence has emphasized the enduring power of patriarchy. Liberal beliefs to the contrary, some feminists argue that many gains have been illusory, and that conservative backlashes with respect to family structures, hiring practices, access to abortion, and other issues foreshadow new ways of treating women as subordinate, or in Simone de Beauvoir's (1970) words, as "the other."

The feminization of poverty, discrimination in workplace settings, exposure to violence in public and private places, and women's lack of political influence are a few examples of the issues addressed by feminist theorists and practitioners. Some of these issues are discussed in more detail in Chapter Nine, where we will examine the politics of family law and reproductive rights.

STUDY QUESTIONS

❏ Many scholars refer to the gap between *formal equality* and *substantive inequality* in law and society. Discuss how this concept can be applied to the issue of legal protections for women.

❏ Review Smart's (1989) discussion of the ways in which legal procedures for allegations of rape and child sexual abuse correspond to male-oriented (phallocentric) culture. Critically assess her arguments. In what ways might her approach be qualified? In what ways could her arguments be extended?

❏ Catherine MacKinnon (1987) advocates a feminist approach that is "unmodified." Address the issue of how women's experiences, discourses, and solutions are co-opted by legal authorities and other agents. In what ways is sex equality limited by gender (MacKinnon 1987, 45)?

NOTES

1. Renzetti and Curran (1989, 202) conclude that the doctrine of "equal pay for equal work" is limited by continued patterns of sex segregation. Therefore, a law such as the Equal Pay Act in the United States does not necessarily reverse occupational segregation. The authors note, however, that a doctrine of "comparable worth"—in which worth is assessed in terms of similarly valued work, even if the jobs are different—may serve to narrow the wage differential between male and female employees.

2. This system was formulated as one vote for an unskilled labourer, two votes for a skilled labourer, and perhaps three votes for a superintendent or foreman (see Eisenstein 1981, 119).

3. Manual workers have to a large extent been disparaged for what is often seen as unskilled or unimportant work. Orwell (1937) challenged this disparagement, but, as is discussed in this chapter, he has also been criticized for disregarding women's work in his paean to male manual workers. Other writers have also depicted the worthiness of working people. More recently, Robert Bly (1987, 16) remarks on the "ascensionism" that separates the higher life of mental work from the lower life of manual labour: "The new attitude centered on one idea: physical labor is bad. [D.H.] Lawrence recalls that his father, who had not absorbed this idea, worked in the mines, enjoyed the camaraderie with the other men, came home in good spirits and took his bath in the kitchen. But around that time the new schoolteachers arrived from London to teach Lawrence and his classmates that physical labour is low, and that boys and girls should strive to move upward into a more 'spiritual' place—higher work, mental work."

4. George E. Babbitt is the central character in Sinclair Lewis's novel, *Babbitt* (1922). The *Canadian Dictionary of the English Language* defines "Babbitry" as the attitudes, beliefs, and conduct of "a member of the American middle class whose adherence to its ideals is such as to make him a model of narrow-mindedness and self-satisfaction."

5. The Cleveland Crisis refers to the extensive press coverage of the practices of a female pediatrician and, to a lesser extent, a male doctor who assessed child sexual abuse by the physical diagnosis of anal dilation. Many have criticized such assessments as unreliable. To use them to recommend removal of the child from his or her home, or to press charges against parents, has been seen as more of a "moral panic" (Smart 1989, 62) than sound medical practice. Smart (1989, 62–64) notes that the diagnosis and the recommendations that children be taken into emergency care were controversial. Smart (1989, 62) cautions that other considerations were also used by the doctors, but this fact was lost in the great criticism directed against them. She adds that the attack on both pediatricians and on the social service personnel who placed the children in care appears to have reinforced the ideology of nonintervention in the nuclear family and the notion that child sexual abuse is a rarity. In other words, the backlash against the Cleveland doctors seems to have taken a conservative twist, highlighting parents' rights and obscuring real difficulties in detecting and prosecuting child sexual abuse. The media line that some doctors may be on a "witch-hunt" for parents who are in fact nonabusing may, in fact, have served to reverse a number of "small advances" (Smart 1989, 63) with respect to child sexual abuse. Again, such conflicts may serve not to address cases of abuse, but to marginalize the issue and restore a sense of complacency.

REFERENCES

Baril, J. (1990) "At the Centre of the Backlash." *The Canadian Forum* 68 (786): 14–17.

de Beauvoir, S. (1970) *The Second Sex*. Translated and edited by H.M. Parshley. New York: Bantam.

Bly, R. (1987) *The Pillow and the Key: Commentary on the Fairy Tale Iron John*. St. Paul, Minnesota: Ally Press.

Boyd, S., and E. Sheehy (1989) "Overview: Feminism and the Law in Canada." In *Law and Society: A Critical Perspective*, edited by T. Caputo, M. Kennedy, C. Reasons, and A. Brannigan, 255–70. Toronto: Harcourt Brace Jovanovich.

Boyle, C. (1991) "Sexual Assault: A Case Study in Legal Policy Options." In *Canadian Criminology: Perspectives on Crime and Criminality*, edited by M. Jackson and C. Griffiths, 99–109. Toronto: Harcourt Brace Jovanovich.

Campbell, B. (1984) *Wigan Pier Revisited*. London: Virago.

Comack, E. (1988) "Justice for Battered Women? The Courts and the 'Battered Wife Syndrome'." *Canadian Dimension* 22 (3): 8–11.

Chrystos (1988) *Not Vanishing*. Vancouver: Press Gang.

Chrystos (1991) *Dream On*. Vancouver: Press Gang.

Clark, L., and D. Lewis (1977) *Rape: The Price of Coercive Sexuality*. Toronto: The Women's Press.

Eisenstein, Z. (1979) *Capitalism, Patriarchy, and the Case for Socialist Feminism*. New York: Monthly Review Press.

——— (1981) *The Radical Future of Liberal Feminism*. New York: Longman.

Garrett, S. (1987) *Gender*. London: Tavistock.

Gavigan, S. (1986) "Women, Law and Patriarchial Relations: Perspectives in the Sociology of Law." In *The Social Dimensions of Law*, edited by N. Boyd, 101–24. Toronto: Prentice-Hall.

Gregory, J. (1979) "Sex Discrimination, Work and the Law." In *Capitalism and the Rule of Law*, edited by B. Fine, R. Kinsey, J. Lea, S. Picciotto, and J. Young, 137–50. London: Hutchinson.

Gunderson, M., and L. Muszynski, with J. Keck (1990) *Women and Labour Market Poverty*. Ottawa: Canadian Advisory Council on the Status of Women.

Harris, M. (1990) *Unholy Orders: Tragedy at Mount Cashel*. Markham, Ontario: Viking.

Held, D. (1984) "Introduction: Central Perspectives on the Modern State." In *States and Societies*, edited by D. Held, J. Anderson, B. Gieben, S. Hall, L. Harris, P. Lewis, N. Parker, and B. Turok, 1–55. London: Martin Robertson.

Kitzinger, S. (1987) *Women's Experience of Sex*. Harmondsworth: Penguin.

Lakeman, L. (1990) "Women, Violence and the Montreal Massacre." *This Magazine* 23 (7): 20–23.

Lewis, S. (1922) *Babbitt*. New York: Harcourt, Brace & Co.

Livesay, D. (1972) "Look to the End." In *The Two Seasons: Collected Poems of Dorothy Livesay*. Toronto: McGraw-Hill Ryerson. Reprinted with permission of the author.

Luxton, M. (1980) *More Than a Labour of Love: Three Generations of Women's Work in the Home*. Toronto: Women's Educational Press.

McCormack, T. (1991) "Politically Correct." *The Canadian Forum* 70 (802): 8–10.

MacKinnon, C. (1987) *Feminism Unmodified: Discourses on Life and Law*. Cambridge: Harvard University Press.

Malarkey, R., and J. Hagan (1989) "The Socio-Legal Impact of Equal Pay Legislation in Ontario, 1946–1979." *Osgoode Hall Law Journal* 27 (2): 295–336.

Mitchell, J. (1973) *Woman's Estate*. New York: Vintage Books.

Morton, M. (1988) "Dividing the Wealth, Sharing the Poverty: The (Re)formation of 'Family' in Law in Ontario." *Canadian Review of Sociology and Anthropology* 25 (2): 254–75.

Orwell, G. (1937) *The Road to Wigan Pier*. Harmondsworth: Penguin.

Pascall, G. (1986) *Social Policy: A Feminist Analysis*. London: Tavistock.

Renzetti, C., and D. Curran (1989) *Women, Men, and Society: The Sociology of Gender*. Boston: Allyn and Bacon.

Robertson, H. (1990) "Sexual Taboo—The M Word." *The Canadian Forum*, 68 (691): 4.

Russell, S. (1987) "The Hidden Curriculum of School: Reproducing Gender and Class Hierarchies." In *Feminism and Political Economy: Women's Work, Women's Struggles*, edited by H. Maroney and M. Luxton, 229–45. Toronto: Methuen.

Seager, J., and A. Olson (1986) *Women in the World*. London: Pluto Press.

Sherman, J., and E. Cohn (1989) "The Impact of Research on Legal Policy: The Minneapolis Domestic Violence Experiment." *Law and Society Review* 23 (1): 117–41.

Smart, C. (1989) *Feminism and the Power of Law*. London: Routledge and Kegan Paul.

Stanko, E. (1990) *Everyday Violence: How Women and Men Experience Sexual and Physical Danger*. London: Pandora Books.

CHAPTER FIVE

The Donald Marshall Case

I.
I remember the obituary
of the Saugeen brave from
the River Credit mission
in the winter of 1830:
"Insane through continued drunkenness,
and eaten by wolves".

II.
I remember, also,
the words of a squaw
from Portage-la-Prairie
as the mounties arrested her
last Christmas:
"You see me on the street,
you don't even know my name—
but back in the bush
with a bottle of wine,
you called me honey".

(Brian Burtch, "The Wolves")

INTRODUCTION

Conviction of people for crimes they did not commit is a subject that is very important in understanding legal processes and principles. Literary works such as *Papillon*—based on the wrongful conviction in 1931 of Henri Charrière in France—and *Les Misérables*—which uses the protagonist, Jean Valjean, to dramatize injustices faced by the poor in nineteenth century, post-Napoleonic France—underscore the reality of wrongful convictions and the difficulties facing people who seek to establish their innocence. In Canada, one can cite a number of cases of wrongful conviction. Neil Boyd (1988) contends that some individuals executed for murder may indeed have been innocent. The execution of Wilbert Coffin in Quebec in 1960, and the conviction of Steven Truscott in Ontario in 1959 (LeBourdais 1966; Burtch 1981) generated great controversy over possible miscarriages of justice.

In recent times, other cases in Canada have been investigated to see if the wrong person was convicted. Of these cases, however, the 1971 conviction of Donald Marshall, Jr. for a murder in Nova Scotia has attracted considerable public and official interest. The conviction of Marshall has not only challenged the legitimacy of the criminal justice system in Canada, especially the administration of justice in Nova Scotia, but has also raised questions surrounding patterns of racism in various sectors of the state: policing, courts, prisons, segregation on and off reserves, and so forth. The process by which Marshall was convicted and later released from prison has been addressed by Harris (1990). The 1989 *Report of the Royal Commission on the Donald Marshall, Jr. Prosecution* will be reviewed in this chapter, along with criticisms of the reforms and assumptions that seem to characterize the Royal Commission Report (e.g., Mannette 1990). To begin with, however, we will use Harris's (1990) work to review the key events in the Marshall case.

The wrongful conviction of Donald Marshall has influenced the ways in which criminal law is understood in Canada. Convicted of the murder of his friend Sandy Seale, Marshall was imprisoned for eleven years before his eventual release and exoneration for the murder. This chapter provides an overview of events in the Marshall case. These events are linked with sociological factors that may have contributed to his conviction, with the ensuing Royal Commission that investigated the Marshall case and, in a wider perspective, with the question of racial discrimination in the Nova Scotia criminal justice system.

BRIEF SUMMARY OF KEY EVENTS

May 28, 1971: Sandy Seale is fatally stabbed by Roy Ebsary. Seale's companion, Donald Marshall, Jr. is wounded. Marshall is treated by police as the murder suspect.

November 5, 1971: Jury finds Marshall guilty; he is sentenced to life imprisonment.

November 15, 1971: Jimmy MacNeil confides to his family that Junior Marshall is innocent of murder. Several people are interviewed, including Roy Ebsary (see Harris 1990, 226–30). Donna Ebsary is *not* interviewed, but Greg and Mary Ebsary are interviewed.

November 1971: RCMP search of Halifax and Ottawa records indicates that Ebsary was convicted of carrying a concealed weapon, as well as violating the Liquor Control Act, following an incident in 1970. This incident occurred less than one year before Sandy Seale's death (Harris 1990, 237).

November 1971: RCMP polygraph experts conclude that Ebsary's responses are generally truthful. Jimmy MacNeil's responses are deemed suspect (Harris 1990, 238). (N.B.: In 1982, eleven years after the polygraph examination, the examiner reported that polygraph results were sent to Donald MacNeil. The examiner assumed, incorrectly, that the results and examination had been conveyed to Marshall and his lawyer (see Harris 1990, 239).

August 1978: Marshall joins Atlantic Challenge wilderness excursion, on a ten-day temporary absence from Springhill Institution. Within a month, his T.A. privileges are suspended for drinking and marijuana incidents (Harris 1990, 286–87).

September 24, 1979: Marshall escapes from Native Brotherhood canoeing expedition. At large for two days, he is arrested at Shelly Sarson's apartment (see Harris 1990, 9–13, 292).

February 3, 1982: RCMP Constable Donald Wheaton is assigned to the Donald Marshall case. Wheaton reviews case files, consults with Sydney police officer "Woody" Woodburn, who investigated the 1981 stabbing of Goodie Mugridge (Harris 1990, 311). RCMP Constable Jim Carroll joins Wheaton in the reinvestigation. (N.B.: The November 15, 1971, statement by Jimmy MacNeil is *not* in the file supplied by John MacIntyre to the RCMP.) Interview with Mitchell Sarson on February 9, 1982, points to possible vindication of Marshall, and to Ebsary's guilt.

March 29, 1982: Marshall is released from Dorchester Prison.

June 16, 1982: Justice minister Jean Chrétien refers Marshall's case to the Nova Scotia Court of Appeal.

July 29, 1982: Stephen Aronson applies to Nova Scotia Appeal Division to determine admissibility of fresh evidence, including recounting of evidence by Chant and Pratico (Harris 1990, 360).

May 10, 1983: Marshall is acquitted of the charge of murdering Sandy Seale (Harris 1990, 370).

November 24, 1983: In his second trial, Roy Ebsary is sentenced to five years in prison for murdering Sandy Seale. Decision is appealed and a new trial is ordered.

1983: Judgement of the Nova Scotia Supreme Court (Appeal Division). Five judges indicate that "any miscarriage of justice is, however, more apparent than real," and "there can be no doubt that Donald Marshall's untruthfulness through this whole affair contributed in large measure to his conviction" (see Harris 1990, 367–68).

September 1984: Donald Marshall instructs his lawyer, Felix Cacchione, to accept compensation offer of $270 000 (with Marshall responsible for his legal fees).

1985: Roy Ebsary is found guilty of manslaughter in jury trial. An appeal seeking a fourth trial is set aside, and his sentence is reduced to one year in county jail (Harris 1990, 383).

September 1987: Provincial Royal Commission is held on the Marshall case.

January 1990: The Commission Report on the Marshall case is released, generating considerable media coverage and commentary. The Commission absolves Marshall entirely of the murder and conviction, while criticizing the justice administration and other individuals. The Report deals with racism generally.

KEY FIGURES IN THE MARSHALL CASE

Maynard Chant: Witness for prosecution. Attempted to recant earlier statement implicating Marshall in murder of Sandy Seale—"Donald Marshall didn't do it" (Harris 1990, 157). Eventually testified against Marshall.

Donna Ebsary: Mary and Roy Ebsary's daughter. Saw her father washing blood off the murder weapon.

Greg Ebsary: Mary and Roy Ebsary's son. Teenager at the time of Sandy Seale's death.

Mary Ebsary: Common-law wife of Roy Ebsary.

Roy Ebsary: Murdered Sandy Seale. History of violence, including wounding with a knife. Tried four times, sentenced to one year in prison. Now deceased.

Roy Gould: A political activist on the Membertou reserve and supporter of Marshall. The first person Marshall contacted when he discovered that Roy Ebsary was the man who murdered Sandy Seale.

Patricia Harris: Witness for prosecution. Provided two contradictory statements, including a statement about an older man (Roy Ebsary) talking to Marshall (see Harris 1990, 90–92 and 151–52 for her testimony).

Simon Khattar: Defence lawyer in 1971 murder trial.

John MacIntyre: Chief of police, Sydney.

Donald MacNeil: Crown prosecutor in 1971 murder trial.

Jimmy MacNeil: Witness to Sandy Seale's murder and friend of Roy Ebsary.

Brought this information forward to Sydney police on November 14, 1971, after encouragement from his brothers, sister, and mother (see Harris 1990, 221–22).

Caroline Marshall: Mother of Donald Marshall, Jr. Worked as a cleaner at St. Rita's Hospital in Sydney.

Donald Marshall, Jr.: Born 1953. Lived on the Membertou Reserve. One of thirteen children, and eldest son. "Failed" twice in public school, left school at fifteen to apprentice with father. Member of the Shipyard Gang. Seventeen years old when charged with murder of Sandy Seale.

Donald Marshall, Sr.: Grand Chief of the Micmac Nation, and employed as a plasterer.

John Pratico: Witness at the 1971 murder trial. His June 4 statement was false, indicating that he had seen Marshall stabbing Sandy Seale. Disavowed the June 4 statement (see Harris 1990, 156–57, 176).

Moe Rosenblum: Defence lawyer in 1971 murder trial.

Sandy Seale: Teenage son of Leotha and Oscar Seale. Fatally stabbed in Wentworth Park on May 28, 1971.

BACKGROUND

Michael Harris's *Justice Denied: The Law versus Donald Marshall* (1990) is a careful reconstruction of the events of the Marshall case and raises a number of serious questions about official conduct in the case and the actions of ordinary people who were aware that Marshall was innocent of the murder charge. Only after years in prison did Marshall's claims of innocence attract the attention of journalists, most notably Michael Harris. Marshall's release from prison in 1982 and compensation award in 1983 vindicated him, but the wider issues of discrimination and illegal conduct by officials remain.

In 1971, Donald Marshall was seventeen years old. He was the eldest son of Caroline and Donald Marshall, Sr. Donald had twelve siblings. The Marshall family lived on the Membertou Reserve, an urban reserve that houses 400 Micmac Indians. Donald Marshall, Sr., was the Grand Chief of the Micmac Nation and worked as a plasterer in the Sydney area. As Grand Chief, Mr. Marshall represented approximately 5000 Micmacs, primarily in Nova Scotia. Caroline Marshall was employed as a cleaner in a nearby hospital. Harris (1990, 17) mentions that the people on the reserve had never shared in the wealth created by the industrial developments in Sydney, Nova Scotia: "Bleak and rundown, Membertou was a world apart, its poverty, alcoholism, and paralyzing social isolation largely ignored by the city in whose midst it existed" (Harris 1990, 17).

The decimated status of the Membertou Reserve contrasts sharply with the vibrancy of the Micmac people prior to European contact. York (1990, 55–57) states that several thousand Micmacs thrived on Canada's east coast in the 1500s. He adds: "The Micmacs had their own political structures, boundaries, laws, and a sophisticated culture and language" (York 1990, 55). Through disease, liquor, and the reserve system (which confined the Micmac to barren ground and eliminated their traditional livelihood of fishing and hunting), the Micmac population fell and many Micmac communities disintegrated (York 1990, 57, 64–65).

A similar portrait of community disintegration has been made of other reserves, in which traditional means of employment and culture have been eroded. Shkilnyk (1985), for example, documents the inordinately high rates of alcoholism, family conflicts, suicide, and other forms of violent death, on the Grassy Narrows Reserve in northern Ontario in the 1970s. Shkilnyk (1985) links these problems to wider changes affecting the Grassy Narrows community: specifically, mercury poisoning of surrounding waters, which has eliminated a source of livelihood for the Ojibwa and poisoned their water supply; the replacement of a hunting, trapping, and fishing economy with a social welfare dependency; introduction of alcohol; and the overall neglect of community life on the reserve.

There are at least three levels of analysis that can be applied in understanding the Marshall case. The *macrosocial* level emphasizes broad political and social structures. Harris's (1990, 17) depiction of the "bleak" character of the Membertou Reserve indicates that the Marshall case must be set in the context of the discrimination and poverty experienced in one degree or another by the Micmac people on the reserve. This macrosocial perspective can be linked with the relative helplessness of individuals in the face of broad economic, cultural, and political changes.

At the *subcultural* level, it can be observed that fighting, drinking, and petty crimes were valued by many of the youth on the reserve. Not all commentators, however, agree with Harris's perspective. Mannette (1990, 507) provides a report by one Micmac that Harris portrayed Membertou and Sydney as "Harlem North" and overemphasized gang violence. Mannette (1990) contends that many journalistic accounts of the Marshall case did not adequately portray traditional tribal values such as esteem for elders and co-operation.

The subcultural portrait corresponds to classic, criminological works on the nature of gang violence and working-class crime. Thus we can see that resistance to dominant, middle-class norms of discipline, respectability, and restraint was prominent among Marshall's peers, with their emphasis on "macho" ideals and violence. This perspective has the advantage of allowing us to trace specific interactions and events in Membertou and elsewhere, while remaining a focus on *social class* as a factor in deviance and social control measures.

The *labelling perspective* could be used to explain how Marshall's identity was increasingly constructed as delinquent, dangerous, and in need of incarceration. This construction of his deviant identity could, in turn, lead to a presumption of his untrustworthiness and likely guilt in the murder of Sandy Seale. Marshall was thus relatively defenceless against the police charge and the resulting prosecution, notwithstanding the formal, due-process protections of the criminal trial. The labelling perspective is rooted in the dynamics of power and social definitions of deviance. It is important to keep in mind, however, that the labelling perspective has been criticized for its lack of a formal "theory" of deviance, poor operationalization of variables, and its limited value in predicting who is labelled deviant and the nature of social reactions to such labels.

JUSTICE DENIED: THE PROSECUTION OF DONALD MARSHALL, JR.

Donald Marshall was born in Sydney, Nova Scotia, in 1953. He had failed school twice by the time he entered sixth grade. Donald remarked that Indians were "treated like dirt" at school. While in grade seven, he was expelled for hitting a teacher. Harris (1990, 21) notes that Marshall could either work as an apprentice plasterer with his father or be sent to a reformatory. Thus, while a teenager, Marshall left school to work with his father.

Marshall was involved with a gang called the Shipyard Gang and became well known to police for several incidents, including underage drinking, vandalizing tombstones, and assaulting a local bootlegger. Marshall was nicknamed "Little Rock" out of respect for his fighting skills.

Marshall's status as a delinquent changed on the evening of May 28, 1971. Marshall had set out for a dance in Sydney. Crossing Wentworth Park, he noticed two men apparently bumming cigarettes from people in the park. Around the same time, Sandy Seale, a black teenager and an acquaintance of Marshall, had unsuccessfully tried to get into the dance. Marshall and Seale teamed up. On the way home, according to Harris (1990, 41), the two agreed to panhandle in the park; if necessary, they could take the money by force.[1]

When the boys approached Roy Ebsary and his younger companion, Jimmy MacNeil, they hinted around for money. Unknown to either Marshall or Seale, Ebsary had been mugged several times in the past. He had "sworn a terrible vengeance on the next person who accosted him" (Harris 1990, 42). Ebsary stabbed Sandy Seale in the stomach, fatally wounding him. Marshall was also cut by Ebsary, but escaped and sought help. Seale was taken to hospital by ambulance. Despite surgery, he died on the evening of May 29.

Marshall was at this time the only witness available to police. Sandy had not recovered consciousness and had not been able to identify the attacker. There was also a lack of physical evidence, including the murder weapon. Marshall was questioned by police. At one point, he reviewed a police line-up of seven men, but indicated that the killer was not in the line-up. He described the attacker (Ebsary) as an older man, about 50 years old. He was small, with grey hair, and dressed like a priest; that is, he wore a dark, hooded cloak (Harris 1990, 40 & 63). In his formal statement to police, two days after the murder, Marshall stood by his description of the assailant and his companion. He did not indicate that either he or Sandy Seale had sought to panhandle or "roll" the two men. The Sydney police force had already designated Marshall as a possible suspect. A telex sent from the Sydney police to RCMP headquarters in Halifax indicated that Marshall was "possibly the person responsible" (Harris 1990, 63).

After the stabbing, Ebsary and MacNeil fled to Ebsary's home. MacNeil was sworn to silence. Nevertheless, Ebsary's thirteen-year-old daughter, Donna, observed her father washing blood from a knife, shortly after they returned to Ebsary's house (Harris 1990, 252). MacNeil did not approach police at this point.

As noted above, there were suspicions by some investigators that Marshall's statement was not credible. Sgt./Det. John MacIntyre headed the murder investigation. Harris (1990) provides considerable detail concerning MacIntyre's efforts to place Marshall at the scene, using the testimony of three teenage witnesses. None of the three were at the murder scene at the time, although all three provided statements that they observed Marshall stabbing Sandy Seale. Harris's point—since reinforced by the Report of the Royal Commission on the Donald Marshall, Jr. Prosecution—is that these witnesses were intimidated into giving false statements. Moreover, information that might have been crucial to Marshall's defence was not released by the police or the prosecutor's office to Marshall's attorneys.

On June 1, 1971, with the murder case still unsolved, a letter from the Black United Front was sent to Sydney police chief Gordon MacLeod (Harris 1990, 67). The police were under great pressure to solve this murder, especially in the wake of an unsolved murder of a Chinese-Canadian man a few years earlier (Harris 1990, 57–58). On June 4, 1971, Marshall was arrested and charged with second-degree murder.

In the ensuing murder trial, no physical evidence was brought forward linking Marshall with the crime. The three key witnesses for the defence testified against Marshall. One of the witnesses—John Pratico—met Donald Marshall, Sr., outside the courtroom during the trial. Pratico confessed that his evidence was incorrect, that he hadn't seen Marshall kill Sandy Seale (Harris 1990, 157–58). Although one of Marshall's lawyers was immediately advised of this, Pratico was not able to recant his statement. Two days after his statement to Marshall's father, apparently afraid of repercussions if he did not implicate Marshall, Pratico testified that he had, indeed, seen Marshall stab the boy.

On November 5, 1971, Marshall was sentenced to life in prison. Because he was still a juvenile, he served some time in jail and then was transferred to the Dorchester maximum-security penitentiary in New Brunswick in June 1972. In October 1974, he was transferred to Springhill, a medium-security penitentiary in Nova Scotia. Marshall spent almost five years in Springhill, before escaping while on a temporary absence. He was recaptured shortly after his escape. On October 30, 1980, Marshall was returned to Dorchester Penitentiary, where he served the next couple of years prior to his release and eventual acquittal.

The second half of *Justice Denied* begins with the central theme of Donald Marshall's innocence and the knowledge of others that he had been wrongfully convicted. Jimmy MacNeil's confession that he had lied about Seale's killer was heard by MacNeil's brothers, sister, and mother in November 1971 (Harris 1990, 222). Even though the Sydney police had heard of this confession the day after MacNeil confessed to his family (Harris 1990, 223), and despite the clear identification of Roy Ebsary as the murderer, Donald Marshall was not cleared of the murder. The subsequent interviews with Mary and Roy Ebsary and their teenage son Greg were interpreted by Sgt./Det. MacIntyre and Louis Matheson, the assistant crown prosecutor, as inconsistent with Jimmy MacNeil's allegation. One result of the allegation, however, was that the director of criminal prosecutions in Nova Scotia, Robert Anderson, was contacted, and a *reinvestigation* of the Marshall case was launched, this time under the auspices of the RCMP (Harris 1990, 232).

The RCMP investigation began on November 16, 1971, and concluded less than a month later. Harris (1990) depicts this reinvestigation as a "rubber stamp," which depended on the dubious results of a polygraph investigation and used "armchair psychology" (Harris 1990, 238) to dismiss MacNeil's allegation as delusional.

Harris (1990) treats Marshall's years in prison thematically: the recurrence of physical violence among prisoners, the contraband drug market in prison, the unsuccessful attempts to have the murder conviction appealed or reviewed. Marshall faced the dilemma of showing remorse and confessing to a crime he did not commit in order to increase his chances for a day parole or full parole. Harris (1990, 305) reviews a visit to Marshall made by Mitchell Sarson on August 26, 1981. Sarson told Marshall that Roy Ebsary admitted that "he killed a black guy and stabbed an Indian in the park in 1971" (Harris 1990, 305). Marshall quickly telephoned his friend Roy Gould. This information about Ebsary's involvement in the murder was passed on to the Union of Nova Scotia Indians who immediately contacted the Sydney Police. In late March 1982 Marshall was released from prison and in May 1983 he was acquitted of the murder of Sandy Seale.

Marshall's suffering did not end with his pardon and release from prison. Harris (1990, 359) documents the adjustments that Marshall faced on release, including legal costs that amounted to $70 000. Harris notes that no convicted criminal had ever had his conviction overturned, with a full pardon, despite provisions for this in the Criminal Code (Harris 1990, 359). This situation underscores a central theme in this text: the gulf between formal legal provisions and the structural barriers to putting these provisions in practice.

PROVINCIAL ROYAL COMMISSION ON THE MARSHALL CASE

On January 26, 1990, the Commission investigating the Marshall case released its Report. The Commission examined the particulars of the case and, more broadly, the question of criminal justice and Natives in Nova Scotia. National media coverage reviewed the recommendations of the Report and discussed whether the recommendations were merely symbolic or designed to change current, discriminatory practices against Native people in the criminal law.

The Report was unusually blunt in its critique of the Nova Scotia criminal justice system: "The criminal justice system failed Donald Marshall Jr. at virtually every turn from his arrest and wrongful conviction for murder in 1971 up to and even beyond his acquittal by the Court of Appeal in 1983" (Nova Scotia 1989, 1). The Report outlined 82 recommendations for improving the justice system in Nova Scotia, including reopening the compensation settlement agreed to by Marshall, and criticizing the prosecutor, the Sydney police chief, the defence lawyers, and the judiciary (trial and appeal). The Report rebutted the "gratuitous defence of the justice system" that was part of the 1983 Nova Scotia Appeal Court's statement that any miscarriage of justice in the Marshall case was more apparent than real (see News Services 1990).

News coverage on the CBC was extensive, with some commentators concluding that, unlike the pardon, the Commission Report was a complete vindication of Marshall and a severe criticism of the parties responsible for the administration of criminal justice in Nova Scotia.

Recommendations

The Royal Commission was chaired by Chief Justice Alexander Hickman, with Associate Chief Justice Lawrence Poitras and Mr. Gregory Evans serving as commissioners. The 82 recommendations covered many aspects of the Marshall case. The recommendations were subdivided into six general categories: dealing with the wrongfully convicted; visible minorities in the criminal justice system; the specific issue of the Nova Scotia Micmac and the criminal justice system; blacks in the criminal justice system; administration of criminal justice; and police and policing. A summary of these recommendations is listed below.

Wrongful Conviction. With respect to the wrongfully convicted, the Commission made several recommendations of a general nature: first, that an independent review mechanism be established to assist in reinvestigation of wrongful conviction cases; second, that this review body have unrestricted access to documents and material in any particular case, and have coercive power to compel witnesses to provide information. The Report also recommended that compensation claims by people who were found to be wrongfully convicted be considered by a judicial inquiry. This inquiry would be "completely independent" (Nova Scotia 1989, 25) of any involvement with the administration of justice in all Canadian jurisdictions, including Nova Scotia. The judicial inquiry would consider all factors pertinent to the case, and there would be no preset limit on the amount of compensation that might be recovered. Legal fees and disbursements of the wrongfully convicted person would be assumed as part of the inquiry's expenses. The report of the inquiry would be made available as a public document.

These general recommendations were followed by a specific recommendation concerning Donald Marshall, Jr., "that Government recanvass the adequacy of the compensation paid to Marshall in light of what we have found to be factors contributing to his wrongful conviction and continued incarceration" (Nova Scotia 1989, 26).

Visible Minorities and Criminal Justice.   The Commission recommended that the Nova Scotia government continue to support the minority admissions program administered by Dalhousie Law School. This admissions program—for Micmacs and indigenous blacks—was designed to provide greater access to legal training for these groups. As such, it recognizes the barrier to postsecondary education for these visible minorities. Other recommendations expressed support for the appointment of members of visible minorities as judges and administrative board members. Crown prosecutors would be exposed to educational programs that would focus on "systemic discrimination toward black and Native peoples in Nova Scotia in the criminal justice system" (Nova Scotia 1989, 26), and to specific measures that prosecutors could employ to reduce the effects of systemic discrimination in Nova Scotia's criminal justice operations. More blacks and Native people would be employed within the correctional services, and institutional programs would emphasize the educational, religious, and cultural needs of Native and black offenders. It was recommended that the two departments most concerned with criminal justice—Attorney General and Solicitor General—adopt and publicize a policy on race relations. This policy would involve *employment equity* and an elimination of racially-based inequalities in these departments and related agencies.

A cabinet committee on race relations was also recommended. The cabinet committee would meet on a regular basis with representatives of visible minority groups to discuss criminal justice matters. The Attorney General would explore measures to reduce the impact of systemic discrimination in the current criminal justice system. Members of visible minorities would be encouraged to join the correctional services. Where a "significant number of Natives and

Blacks are incarcerated" (Nova Scotia 1989, 27), institutional programs would respect the cultural, educational, and religious needs of these offenders.

Nova Scotia Micmac and Criminal Justice.
A five-year pilot project was recommended for the Nova Scotia Micmac. A Native criminal court would appoint a Native justice of the peace with jurisdiction to hear summary conviction offences. Diversion, mediation, and community work projects would be included in the mandate of this community-controlled court. The court would be designed to encourage "resolution of disputes without resort to the criminal courts" (Nova Scotia 1989, 28). Aftercare services, community input into sentencing decisions, and courtwork services would be made available as part of the court's resources.

The Report recommended a Native justice institute to provide research on Native customary law, to funnel community needs and concerns to the Native criminal court, and to train court workers and other personnel. It would also work with the professions and law schools and monitor discriminatory treatment of Native people in the criminal justice system.

All courts in Nova Scotia would have the services of an on-call Micmac interpreter. Legal aid provisions would be strengthened, and regular sittings of provincial courts would be held on reserves. Recruitment of Native constables would be encouraged within the RCMP and municipal police forces. The spirit of these recommendations thus centred on providing a stronger ratio of Native personnel in the criminal justice system. Beyond this orthodox approach to criminal justice, the Commission recommended experiments with community-controlled dispositions. These experiments were, however, limited by the summary conviction caveat. Overall, there was a call for greater sensitivity to the unequal treatment of Micmacs and other Native people in criminal justice.

Blacks in the Criminal Justice System.
Before we discuss the specific recommendations of the Marshall Commission with respect to black people, it is important to note that discrimination against blacks in Canada has become a major political issue. In Toronto and Montreal, for example, police forces have been strongly criticized for their treatment of black people. The Black United Front in Nova Scotia has been active in publicizing cases of discrimination in work, education, and in various other settings (e.g., restaurants, retail stores) in order to underscore the extent to which racism is, for many blacks, an everyday occurrence. (The prevalence of discrimination against visible minorities was also emphasized throughout the National Symposium on Visible Minorities and Native Youth, held at Ottawa's Carleton University in the summer of 1990.)

The Marshall Commission made only four recommendations concerning blacks in the criminal justice system, among them the establishment of a race relations division within the provincial Human Rights Commission. One of the full-time commissioners would be designated a race relations commissioner. This commission should be adequately funded in order to provide (1) independent legal counsel and (2) a public awareness program, with particular emphasis on Native and black concerns.

Other recommendations involved improvements to legal aid funding for black clients. The Commission recognized that there was a "dependence of Black clients on legal aid services" (Nova Scotia 1989, 30). This dependence could be understood in the context of patterns of lower incomes for black people and other structural limits that impeded equal access to lawyering. Instead, the Marshall Commission appears to have opted for a reinforcement of legal aid services rather than more dramatic reforms in race relations.

Administration of Criminal Justice.   The Marshall Commission made fifteen general recommendations for criminal justice administration. The office of director of public prosecutions should be created. The director would be appointed by the provincial Governor in Council. Employment benefits and salary would be equivalent to those of a county court judge. The director would provide an annual report to the Attorney General concerning public prosecutions in Nova Scotia.

The Marshall Commission went on to outline sixteen general factors that might be considered in determining whether specific prosecutions are in "the public interest" (Nova Scotia 1989, 33). These involved a blend of considerations of general deterrence, special infirmities and age of the accused person, triviality (or seriousness) of the offence, and so forth. A key point is that the discretion to prosecute remained with the powers of the Attorney General's office. It was clearly recommended that prosecutorial decisions should not rest on such factors as race, religion, political beliefs, and the prosecutor's "personal feelings" concerning either the alleged offender or victim. In this discussion, we see the Commission exhorting a fully rational, nonpartisan approach to criminal justice administration. This approach is nevertheless clearly challenged by arguments that racial discrimination is not confined to particular individuals but is, rather, part of the history and everyday experience of Native people and blacks in Nova Scotia.

This issue of disclosure by the Crown was a key factor in the Marshall case. The Commission recommended that accused persons be entitled to receive various kinds of information before electing the mode of trial (jury or judge as trier of fact) and before entering a plea. The information would include verbal and written statements, exhibits contemplated by the prosecutor, copies of witnesses' statements, criminal records of witnesses who might be called to testify, and so forth. The general spirit of the recommendations is that the accused should have access to such information and "any other material or information known to the Crown and which tends to mitigate or negate the defendant's guilt," or which might reduce the accused's punishment (Nova Scotia 1989, 34). Again, it is significant that government discretion would be provided for; specifically, that applications to limit disclosure by the Crown could be considered. A formal application by the prosecutor, coupled with evidence that disclosure would threaten the safety of a person or "interfere with the administration of justice," might therefore be supported.

Police and Policing.   The Marshall Commission's tendency to reinforce official state institutions is evident in its recommendation that the resources of the provincial police commission be sufficient to its mandate. Co-ordination of different levels of state agencies was recommended with respect to the "municipal-provincial partnership" (city police and RCMP forces) in Nova Scotia (Nova Scotia 1989, 36). Adequacy of resources, liaison between different levels of police operations, and co-ordination of police information were highlighted in these recommendations.

In addition, recruitment of visible minorities should be "actively encouraged" by both RCMP and municipal police authorities. Emphasis here is given to establishing a more multiracial composition at all levels of policing. In this spirit, a specific recommendation stated that members of visible minorities should be part of police management positions (Nova Scotia 1989, 37). The Commission seems to have placed faith in the power of policies and guidelines. For example, in order to eradicate racial slurs and stereotyping in municipal police departments throughout Nova Scotia, it was suggested that official policies be developed akin to those adopted by the RCMP and the Metropolitan Toronto police force (Nova Scotia 1989, 38).

The Marshall Inquiry has been described as a forum in which the tribal values of the Micmac people prevailed "within the context of segregationist social reality" (Mannette 1990, 522). Mannette (1990, 506) emphasizes the irony of an Inquiry whose discourse could be read as an ideological defence of "an essentially reformable system," yet which allows members of the Micmac and other groups outside of the dominant culture some voice in the Inquiry proceedings. While the Inquiry did not result in criminal sanctions against anyone implicated in the wrongful conviction of Donald Marshall, Jr.—it has been described as a trial "in which no one goes to jail" (Mannette 1990, 522)—it does underscore the vitality of tribal culture in the face of racial segregation and attempts by the provincial government to assimilate tribal cultures. That said, the aftermath of the Marshall case has left serious questions about the links between politics and justice in Nova Scotia; not the least of which is the tremendous discretionary power of police, judges, and other government officials in withholding information (Harris 1988). Another aspect of the case that is troubling is the state authorities' resistance to efforts to see the Marshall case as part of a structural problem within the administration of justice. Leonard

Pace, the attorney general of Nova Scotia at the time Marshall was convicted, was subsequently appointed to the judiciary and served as one of the judges in Marshall's 1982 hearing (see Harris 1990, 369). Many have argued that it was inappropriate for someone so closely connected to the administration of justice at the time of Marshall's prosecution to sit in judgement not only of Marshall, but of the justice system. This aspect of the Marshall case challenges the liberal notion of impartiality in the administration of justice.

NATIVE PEOPLE AND JUSTICE

The wrongful conviction of Donald Marshall, Jr. received national attention, culminating in the Report of the Marshall Commission and a compensation arrangement for Donald Marshall and his parents. In a sense, this miscarriage of justice could be seen as an example of proverbial "rotten apples" in the police and prosecutorial services. The solution for such episodes could thus centre on better recruitment, selection, and training of officials. In quite another sense, however, it has been argued that the Marshall case is part of a much wider pattern of social and economic discrimination against people of colour.

That the Marshall case is more than just an isolated example of malfeasance and lack of co-ordination among state agencies is confirmed by a recent case in Alberta. Currently, the Alberta Ministry of the Attorney General is reviewing the conviction of William Nepoose for second-degree murder. Nepoose has—at the time of writing—served nearly four years of a fifteen-year sentence for the murder of a young woman. It has been alleged that Nepoose was not involved in this murder; in fact, one witness claims that she was intimidated by RCMP officers into testifying that she saw Nepoose discard the victim's body (Canadian Press 1991). The 1971 killing of Helen Betty Osborne, a Native teenager in The Pas, Manitoba also sparked concerns over racism and criminal justice. It was not until 1987 that charges were laid, with only one of four suspects in the murder eventually convicted. Priest (1990) links this killing—and the difficulties in transforming common knowledge about the likely murderers into a conviction—to factors that include community disorganization and racial conflicts.

The lengthy recommendations of the Commission investigating the Marshall case seem to reinforce state powers. The Commission implies that the administration of justice is fundamentally sound within Nova Scotia, and that through a series of improvements to existing services, the ideal of equal justice can be realized. Many commentators on criminal justice are not convinced by this reformist approach. Glasbeek (1989, 133–35) argues that the state is not committed to the ideal of justice for individuals, but rather to intervening in ways that legitimate a competitive market economy and social structure. Calls for better co-ordination of services, expansion of government inspectorates, and stronger penalties for serious activities (e.g., workplace accidents) must be juxtaposed with the reality that considerations of property and authority often outweigh attention to principles of justice. In the Marshall case, the question is clear: To what extent will the publicity and the Commission's recommendations lead to concrete changes in social ordering?

The issue of white justice and Native people has received considerable media attention in recent years. Nevertheless, many researchers have noted very slow progress in attempts to improve conditions for Native peoples. In 1970, Ian Adams's *The Poverty Wall* documented the impact of chronic poverty on many Canadians. One chapter of this book gives an account of the death of Charlie Wenjack, an Ojibwa youth who had been transported 400 miles from his reserve in northern Ontario to a residential school in Kenora, Ontario. The boy tried to return home on foot but died of exposure on October 22, 1966. This example dramatizes the plight of many Native youths who have been taken from familiar surroundings and placed under the tutelage of white teachers and other authorities.

Fifteen years after Adams's book, Shkilnyk (1985) published a critical account of the destructive effects of relocation and pollution on an Ojibwa community at Grassy Narrows, near Kenora, Ontario. Shkilnyk (1985) combined her observations of life at Grassy Narrows with official statistics to document a host of social problems that had troubled the residents of Grassy Narrows. These problems included high rates of violent death, increased admissions for care at psychiatric hospitals and detoxification centres, widespread unemployment (and hence, welfare dependency), increased rates of assault, and high levels of alcoholism and other drug abuse. Shkilnyk (1985) points to several structural factors that contributed to the decline of a previously isolated and stable community structure, especially the relocation of the Grassy Narrows people from the English-Wabigoon river site to a new reserve 8 kilometres away. This relocation was instigated by the Department of Indian Affairs office in Kenora. The new reserve was close to a logging road, and government authorities thought that the Ojibwa would have better access to electricity, running water, professional health care, and schooling (Shkilnyk 1985, 53). This forced "exodus" had a dramatic effect on the long-established kinship ties among the Ojibwa and this was compounded by a drastic environmental problem: mercury contamination of the English-Wabigoon river, and subsequent poisoning of some members of the Grassy Narrows band.

A number of Canadian musicians—among them Buffy Sainte-Marie, Bruce Cockburn, and Gordon Lightfoot[2]—have written of the effects of white regulation of Native culture and misappropriation of Indian lands. Buffy Sainte-Marie's song, "My Country 'Tis of Thy People, You're Dying," speaks of the continued destruction of Native cultural integrity. Mannette (1990, 511) points out that, despite efforts to physically isolate tribal members and to assimilate these cultures—for example, through inculcation of English as the preferred language, or social practices that discourage the "cultural integrity" of groups such as the Micmac—the vitality of Native culture is evident in the proceedings of the Marshall Inquiry. The co-existence of a renaissance of tribal culture and the continuing patterns of discrimination against Native people points to a lack of certainty as to whether Native cultures will be marginalized, will disappear, or will flourish.[3] There are many Native artists, however, who have overcome the barriers of discrimination—the work of painter Norval Morrisseau, sculptor Bill Reid, and architect Douglas Cardinal (designer of the Museum of Civilization in Hull, Quebec) are outstanding examples (Robertson 1989, 4–6).

Politically, the decisive actions of Native leaders that led to the failure of the Meech Lake Accord speak of the greater militancy and political organization of aboriginal peoples. Elijah Harper, a member of the Manitoba legislature and former chief of the Red Sucker Lake band in Manitoba, stalled the Meech Lake proposal on June 23, 1990, and thereby succeeded in killing it. Native leaders have also made progress in their claims for a Native sovereignty that is distinct from federal and provincial civil jurisdictions. If successful in their claims, aboriginal peoples would constitutionally be able to determine their own future and to manage their own resources and communities.

In recent years, a number of studies have critically assessed the process of colonization in Canada. Thatcher (1986) notes that Native peoples have tended to be labelled as a problem population in the official statistics of various control agencies: social welfare, courts, policing, prisons, and the practice of adopting-out of Native children to white families. LaPrairie (1987) found that Native women were "heavily overrepresented" in jails and prisons in Canada. In B.C., for example, while Native women made up only five percent of the population, they constituted 20 percent of all incarcerated women in the province (LaPrairie 1987, 103). The author adds that this incarceration rate reflects not individual pathology as such, but rather substantial disparities embedded into Canadian society (LaPrairie 1987, 110). Thatcher (1986) concludes that the perception of Native peoples as essentially "deviant" serves a useful function for economically and politically dominant groups in modern Canada. He contends that such negative stereotyping of Indians, Inuit, and Métis serves (1) to justify a history of colonization and racism in Canada, and (2) to rationalize the government's failure to deal with longstanding Native land claims.

Tennant (1990) provides a detailed account of the events that have led up to the current struggles to resolve land claim disputes in British Columbia. He notes that whites tend to occupy key positions in provincial (and federal) government despite the increase in the number of "non-white" peoples in modern British Columbia. The author points out that aboriginal peoples were clearly a majority at the time of the first contact with European settlers. Despite the initial co-existence between Native people and Europeans, a gradual pattern of white cultural dominance came into effect—Native names became anglicized, for example, and such cultural rituals as the potlatch ceremony were banned by law.

Tennant notes that, despite a tradition of recognizing some Native land claims in the 1860s, official policies worked in such a way as to worsen the prospects of negotiated settlement of these claims. When James Douglas was governor of B.C. (1858–1864), the government established a policy that confined Native people only to the restricted area of villages and fields (not the wider lands they used). Also, pre-emption of vacant land was available through law, thus allowing governments to appropriate land without negotiating with the aboriginal people affected by such transfer of land. This process was accelerated under the subsequent regime of Joseph Trutch. While Douglas had at least left a legacy whereby Native title to lands had not been formally extinguished, Trutch, chief commissioner of lands and works from 1864 to 1871, helped to implement policies that reduced the size of virtually every reserve in the colony (Tennant 1990, 42).

Tennant thus documents a legacy of failure of the B.C. government to resolve land claims beginning in the mid-nineteenth century. He notes that, in modern times, many Native groups have taken actions to settle these land claim disputes. Such organizations as the church and the B.C. Federation of Labour, as well as some municipal officials, have offered Native leaders support in resolving land claim disputes and other longstanding injustices. Ironically, Tennant's book had barely reached the booksellers when the B.C. Supreme Court presented a controversial decision against the Gitksan-Wetsuwetén people. On March 8, 1991, B.C. Chief Justice Allan McEachern ruled that the plaintiffs—the Gitksan Wetsuwetén—were entitled to use "occupied or vacant Crown land" in the region for aboriginal sustenance. However, the thrust of the plaintiffs' case, extending well beyond the issue of reserve lands and Crown lands, was set aside. Chief Justice McEachern put this bluntly: "As the Crown has all along had the right to settle and develop the territory and to grant titles and tenures in the territory unburdened by aboriginal interests, the plaintiffs' claim for damages is dismissed" (*Delgamuukw et al. v. the Queen*, 1991). This court case, which was estimated to cost 25 million dollars over the three years of litigation and hearings, was clearly a setback for Native people seeking exclusive title to land (Still 1991, A1; Glavin 1990). Nevertheless, there are ongoing efforts to settle land claims through the courts and through negotiations with provincial and federal governments. A particularly bold legal initiative has been made by Bruce Clark, a lawyer who has been active in struggles for aboriginal rights in Canada. Clark has made a constitutional argument that the British Crown acknowledged a right of Indians to govern lands not ceded to the Crown. Clark also maintains that the 1982 Constitution Act secured a "constitutional protection" of aboriginal rights (Raphals 1991, 12). Thus, notwithstanding the negative judgement as perceived by the Gitksan-Wetsuwetén people, there are ongoing efforts to establish Native title to land and claims to self-government.

STUDY QUESTIONS

❑   To what extent do the recommendations of the Provincial Royal Commission on the Donald Marshall, Jr. Prosecution address structural problems facing Native people in Canada? Do these recommendations tend to treat the Marshall case as an anomaly—as a case of an individual being mistreated within a fundamentally sound criminal justice system?

❑   Sociologists recognize the importance of placing legal powers in a wider social context. Discuss the ways in which land claims and efforts to secure Native self-government have been facilitated or hindered by legal policies.

NOTES

1. It is not clear whether or not the two boys actually sought to mug Ebsary and MacNeil. Harris (1990) indicates that this was the case, but the Royal Commission Report (1990) challenges this assumption.

2. Excerpt from *Cherokee Bend*:

> *His father was a man*
> *who could never understand*
> *the shame of a red man's face,*
> *so they lived in the hills*
> *and they never came down*
> *but to trade in the white man's place.*
>
> ...
>
> *CHORUS:*
> *Daddy didn't like what the white man said*
> *about the dirty little kid at his side,*
> *Daddy didn't like what the white man did*
> *nor the deal, or the way that he lied.*
> *There was blood on the floor*
> *of the Government store*
> *when the men took his Daddy away*
> *And the boy stayed back, and he come to his end,*
> *and he run like the wind from Cherokee Bend.*

Lyrics and music by Gordon Lightfoot, published by Moose Music, CAPAC. From the LP *Cold on the Shoulder* (1975). Warner Bros. DISC MS 2206.

3. Mannette (1990, 514 & 525) reports that some Micmac people "internalize the dominant definition" of Indianness, and that "most households" on the Membertou reserve speak English, not Micmac. Mannette's article nonetheless emphasizes the ways in which tribal culture has prevailed, or is beginning to resurface, in Nova Scotia.

REFERENCES

Adams, I. (1970) "Why Did Charlie Wenjack Die?" In *The Poverty Wall*, 27–44. Toronto: McClelland and Stewart.

Boyd, N. (1988) *The Last Dance: Murder in Canada*. Toronto: Prentice-Hall.

Burtch, B. (1981) "Reflections on the Steven Truscott Case." *Canadian Criminology Forum* 3 (2): 131–45.

────── (1978) "The Wolves." *The Canadian Forum* 58 (684): 12.

Canadian Press (1991) "Accused Killer Claims Innocence." *The Regina Leader-Post* (February 13).

Delgamuukw et al. v. the Queen, 3 W.W.R. 97, 79 D.L.R. (4th) 185 (B.C.S.C.) (1991).

Glasbeek, H.J. (1989) "Why Corporate Deviance Is Not Treated as a Crime: The Need to Make 'Profits' a Dirty Word." In *Law and Society: A Critical Perspective*, edited by T. Caputo, M. Kennedy, C. Reasons, and A. Brannigan, 126–45. Toronto: Harcourt Brace Jovanovich.

Glavin, T. (1990) *A Death Feast in Dimlahamid*. Vancouver: New Star Books.

Harris, M. (1990) *Justice Denied: The Law versus Donald Marshall* (2nd edition). Toronto: Totem/Collins.

────── (1988) "Warts and All." *Saturday Night* (November): 20–25.

LaPrairie, C. (1987) "Native Women and Crime in Canada: A Theoretical Model." In *Too Few to Count: Canadian Women in Conflict with the Law*, edited by E. Adelberg and C. Currie, 103–12. Vancouver: Press Gang.

LeBourdais, I. (1966) *The Trial of Steven Truscott*. Toronto: McClelland and Stewart.

Mannette, J. (1990) "'Not Being a Part of the Way Things Work': Tribal Culture and Systemic Exclusion in the Donald Marshall Inquiry." *Canadian Review of Sociology and Anthropology* 27 (4): 505–30.

News Services (1990) "Marshall Case Could Spark Legal Changes." *The Vancouver Province* (January 28): 16.

Nova Scotia (1989) Provincial Royal Commission on the Donald Marshall, Jr., Prosecution. *Digest of Findings and Recommendations*. Halifax: The Commission. Released January 1990.

Priest, L. (1990) *Conspiracy of Silence*. Toronto: McClelland and Stewart.

Raphals, P. (1991) "Nations in Waiting." *The Canadian Forum* 69 (799): 10–14.

Robertson, H. (1989) "Native Artists: Against All Odds and Expectations." *The Canadian Forum* 68 (782): 4–6.

Shkilnyk, A. (1985) *A Poison Stronger Than Love: The Destruction of an Ojibwa Community*. New Haven: Yale University Press.

Still, L. (1991) "Indians Lose Case: B.C. land not theirs to use exclusively, chief justice rules." *The Vancouver Sun* (March 8): A1 and A12.

Tennant, P. (1990) *Aboriginal Peoples and Politics: The Indian Land Question in British Columbia, 1849–1989*. Vancouver: University of British Columbia Press.

Thatcher, R. (1986) "The Functions of Minority Group Disrepute: The Case of Native Peoples in Canada." In *The Political Economy of Crime*, edited by B. MacLean, 272–94. Toronto: Prentice-Hall.

York, G. (1990) *The Dispossessed: Life and Death in Native Canada*. London: Vintage.

CHAPTER SIX

Racial Discrimination in Law: An International Perspective

INTRODUCTION

To this point, our attention has focused on general perspectives in understanding legal processes and specific events or incidents surrounding law. In this chapter we assess the concept of discrimination in law, using a range of international cases and studies. Particular attention is paid to racial discrimination, a phenomenon that has generated protest and litigation in an attempt to reduce ongoing patterns of exclusion and repression. This comparative approach underscores two key findings: first, that law is applied unevenly to various racial groups, even when measures are in place to guard against discrimination; and second, that there is substantial controversy over how (or if) law can be used to protect the interests of those who are discriminated against. This chapter provides a discussion of materials that pertain to racial discrimination—and the efforts to reduce discrimination through law—in Canada, England, the United States, and Australia and the South Pacific.

Let us begin by returning to the Dreyfus affair, which was mentioned in Chapter Two. The Dreyfus affair was a travesty of justice, involving the now-infamous scapegoating of Alfred Dreyfus, the French captain who was convicted of treason and imprisoned on Devil's Island. Dreyfus had been falsely accused of selling military information to the Germans. Arrested in October 1894, Dreyfus was convicted in December of the same year and transported to the penal colony of Devil's Island. Dreyfus remained in prison until 1906, when his conviction was annulled by the United Appeal Court. Ironically, Dreyfus was eventually decorated with the Legion of Honour and reinstated in the French army. Dreyfus died in 1935.

It is significant that, despite the 1898 confession of the major who had forged the documents that helped convict Dreyfus, Dreyfus remained in prison for another eight years. It is also significant that this miscarriage of justice did not go unchallenged. Several leading intellectuals, artists, and other figures agitated for Dreyfus's release. When Emile Zola's famous statement, *J'Accuse*, was published in 1898, it sold 200 000 copies on the first day of publication. The Dreyfus case has been widely associated not only with military corruption but also with a strong undercurrent of anti-Semitism in French society. The widespread mobilization of the *Dreyfusards* provided some counterbalance to the corruption and prejudice associated with the case.

On a wider scale, one can say that there has been a steady legacy of discrimination against racial minorities in Western societies. In *The Mismeasure of Man* (1981), Stephen Gould addresses the ways in which Western science has reinforced negative, paternalistic stereotypes of non-Caucasian races. Gould (1981, 32 & 35) notes that such American heroes as Benjamin Franklin, Thomas Jefferson, and Abraham Lincoln expressed racial views that would today be viewed as embarrassing. Scientific doctrines of racial inferiority and undesirability were applied throughout the world. As Gould (1981) suggests, this led to an ideology of blacks and Indians as "separate and inferior." The ideology of racial superiority was used by eighteenth and nineteenth century politicians and scholars to justify slavery and denial of civil rights for aboriginals and people of colour. As noted in Chapter Three, Kennedy (1989) has documented how a variety of colonial regimes sought to impose a money economy and other measures on sub-Saharan societies, many of which were already economically and culturally self-sufficient. Underlying these developments, however, is the play of racial ideologies. Even those who favoured greater rights for nonwhite peoples tended to accept some aspects of the racial inferiority doctrine. Thomas Jefferson ventured: "Whatever be their degree of talents, it is no measure of their rights" (Gould 1981, 31).

This labelling of human beings as inferior or superior, as advanced or defective, was bolstered by many legal and administrative policies that would today be dismissed as uncivilized and racist. Some proponents of the theory of racial superiority advocated distinct forms of education, with blacks streamed into manual work and whites into more academic work (Gould 1981, 47). Gould (1981, 323) examines scientists' efforts to debunk these theories of racial inferiority and the radical measures designed to deal with those who were considered inferior:

> When American eugenicists attributed diseases of poverty to the inferior genetic construction of poor people, they could propose no systematic remedy other than sterilization. When Joseph Goldberger proved that pellagra was not a genetic disorder, but a result of vitamin deficiency among the poor, he could cure it.

The key point in Gould's work is the way in which quasi-scientific methods were employed not to understand racial diversity but, rather, to classify racial groups by Eurocentric standards. Viewing certain races as inferior was widely accepted throughout the dominant culture and was a useful way of promoting assimilation of the so-called inferior races, or alternatively, implementing policies that segregated aboriginal peoples from white people (Gould 1981, 31). Gould's work challenges the notion of science as a neutral field and suggests, instead, that science is deeply involved in political interests, even to the extent of generating and perpetuating mythologies disguised as scientific verities. In the case of the racial inferiority doctrine, quasi-scientific theories supported and justified discrimination against various groups on the grounds of their intellectual, moral, and social inferiority. Science and popular culture thus promoted doctrines of racial inferiority, but not without ongoing challenges to these pseudo-scientific claims.

This historical backdrop is useful in understanding how laws and state policies have been formulated in colonial societies. Today, the very survival of groups whose economic resources have been weakened through racially-inspired policies and laws may hang in the balance. Turk (1982, 13), for example, draws our attention to the growing power of multinational corporations worldwide. Multinational corporate power presents a world view that is vaunted above others and that seeks to gain even greater control of resources. Turk sees the survival of some politically weaker groups as an object lesson in power:

> While it has been understood that rapid, and especially uneven economic development is incompatible with many traditional beliefs and ways of life . . . it is even clearer—from the history of colonized and exploited peoples everywhere—that impoverishment corrodes and ultimately destroys the faiths, moralities, sensibilities, and knowledge by and for which people live (Turk 1982, 13).

Turk's point could be applied to many countries and epochs. Turk has addressed issues of power and legal order in South Africa, for example, and others have addressed the political economy of underdevelopment worldwide.

Racial Discrimination and the Law

Canada

Focusing on the issue of racial discrimination and the law allows us to address the key aspects of the ideal liberal-democratic state: equality before the law, equality of opportunity, and fair treatment of people regardless of racial origin. The Donald Marshall case, discussed in Chapter Five, is an example of discrimination against one person. We also saw how the Micmac and other indigenous peoples in Canada face various kinds of systemic discrimination in employment, education, and other areas. Despite this often bleak outlook on the situation of indigenous peoples, there are examples in which the state has implemented laws and policy initiatives to move beyond exclusion and neglect of Native peoples. Hunter (1981, 160) assesses patterns of social inequality in Canada and concludes that aboriginal peoples in Canada experienced the greatest increase in educational involvement between 1951 and 1971. Hunter (1981, 160) is critical, however, of the federal government's greater involvement in promoting such educational participation and its agenda of acculturation and social integration of aboriginal peoples. He notes also that, despite some gains in educational participation, aboriginal peoples continue to lag well behind average rates of participation.[1] Even today, in spite of successful programmes run by Native bands in many provinces (see York 1990, Chapter 2), many Native students—and low-income children generally—do not complete school, college, or university studies (Canadian Council on Social Development 1991).

Another controversial issue in the history of discrimination and the law in Canada is the treatment of Native families. In recent years, for example, there has been considerable criticism of legally-sanctioned assimilation policies, including the replacement of tribal language and customs with European languages (primarily English) and the forced relocation of Native children to residential schools. As noted in the previous chapter, the continuing difficulties surrounding aboriginal land claims testify to the state's reluctance to resolve these longstanding demands.

The issue of transracial adoption underscores the fundamental power imbalance between whites and Natives in Canada. McGillivray (1985, 450) notes the polarized, conflicting values implicit in debates over transracial adoption. Interracial adoption procedures are seen by some as desirable—a reflection of racial integration—while others associate legitimation of such practices as tantamount to cultural genocide. For the latter, "each child 'lost' by adoption outside the ethnic group represents an incalculable drain of cultural resources" (McGillivray 1985, 450). McGillivray (1985, 451–52) reports that, for over a decade, adoption of Native children in Saskatchewan was primarily approved for nonstatus adoptive parents, many of whom were white. Between 1972 and 1981, the ratio of nonstatus adoptive parents to status adoptive parents was 6 to 1 (722 adopted children versus 120 adopted children, during this period). The author notes, however, that adoption policy has shifted recently toward a stronger appreciation of cultural integrity of Native peoples, with priority given to minority group rights over rights of prospective adoptive parents outside of the minority group.

Formal and nonformal discrimination against the Chinese in Canada has long been associated with Canadian public policy. Li (1988, 23) notes that in the 1850s and 1860s, Chinese immigrants were generally well-regarded for their industriousness and general value to a frontier society. Nevertheless, as the British Columbia economy experienced decline in the 1860s and 1870s, various steps were taken against the Chinese, including legislation to take away the right to vote and a ban on hiring Chinese workers for government projects (Li 1988, 23). Even though anti-Chinese sentiments seemed "especially strong" in B.C., Li (1988, 27) found that several attempts to discriminate against the Chinese in Canada—for example, by imposing an annual tax on the Chinese and preventing immigration from China altogether—were defeated or disallowed, although a "head tax" eventually came into force.

Anti-Chinese measures were also applied with respect to labour issues. Comack (1986, 72–75) offers a theoretical explanation of organized labour's broadly based opposition to competition from Chinese labourers. She notes that much of the anti-Chinese action in the late nineteenth century stemmed not simply from racism, but also from an effort by organized workers to keep and improve their conditions of work. Labour organizations in Canada opposed greater use of unskilled labour. In this sense, then, Chinese labourers could be seen as pawns, used by industrial capitalists to divide the labour force and undermine efforts by organized labour to realize better working conditions and wages. Comack (1986, 73) concludes that the " . . . anti-Chinese posturing of organized labour in British Columbia was therefore not a purely racist reflex but part of a general strategy to oppose the immigration of the unskilled."

One of the most criticized legal enactments in Canada in this century was the internment of Japanese Canadians during the Second World War. By 1943, it was estimated that over 12 000 adults and children of Japanese descent were kept in internment camps, officially sugar-coated as "interior settlements" (Adachi 1976, 252). The financial losses and general strain of internment have been well documented in autobiographical accounts and fiction (Kogawa, interviewed by Redekop 1989; Nakano 1980). In 1988, the Canadian government issued an apology for the internment decision, and financial compensation was offered to those who had endured the evacuation and financial losses.

England

In England, discrimination against black people has been criticized throughout the criminal justice system and other facets of the legal structure. Gordon (1983, 9–10) outlines how immigration law became tightened as the need for cheap labour from India, the Caribbean, and Africa was no longer urgent. Thus, while Commonwealth citizens were entitled, under the provisions of the British Nationality Act of 1948, to work and settle in Britain if they desired, new restrictions on immigration were implemented in the 1962 Commonwealth Immigrants Act. Gordon (1983) uses a variety of instances and legal decisions to strengthen his argument that law is often discriminatory toward racial minorities. He notes that racism is not a process that is outside the law but is, rather, accepted officially and enshrined in British law (Gordon 1983, 10–11). Gordon's (1983, 24) account of discrimination against black people in England reveals a deep-seated animosity between the dominant white culture and the growing number of nonwhite residents.

Gordon (1983, Chapter 2) sketches the deterioration of police-community relations in many jurisdictions. This deterioration is linked with various police practices, including harassment of suspects, abuse of the Judges' Rules (to be applied when suspects are taken into police custody), and abuse of police stop-and-search powers. Gordon (1983, 35) observes that black people experience police intervention even in their homes and at work. Black people are prone "to be stopped, searched, questioned and detained under the provisions of the Immigration Act," and furthermore, police officers as well as immigration officers are empowered to question people suspected of breaking immigration law. Gordon (1983, 38) recognizes that such intrusions could be directed at anyone thought to be foreign, but "the brunt of such harassment falls on the black community."

Gordon (1983) provides ample accounts of racism throughout the criminal justice spectrum in England: suspicion, interrogation, arrest, trial, conviction, incarceration, and so forth. In his conclusion, he suggests that the formulation of "the black problem" was a reaction by the government of the day to growing crises of legitimacy. The ensuing law-and-order campaigns were used to consolidate state powers, without directly addressing the underlying problems of white racism (Gordon 1983, 137). These established patterns of racism have been subject to increasing criticism and lobbying for reforms. The National Council for Civil Liberties has taken action against various manifestations of racism, be they discriminatory hiring practices, abuse of police authority, or what are seen as unconscionable modifications to immigration-related legislation[2] (Lilly 1984, 82–88).

Discrimination has generated considerable attention among *realists*—or *left realists*—who are concerned with reforming policing practices and other aspects of official control of citizens. In England, left realists address specific populations that are at greatest risk of criminalization, including racial minorities, the unemployed, the elderly, women, and youth. Despite the rhetoric of equal opportunity associated with liberal and conservative ideologies, it has been pointed out that English social structures reflect considerable discrimination in the area of social control. Kinsey, Lea, and Young (1986, 44–45) indicated that in London, approximately 99 percent of police officers were white, and a significant minority of persons surveyed perceived police practices to be discriminatory. Studies and surveys conducted in London revealed that 29 percent of Londoners surveyed believed that police discriminated against certain groups (most notably, youth and ethnic minorities). Similar studies in Merseyside showed that, in "areas with little crime," over 70 percent of persons surveyed registered support for the impartiality of the police.

United States

> *What happens to a dream deferred?*
>
> *Does it dry up*
> *like a raisin in the sun?*
> *Or fester like a sore—*
> *And then run?*

Does it stink like rotten meat?
Or crust and sugar over—
like a syrupy sweet?
Maybe it just sags
like a heavy load.

Or does it explode?

(Langston Hughes, "Montage of a Dream Deferred")

Racial injustice is often presented as one of the most intractable and telling indictments of American politics. Worsley (1984, 344), in his wide-ranging discussion of world development, refers to the "social battlefields" and poverty within major American societies and the vast imbalance of wealth in "a society where the race goes to the strong and the weak to the wall." In the view of Hall and his associates (1978, 387), it has been the nature of American capitalism to force American blacks into a "distinct, super-exploited class" within the larger working-class population and to limit them to the lowest reaches of poorly paid "marginal work."

It is well documented that black Americans are, on average, disadvantaged with respect to education, income, access to health care, and so forth. This tendency to *substantive inequality* has been offset, not by any dramatic social and economic gains, but by the reinvocation of an ideology of equal opportunity in the social structure, ostensibly backed by legal powers to combat discrimination.

Bond (1987) chronicles the civil rights movement in the United States between 1954 and 1965, a movement which was founded to reverse established patterns of racial discrimination. Bond (1987, 11) notes that black Americans were excluded from higher education at university. Other schools—public schools, high schools, and colleges—were divided along racial lines in states with Jim Crow laws.[3] These laws applied to virtually all aspects of life in these states: public transportation, theatres, schooling, restaurants, and so forth (Bond 1987, 12–13).

In the 1953 legal case *Brown v. Board of Education*, the judges held that the separate-but-equal doctrine of Jim Crow policies was unjust: "Separate educational facilities are inherently unequal" (Bond 1987, 32–34). This landmark case was seen as a major victory for equal rights; however, many were unconvinced that the legal victory in *Brown* would translate into equality of opportunity and resources.[4] The spirit of the *Brown* decision—that the nature of racial segregation in American schools was injurious for black children—was thus but one step in the overall movement against racism in American life.

The struggle for equality also targeted the practice of racial segregation on public transportation, especially in southern states. In 1953, a one-day boycott of the segregated seating system on buses in Baton Rouge, Louisiana ended unsuccessfully. Nevertheless, partial success was recorded there a few months later, with a compromise result in which one back seat was reserved for blacks, and two front seats were reserved for whites (Bond 1987, 60). In Montgomery, Alabama, in the early 1950s, white passengers enjoyed the privilege of reserved seating. This arrangement prevailed, even though 75 percent of the ridership was black. Bond (1987, 62) recalls that "as the whites took their seats, black riders had to get off the bus and re-enter through the back door." In 1955 a protest was launched in Montgomery against segregated seating following the ejection and arrest of Claudette Colvin, a black teenager who refused to give up her seat to a white person (Bond 1987, 62–63). By the 1960s, the scale of the civil rights movement was unmistakable: in 1963, approximately 800 demonstrations took place across America, culminating on August 28, when nearly a quarter-million people marched on Washington to demand action on civil rights (Edwards 1981, 95).

The civil rights movement has, as expected, suffered some reversals, and in virtually all areas of life, black Americans continue to be discriminated against. In more recent times, some researchers have reported substantial differences in perceptions of criminal injustice in the United States. Hagan and Albonetti (1982, 352) conclude that the black Americans sampled in their study were much more likely to perceive injustice in criminal law practices than were white Americans. In contrast to some earlier studies, which indicated no significant differences in such perceptions of injustice, there was clearly an increased perception of "race and class conflict" surrounding criminal injustice in the United States.

Freeman (1982) is very critical of the argument that Supreme Court decisions have improved the overall pattern of racial discrimination in America. Reviewing U.S. Supreme Court decisions concerning antidiscrimination law, he concludes that they have not substantially altered the relatively subordinate position of black Americans with respect to education, voting rights, and housing. Freeman (1982, 210) argues that antidiscrimination law ironically serves to legitimize racially based practices, even while it claims to be against such practices:

> As surely as the law has outlawed racial discrimination, it has affirmed that Black Americans can be without jobs, have their children in all-black, poorly funded schools, have no opportunities for decent housing, and have very little political power, without any violation of antidiscrimination law (Freeman 1982, 210).

Freeman (1982) outlines two theoretical perspectives that are crucial to an understanding of discrimination and the limits of antidiscrimination law: the perpetrator perspective and the victim perspective. The *perpetrator perspective* is used to address racial discrimination as an isolated event, unconnected with the wider conditions of life for minorities. It is a remedial perspective, seeking to correct or punish misbehaviour by racist individuals. This perspective is ahistorical, meaning that it ignores or minimizes any sense of historical connection between racial policies in the past and racist expressions in the present. The perpetrator perspective implies that, aside from the inappropriate actions of a minority of perpetrators, the social system is fundamentally fair, affording opportunities for those seeking them. The courts are able to act as a watchdog, correcting instances of discrimination.

The *victim perspective*, while acknowledging that individual perpetrators victimize other individuals, suggests that racial discrimination is an everpresent force for subordinated groups. Freeman (1982, 211) thus refers to the existence of a perpetual underclass, who are often denied such basic necessities as adequate housing, employment, and income, and even a sense of their own human dignity and self-worth. Racial problems will not be eliminated by isolated court decisions; rather, affirmative action is needed to correct systemic discrimination against minorities. The victim perspective, with its holistic approach to understanding and addressing racial discrimination, is nonetheless far from a dominant perspective. Freeman (1982, 211) notes that antidiscrimination law in the United States is "hopelessly embedded" in the reformist ideology of the perpetrator perspective.

One weakness of Freeman's approach is its lack of attention to the dialectics of human rights struggles and political response. It fails to take into account the greater representation of blacks and Hispanics on some city councils and other political bodies in the United States or the successful efforts to block conservative initiatives. The failure to appoint conservative nominee Robert Bork to the Supreme Court is one example of this latter trend. On July 1, 1987, Bork was nominated by then President Ronald Reagan to replace liberal Justice Lewis Powell, who had resigned from the U.S. Supreme Court. A broad coalition of interests—among them the American Civil Liberties Union and groups representing women's issues, the handicapped, racial minorities, and environmental groups—mobilized against this nomination of a conservative candidate. On October 23, 1987, following 12 days of hearings by the senate Judiciary committee, the Bork nomination was defeated 58 to 42 (see Pertschuk 1989). Due to the malleability of the Supreme Court—liberal in the 1960s and 1970s, more conservative in recent years—it may adopt an even more liberal approach in years to come. Freeman's (1982) work can also be questioned since it was written over a decade ago. There is, however, ample evidence to support his premise that formal legal protections, even those affirmed by the U.S. Supreme Court, have not reversed patterns of substantive inequalities along racial lines.

Walzer (1983, 221–24) discusses these complexities of social policy. He points out that the character of compulsory laws, exemplified by the busing of children to achieve racial integration in schools, is laudable in some respects. Nevertheless, the American experience proves that underlying problems—for example, the "tyrannical distributions in the spheres of housing and employment" (Walzer 1983, 224)—cannot be overcome by slight improvements in educational opportunities for racial minorities. Walzer also notes that even in the sphere of education, there have been considerable barriers to the recruitment of school teachers and administrators from visible minorities.

A recent study of 45 major metropolitan areas by the National Bureau of Economic Research (NBER 1990) confirmed that unemployment among young black American men was higher than among their white counterparts. This differential increased dramatically when overall economic conditions worsened. Specifically, in areas where the unemployment rate was less than 4 percent, the unemployment rate for young whites and young blacks, respectively, was 5.8 percent and 7.2 percent. For areas where unemployment exceeded 7 percent, the respective figures were 9.7 percent and 24.6 percent. All figures were drawn from 1987 statistics. The study also found that in better labour markets, young black males benefited from higher wages. This meant that "a 1 percent fall in the overall unemployment rate raises the average wage of black youth by 4 to 7 percent, and all youth by 3 to 4 percent" (NBER 1990).

Edwards (1981, 97–99) offers a cogent argument that the initial successes of the civil rights movement have not been followed up to a significant extent after the 1964 Civil Rights Act. Supreme Court rulings against affirmative action policies and cutbacks in education are two of the factors working against the underclass of black citizens in the United States. The ideology of self-improvement faltered in the face of these structural limitations. Edwards (1981, 95) concludes that the politics of race and work blocked efforts to substantially improve employment opportunities for black people:

> White America was not willing, in the main, to submit to the proposition that the problems of Blacks were rooted in the nature of the social structure. Equality was perceived as a right due to the individual as a matter of principle; for Blacks to demand an alteration in their group position was considered unacceptable.

Legally, socially, economically, and culturally, discrimination against certain minorities in the United States continues.

Australia and the South Pacific

The use of the criminal sanction against aboriginal peoples is for some researchers a form of paternalism: the imposition of a European-derived system of justice on a people who already had established longstanding tribal customs of dispute-resolution. Foley (1984, 164) states that there has been a pattern of gross overrepresentation of Aborigines in the Australian system of criminal justice and uses official statistics from 1976 to indicate that, nationwide, the rate of incarceration of Aborigines is approximately twelve times that of the population as a whole. Foley (1984, 168–72) outlines a *gestalt* of difficulties facing many of Australia's Aborigines: poor health, including significant hearing loss, which in turn compounds linguistic differences and communication problems during interrogation and trial; discriminatory attitudes and practices among Australian police officers; and the "chronic" problem of serious alcohol abuse.

Ligertwood (1984, 193) outlines the problem of crime, particularly juvenile crime, among the Pitjantjatjara tribe in southern Australia. He cites the erosion of "community authority," including broken rituals and ties with Pitjantjatjara elders as the reason for this problem. Given this weakening of traditional authority, Ligertwood acknowledges that this group, and other aboriginal groups, may need to rely on an outside authority to settle disputes. This process would not, however, require complete abdication of local powers in settling some, or conceivably all, disputes. Ligertwood (1984, 210–11) proposes a number of justice-related options, in order that aboriginal peoples might devise their own systems of justice in accordance with their own traditions, with European systems or possibly with modifications and combinations of the two.

Nettheim (1984, 50) points out that the focus of much of international law has been on individual rights. This rather narrow focus has interfered with the full implementation of indigenous peoples' claims for land settlements, cultural survival, and self-determination. Nettheim (1984, 50) observes, however, that both international standards and related structures have been evolving and becoming more relevant to the question of human rights for indigenous peoples. Nettheim (1984, 57) points out that the dominant practice of assimilation of aboriginal peoples in Australia was abandoned in the mid-1970s, although efforts to respect aboriginal legal claims and cultural identities remain inconsistent. He notes that there is also considerable variation among state and territorial governments in the treatment of aboriginal rights; nevertheless, some infringements of human-rights standards can be taken before international bodies.

The history of colonization in the South Pacific highlights the ways in which minority economic interests have transformed many societies. Moorehead (1974) refers to this transformation as "the fatal impact." Societies such as Tahiti were influenced dramatically by European contact in the eighteenth and nineteenth centuries, especially by such Western institutions and concepts as law and private property.[5] As the Australian continent was claimed as an extension of European society, the aboriginal peoples were generally seen as a hindrance to the newly established colonial regime. Once the tribal laws of the Aborigines were subordinated to English legal structures, their numbers dwindled. One estimate shows that the population of 1500 Aborigines near Sydney in 1788 fell to a few hundred by 1830 (Moorehead 1974, 211).

The inhabitants of what came to be known as Bikini Atoll are still affected by the U.S. government's decision to evacuate the island for nuclear testing in the 1940s. In total, 23 bombs were detonated on Bikini Atoll, with the largest bomb, detonated in March 1954, representing an explosion 1000 times stronger than the atomic bomb dropped on Hiroshima (Ellis 1986, 813–15). The Bikini families had earlier been moved to another atoll, where they faced starvation.

Shortly thereafter, they were housed at a U.S. naval base and eventually relocated to the island of Kili. The islanders subsequently suffered various health problems, including diabetes, and also lost their traditional livelihood of fishing and seafaring. The government promise to relocate the Bikinians on their original atoll is, to this day, unfulfilled, largely due to the radioactive waste that has contaminated the soil, water, and crops (Ellis 1986, 815–19).

There are many other examples of conflicts between different races and nationalities beyond the examples set out here. The territorial conflict between Israel and Palestine has generated concerns about the living conditions of the Palestinians (Mulhallen 1984; Gonick 1988). David Grossman's *The Yellow Wind* (1988) is a powerful statement about the hatred that festers under the circumstances of occupation and especially the damage that is done to very young children.

Conflict between racial groups challenges the validity of what some see as a fictionalized social contract in given societies. For Canadians, the social contract approach was certainly put to the test during the Second World War. Abella and Troper (1983) provide a detailed, historical account of the plight of European Jews in the years prior to the Holocaust and throughout the Second World War (see also Lanzmann 1985; Dawidowicz 1986).[6] Between 1933 and 1945, even as the Jews faced escalating repression and the eventual implementation of the "final solution" (genocide), Canada's record of admitting Jewish refugees was, arguably, "the worst" of all nations that were in a position to accept them (Abella and Troper 1983, v). Approximately 200 000 Jews were admitted to the United States, 70 000 to the United Kingdom, and another 125 000 were allowed to emigrate to Palestine (then administered by Britain). Canada admitted only 5000 Jews between 1933 and 1945, under an implacable doctrine that stated, as far as Jewish immigrants were concerned, "none is too many" (Abella and Troper 1983).

Today, these historical legacies of racial discrimination and anti-Semitism in Canada (see Bolaria and Li 1988) have not been forgotten. We can look to official policies by the federal government favouring multiculturalism in Canada, and to attempts by governments to redress some of the more shocking examples of racism and anti-Semitism. Action by the Crown and by school boards have been taken against some individuals who have denied that the European Holocaust before and during World War II took place. For example, Jim Keegstra, formerly a high school teacher in Alberta (Appelbaum 1985, 7; Bercuson 1985), was charged with the willful promotion of hatred, under section 319 of the Canadian Criminal Code. The Supreme Court of Canada recently ordered a retrial of this case. In New Brunswick, school teacher Malcolm Ross was relieved of teaching duties following complaints after he published material alleging that the Holocaust had not occurred, and in Toronto, Ernst Zundel, who had also denied the existence of the Holocaust

(Weimann and Winn 1986, 19–20), was convicted on the criminal charge of "spreading false news," section 181 of the Canadian Criminal Code. Such examples can be seen as a signal by governments that extreme forms of anti-Semitism will not be tolerated. Financial compensation and an official apology to Japanese Canadians interned during the Second World War (Adachi 1976) can be seen as another example of a more tolerant outlook in Canada.

SUMMARY

This chapter has attempted to show that despite formal measures to ensure racial equality in law and society, scapegoating of minorities, especially visible minorities, has a long tradition in Western societies and elsewhere. The white hegemonic domination of politics has been slow to react to the situation of minorities. The legacy of colonization, and of more modern patterns of immigration in some societies (Gordon 1983), is not easily transformed in modern political economies. Again, we should stress the importance of a dialectical approach that allows for changes in laws and state policies, along with changes in society. Thus, while legal changes are important in antidiscrimination struggles, changes in culture are also very important as far as racial tolerance, and actual improvements (or worsening of) standards of living for racial groups are concerned. Turk (1982, 209) suggests that the character of modern political resistance has shifted somewhat, away from material measures of deprivation to renewed interest in cultural resources. Local and national forms of resistance have also attracted broader sources of support, which Turk (1982, 209) describes as "the internationalization of resistance."

We are also witnessing a fairly broad-based movement to achieve equality—in law, and in social life generally—by many groups that have long been placed on the margin. Young (1990, 122–23) draws our attention to struggles by disabled people, blacks, Hispanics, Asians, and women to achieve a full measure of legal and social equality. As set out in this chapter, however, there remain many structural barriers—including hiring practices, and limits of legal reforms—that impede these efforts against racial discrimination.

STUDY QUESTIONS

❑   Contrast the perpetrator perspective and the victim perspective, in the context of Freeman's (1982) essay on U.S. antidiscrimination law.

❑   Discuss the treatment of aboriginal peoples in Canada, Australia, and the South Pacific. In what ways might law be shaped to suit particular cultural and economic interests in these nations?

❑   Canada is frequently portrayed as a pluralistic country, welcoming different races, faiths, and political beliefs. Discuss ways in which laws have been used to meet this liberal-pluralist ideal, and ways in which laws have contradicted this ideal.

NOTES

1. Hunter (1981, 160–61) emphasizes that aboriginal peoples in northern rural communities who have completed their education often do not get jobs related to their formal education.

2. The National Council for Civil Liberties has interpreted a series of legislative measures and policies as a serious threat to civil liberties in England. Lilly (1984, 87) argues that the passage of three immigration acts—in 1962, 1968, and 1971—dramatized the extent to which "major political parties of the time were quite ready to appease popular racist sentiment . . . "

3. The segregationist system of Jim Crow laws referred to "day-to-day segregation" of whites and blacks. The name Jim Crow was taken from the caricature of a black minstrel, circa 1830 (Bond 1987, 10). The Jim Crow laws were in effect from the 1890s to the 1960s in southern states. Fredrickson (1981, 239 & 249) notes that Jim Crow laws not only disenfranchised blacks, blocking their participation in electoral systems, but also provided a legal basis for socially segregating blacks and whites. The result was a system that was formally equal, but in which resources for blacks were typically inferior to those provided for whites (Fredrickson 1981, 239).

4. Bond (1987, 35) cites the prominent black lawyer Charles Houston as saying: "Nobody needs to explain to a Negro the difference between the law in books and the law in action."

5. The English explorer Capt. James Cook (1728–1779) wrote of the Tahitians: "Upon the whole these people seem to enjoy liberty in its fullest extent, every man seems to be the sole judge of his actions and to know no punishment but death, and this perhaps is never inflicted but upon a public enemy" (Moorehead 1966, 52).

6. Dawidowicz (1986, xxvii) documents the events surrounding the "war" against European Jews. She also offers a clear rejection of some versions of structuralism that purport to explain politics. She criticizes such mechanistic approaches and the view of faceless bureaucratic structures proceeding without significant influence from human will or agency: "No human agent can then be held responsible for decisions or for their consequences. The structuralists have thus eliminated the exercise of free will in human society and deprived men and women of their capacity to choose between good and evil" (Dawidowicz 1986, xxvii).

REFERENCES

Abella, I., and H. Troper (1983) *None Is Too Many: Canada and the Jews of Europe, 1933–1948*. Toronto: Lester & Orpen Dennys.
Adachi, K. (1976) *The Enemy That Never Was*. Toronto: McClelland and Stewart.

Appelbaum, I. (1985) "The Keegstra Case." *The Canadian Forum* 65 (749), 7–15.

Bercuson, D. (1985) *A Trust Betrayed: The Keegstra Affair*. Toronto: Doubleday.

Bolaria, B., and P. Li (1988) *Racial Oppression in Canada* (2nd edition). Toronto: Garamond Press.

Bond, J. (1987) *Eyes on the Prize: America's Civil Rights Years*. New York: Viking.

Canadian Council on Social Development (1991) "The Poverty Connection." *Social Development Overview* 1 (Fall): 9–10.

Comack, E. (1986) "'We Will Get Some Good out of This Riot Yet': The Canadian State, Drug Legislation and Class Conflict." In *The Social Basis of Law: Critical Readings in the Sociology of Law*, edited by S. Brickey and E. Comack, 67-89. Toronto: Garamond Press.

Dawidowicz, L. (1986) *The War against the Jews: 1933–1945*. New York: Bantam Books.

Edwards, W. (1981) "Civil Rights, Affirmative Action: An Incomplete Agenda." In *Pluralism, Racism, and Public Policy: The Search for Equality*, edited by E. Clausen and J. Bermingham, 83–113. Boston: G.K. Hall.

Ellis, W. (1986) "A Way of Life Lost: Bikini." *National Geographic* (June): 813–34.

Foley, M. (1984) "Aborigines and the Police." In *Aborigines and the Law*, edited by P. Hanks and B. Keon-Cohen, 160–90. Sydney, Australia: George Allen and Unwin.

Fredrickson, G. (1981) *White Supremacy: A Comparative Study in American and South African History*. Oxford: Oxford University Press.

Freeman, A. (1982) "Legitimizing Racial Discrimination through Antidiscrimination Law: A Critical Review of Supreme Court Doctrine." In *Marxism and Law*, edited by P. Beirne and R. Quinney, 210–35. New York: John Wiley & Sons.

Gonick, C. (1988) "The Palestinian Uprising." *Canadian Dimension* 22 (3): 23–27.

Gordon, P. (1983) *White Law: Racism in the Police, Courts, and Prisons*. London: Pluto Press.

Gould, S. (1981) *The Mismeasure of Man*. New York: W.W. Norton.

Grossman, D. (1988) *The Yellow Wind*. Translated by Haim Watzman. Toronto: Collins.

Hagan, J., and C. Albonetti (1982) "Race, Class, and the Perception of Criminal Injustice in America." *American Journal of Sociology* 88 (2): 329–55.

Hall, S., C. Critcher, T. Jefferson, J. Clarke, and B. Roberts (1978) *Policing the Crisis: Mugging, the State, and Law and Order*. London: Macmillan.

Hughes, L. (1968) *Selected Poems*. New York: Alfred A. Knopf.

Hunter, A. (1981) *Class Tells: On Social Inequality in Canada*. Toronto: Butterworths.

Kennedy, M. (1989) "Law and Capitalist Development: The Colonization of Sub-Saharan Africa." In *Law and Society: A Critical Perspective*, edited by T. Caputo, M. Kennedy, C. Reasons, and A. Brannigan, 30–53. Toronto: Harcourt Brace Jovanovich.

Kinsey, R., J. Lea, and J. Young (1986) *Losing the Fight against Crime*. London: Basil Blackwell.

Lanzmann, C. (1985) *Shoah: An Oral History of the Holocaust*. New York: Pantheon Books.

Li, P. (1988) *The Chinese in Canada*. Toronto: Oxford University Press.

Ligertwood, A. (1984) "Aborigines in the Criminal Courts." In *Aborigines and the Law*, edited by P. Hanks and B. Keon-Cohen, 191–211. Sydney, Australia: George Allen and Unwin.

Lilly, M. (1984) *The National Council for Civil Liberties: The First Fifty Years*. London: Macmillan.

McGillivray, A. (1985) "Transracial Adoption and the Status Indian Child." *Canadian Journal of Family Law* 4 (4): 437–67.

Moorehead, A. (1974) *The Fatal Impact: An Account of the Invasion of the South Pacific, 1767–1840*. Harmondsworth: Penguin.

Mulhallen, K. (1984) "Jane Storey's Palestine." *The Canadian Forum* 64 (745): 11–13.

Nakano, T., with L. Nakano (1980) *Within the Barbed Wire Fence: A Japanese Man's Account of His Internment in Canada*. Toronto: University of Toronto Press.

National Bureau of Economic Research (NBER) (1990) "Black Youths Aided by Tight Labor Markets." *The NBER Digest* (December): 1.

Nettheim, G. (1984) "The Relevance of International Law." In *Aborigines and the Law*, edited by P. Hanks and B. Keon-Cohen, 50–73. Sydney, Australia: George Allen and Unwin.

Pertschuk, M. (1989) *The People Rising: The Campaign Against the Bork Nomination*. New York: Thunder's Mouth Press.

Redekop, M. (1989) "The Literary Politics of the Victim." *The Canadian Forum* 68 (783): 14–17.

Turk, A. (1982) *Political Criminality: The Defiance and Defence of Authority*. Beverly Hills: Sage Publications.

Walzer, M. (1983) *Spheres of Justice: A Defence of Pluralism and Equality*. New York: Basic Books.

Weimann, G., and C. Winn (1986) *Hate on Trial: The Zundel Affair, the Media, and Public Opinion in Canada*. Oakville: Mosaic Press.

Worsley, P. (1984) *The Three Worlds: Culture and World Development*. London: Weidenfeld and Nicolson.

York, G. (1990) *The Dispossessed: Life and Death in Native Canada*. London: Vintage.

Young, I. (1990) *Justice and the Politics of Difference*. Princeton: Princeton University Press.

CHAPTER SEVEN

Studies of the Judiciary and the Legal Profession

INTRODUCTION

The link between society and the exercise of law is a central focus in the sociology of law. It follows that the profession of lawyering and the nature of the judiciary are important aspects of legal domination and legal reform. In this chapter, we will review several studies of the judiciary and the legal profession. One of our key themes will be the differences and conflicts between lawyering and judging as well as conflicts within the legal profession, including efforts to reverse some elements of professional privilege and to promote a more community-centred approach.

THE JUDICIARY

Judges are among the highest-paid public servants. There are approximately 800 provincial judges at the superior, county, and district court levels across Canada. Superior court judges earn over $140 000 annually, while justices with the Supreme Court of Canada earn over $166 000 a year (McCormick and Greene 1990, 14 & 16). It has been estimated that over 90 percent of court cases are heard in the provincial courts (excluding the appelate courts). McCormick and Greene (1990, 18) add that a substantial proportion of these cases involve criminal offences as well as a variety of provincial offences and other actions stemming from the federal Young Offenders Act.

The judiciary is often presented as a bulwark against a totalitarian state or a complacent society, accustomed to the various injustices of everyday life. In the democratic tradition, the courts are ideally "above the law" and nonpartisan in deciding a multiplicity of legal cases. In keeping with the principles of judicial independence and the rule of law, the workings of the courts would seem to be free from outside interference. In his account of the civil courts in Upper Canada in the late eighteenth and early nineteenth centuries, Wylie (1983), however, concludes that the supposedly impartial administration of justice was, in effect, influenced by prominent merchants and by provincial government administrators. These two elites were united in their search for social and economic stability, and in their belief in the importance of British justice in establishing this stability. Both groups favoured the accumulation of wealth through land and trade policies for the elite as well as a stronger legitimation of the social structure of the day. Beyond this, however, Wylie (1983, 4) notes that there were strong differences in strategies to effect accumulation and legitimacy. The government administrators were more likely to rely on British-based administrative structures and policies, while the merchants lobbied against such an importation of structures and policies.

Wylie (1983, 9) documents how judges in Upper Canada dispensed with legal technicalities that were established in Britain. The use of notaries to launch a suit was not always practised in Upper Canada (where there were few notaries). Similarly, the requirement that commercial accounts have the testimony of a third party—usually a clerk—was often waived, since few frontier traders could afford clerks. Even legal terminology commonly used in Britain was altered for the sake of comprehension. Latin words might thus be translated into such phrases as "in debt" or "breach of agreement" (Wylie 1983, 9).

One source of conflict between judges, administrators, and merchants was the problem of delay in legal business. Wylie (1983, 28–35) identifies several sources of delay in legal proceedings. These included provincial geography and weather, the delays in formally entering a verdict, the centralization of procedures at York (now Toronto), a shortage of attorneys to complete the procedural work required for the courts, and so forth. For judges, adherence to proper court procedures, such as ensuring that defendants had been properly served, meant that court proceedings could be delayed. Merchants who acted as plaintiffs in such cases were thus faced with delays. Efforts to expedite court proceedings met with considerable resistance from court administrators who were concerned with maintaining procedural fairness for defendants.

Unlike the English Superior Courts, the Court of King's Bench in Upper Canada relied more extensively on juries to try questions of fact. This situation was further complicated by the limited number of assizes per year in Upper Canada. Only one circuit per year was held in all regions, whereas in England, two to three yearly assizes were common. Wylie (1983, 8) noted that these travelling (circuit) courts were not always relied on in the late eighteenth century in Upper Canada: " . . . the judges failed to take advantage of the provision permitting circuits around the district and met almost exclusively at Kingston. This practice effectively placed the machinery of justice out of reach of most rural settlers and reflected the limited horizons of the prominent residents of Kingston. . . . "

Wylie notes that there were swift calls for reforms to the Court to allow creditors to recover debts and to generally resolve civil matters. Although the efficiency of the King's Bench was eventually improved, it was not completely to the liking of the merchants. Nevertheless, the more influential merchants could survive the court delays, and there were other mechanisms for resolving economic troubles, most notably out-of-court settlements and greater access to credit (Wylie 1983, 36).

O'Malley (1988, 72–74) argues that analyses of judicial decision-making should take contradictions within the capitalist state into account. That is, instead of applying a simplistic theoretical analysis of links between the judiciary and powerful economic interests, it is important to consider the multiplicity of interests at play, including differences among capitalists as a whole. O'Malley stresses the importance of incorporating the concept of the relative autonomy of the state as a factor in judicial reasoning. The concept of historical specificity refers to nuances and variations within particular jurisdictions or locations, during specific historical periods. Historical specificity is used to render a more precise account of historical forces at play, rather than working toward a general theory of law, economy, or society. In capitalist societies, even though judicial procedures and decisions are largely congruent with capitalist economic and political interests, there is nevertheless a measure of autonomy exercised by judges in deciding cases (O'Malley 1988, 74).

Martin (1986) provides a critical assessment of the role of Canadian judges in the context of the Canadian Charter of Rights and Freedoms. The proclamation of the Charter has been hailed as a great advance for citizens' freedoms, and has been tied with "judicial activism" on a variety of social issues. Martin (1986, 210–15) makes a number of points against this celebratory approach to judicial activism, using the American experience of Supreme Court decisions in labour, welfare, and civil liberties cases. He notes that judicial activism in the United States was used against attempts to establish a mixed economy, that is, to balance the private-sector emphasis on individualism and market forces with public resources to fight racial discrimination, to establish a minimum wage and maximum hours of work, and to impose limitations on child labour. Second, Canadian judges are more likely to be influenced by Commonwealth case law and international documents such as the Universal Declaration of Human Rights (1908) than by the Charter. Martin's third point is that further reliance on the judiciary to set social policy only contributes to greater bureaucratization in Canadian society. Individuals become atomized in this process, and personal and traditional methods of conflict resolution are usurped by state authorities (i.e., the judiciary).

Martin (1986, 215–17) adds that the Canadian courts are largely shielded from public criticism and surveillance. The legacy of the courts has been "most dismal" with respect to modern social and political problems. The reasoning of Supreme Court decisions compounds this record: the written reasons are often unintelligible, lacking coherence for both professional lawyers and legislators, let alone the nonspecialist citizen.

Mandel (1989) also provides a critical look at the *realpolitik* of the Charter. His approach challenges romanticized views of the Charter and, more generally, the ostensibly democratic nature of the judiciary and other players in the legal system. Far from restoring a popular basis to legal decision-making in Canada, Mandel argues that the Charter has instead revived many of the inequalities that existed in the years before its enactment. Specifically, reviewing cases that have been brought forward for Charter consideration, Mandel (1989, 4) concludes that it has in fact "undermined" a variety of popular movements: the women's movement, aboriginal rights struggles, the labour movement, and the peace movement, among others.

Mandel also draws attention to the intricacies and the impenetrable logic of a number of Supreme Court decisions. Using the 1988 *Morgentaler* case for illustration, he points out that the course of appeals in this case has resulted in a variety of unanimous and split decisions between the Ontario Court of Appeal and the Supreme Court of Canada (Mandel 1989, 38).

The judiciary in much of the Western world has traditionally been a male preserve. In 1982, Justice Bertha Wilson was the first woman appointed to the Supreme Court of Canada (Martin 1986, 216). McCormick and Greene (1990, 63) estimate that, as of 1990, less than eight percent of Canadian superior court judges were women; and of the provincially-appointed judges, women made up only six percent of the total. McCormick and Greene describe this as a "gross underrepresentation" of women. The history of court appointments confirms critics' charges that certain groups have been excluded from elite positions in the Canadian political structure. Mandel (1989, 43) refers to the survival of "class bias" in the legal profession and the judiciary, professions dominated by white, middle- to upper-middle-class males. McCormick and Greene (1990, 66–68) found that among Alberta judges, only 37 percent had fathers who worked as labourers or in agriculture. In contrast, approximately half of the Alberta judges had fathers who were lawyers, businessmen, or other professionals.

Racial imbalance in the appointment of state and federal judges in the United States is a historical fact. In 1852, Robert Morris of Boston was the first black judge to be appointed in the United States. Nonetheless, few black judges were appointed during the next century. This trend was reversed somewhat by the gains of the civil rights movement in the 1960s and 1970s. As of 1990, 500 black judges were active at the state or federal level (Spohn 1990, 1196). At the higher levels of the U.S. judiciary, blacks and women remain underrepresented. Neubauer (1988, 171) shows that, of 300 state Supreme Court judges, only 0.6 percent were black and only 3.1 percent were female. At the federal Appeals Court level, these percentages increased to 16.1 percent black and 19.6 percent female (Neubauer 1988, 171). Neubauer (1988, 170) echoes other reports in his depiction of the homogeneity of the judiciary in Western societies. He finds that judges tend to be upper-middle-class white males with above average education.

Some research tends to contradict the argument that greater judicial representation of blacks is needed to counter discrimination against black defendents. Spohn (1990, 1209) studied sentencing decisions of black and white judges in Detroit and found that black offenders convicted of "violent felonies" tended to receive harsher sentences than white offenders, whether they were sentenced by a black judge or a white judge. Canadian research suggests that judges from working-class origins may be *less* sympathetic to workers than judges from upper-class or upper-middle-class backgrounds (McCormick and Greene 1990, 67).

Mandel (1989, 44–46) does not adhere to a static analysis of the judiciary. He refers to current changes in the style and objectives of the Supreme Court, including improvements in the writing of judicial opinions and in various means of communicating its decisions to the mass media and the public at large. Mandel (1989, 45) also points to greater access to lawyering and judicial hearings through increased government funding of certain legal challenges. For example, the Women's Legal Education and Action Fund (LEAF) has received one million dollars from the Ontario government. LEAF has been involved in the litigation of test cases on behalf of women. These cases have exposed such issues as male bias in the conduct of sexual assault trials, the social context of sexual harassment of women, and employment-related discrimination against pregnant women (see Razack 1991).

Other concerns with the judiciary include the ways in which court structures that are ostensibly oriented toward "grass-roots" people—most notably the small claims courts throughout Canada—actually tend to service disputes brought forward, more often than not, by larger players, including collection agencies, large retail stores, insurance companies, and the like (see Olsen 1980). Hagan (1985) also points out that corporate actors, with their superior economic resources and social power, are more likely to obtain successful results when they initiate prosecutions. Hagan dubs this "the corporate advantage," which has often been applied to defend corporate property interests.

Zander (1980, 204–205) discusses some of the competing studies over the role of judges in lawmaking. While judges in most societies are drawn from a "relatively narrow social class"—primarily from executive, professional, or managerial backgrounds—there is some evidence that judges are not especially biased against workers' organizations, or in favour of management interests, as reflected in civil court actions in England. Zander (1980, 224–25) reports that judges have tended to move away from formalism and inflexibility in interpreting law, and toward a more considered, "active" stance in interpreting law. This shift leads to "a greater flexibility of approach and, in particular, an emphasis on principle rather than the rule and precedent and a noticeably greater inclination to talk about policy" (Zander 1980, 224). Abstract decision-making is thus under question, as social aspects of justice are brought into clearer focus. These aspects include not only social class, race, and gender but also the discrepancy between offenders' needs and social resources. Recently, the discharge of some offenders without provision for aftercare services has generated controversy in England (see Brindle 1991). Peay (1989, 231) draws our attention to the need to look more deeply into the social impact of judicial and quasi-judicial decision-making (e.g., in tribunals assessing mentally disordered offenders): ". . . legal safeguards are only likely to be effective in the context of adequate resource provision." The changing role of the judiciary and the diverse interpretations of the politics of judging are also evident in assessments of the legal profession, to which we now turn.

THE LEGAL PROFESSION

The increased complexity of legal terminology and procedures in Western societies has contributed to the growth of the legal profession. In England, by the thirteenth century, the practice of laypersons representing themselves was gradually replaced by "technical pleading" by "narrators," a practice that in turn led to formal lawyering (Louthan 1979, 80). Worldwide, there is considerable variation in the nature of lawyering, with lawyers playing a less prominent part in business transactions and other work in Japan, for instance, than in North America. Moreover, the number of practising lawyers in Japan is low, compared with North America (Kidder 1983, 214–16).

Today, lawyering is considered one of the most prestigious and well-paid professions. Lawyers are often regarded as especially influential in seeing that justice is done through their legal practices, legal teaching, and involvement in virtually all sectors of political life. They continue to play a pivotal role in American political life, in local constituencies, Congress, state governorships, and even the presidency (Louthan 1979, 83). The overrepresentation of lawyers in government and corporate elites helps to secure their reputation as the most powerful of the professions in North America (Hagan, Huxter, and Parker 1988, 11). A dominant ideology of the legal profession is that it has evolved in the context of a "bargain" with the wider society: in return for the right to regulate itself as a profession, including restrictions on who may enter the profession and practise as a lawyer, the legal profession agrees to act in a manner consistent with clients' best interests and the good of society as a whole. Observers have criticized the contradictory nature of this ideology, particularly the gulf between social altruism on the one hand and privileged self-interest on the other (Fennell 1980, 10–11). Using the Law Society of B.C. as their focal point, Brockman and McEwen (1990) report that the ideal of professional self-regulation is undermined in practice. In B.C. telephone directories, for example, references to complaint procedures against lawyers were abbreviated in the yellow pages, and deleted in another directory, *The Pink Pages*. Lack of public awareness about the mechanisms for complaining about professional misconduct or incompetence is a large factor in reducing actual formal complaints against lawyers. Furthermore, other people who are regularly in contact with lawyers—other lawyers and paralegals—rarely avail themselves of complaint procedures, except as a last resort (Brockman and McEwen 1990, 10–13). Threatening or launching complaint procedures is often seen as unprofessional or unbecoming conduct within legal and paralegal occupations.

There is tremendous variation among lawyers with respect to income, status, power, and level of specialization. Galanter (1983) has coined the terms *mega-law* and *mega-lawyering* to refer to extraordinarily large legal practices. In the United States, for example, the twenty largest law firms in 1979 had, on average, 234 lawyers on their staff. Galanter (1983, 155) carefully traces a broad shift in the United States toward larger "units of practice," with a corresponding decline in small units. He also notes that, while mega-law is frequently linked with corporate clients, the expanding field of public law has also provided substantial work for these elite, large-scale firms. Mega-law firms are distinctive for the wide range of their practices, moving far beyond their headquarters to many regions of the United States, and throughout the world as well. These firms also do highly specialized work and use sophisticated technology for storing and processing information. Mega-law firms use expert advice routinely, whereas many smaller firms cannot afford such highly specialized consultants. Other studies have found differences in legal practices, with corporate lawyers working in a rather uncertain context with their corporate clients, in contrast to "personal plight" lawyers such as divorce lawyers, whose interaction with clients tends to be relatively short-term (Flood 1991, 67–68).

Studies of stratification in the American legal profession also emphasize the relatively narrow composition of elite lawyering. Kidder (1983, 217) notes that the typical elite lawyer is almost invariably male, and usually from a "White, Anglo-Saxon, Protestant background." He adds that most of these lawyers graduated from premier law schools, often with very high standing among their graduating class. Although they make up a small percentage of all practising lawyers, these corporate lawyers "dominate" professional bar associations, which, in turn, are responsible for regulating all lawyers within the state (Kidder 1983, 217).

Porter's classic study of power and social class in Canada, *The Vertical Mosaic* (1965), provides a critical analysis of the structure of the Canadian economic elite. The book underscores the role of lawyers, inasmuch as certain corporate and business lawyers have played a facilitative role in "guiding corporations through the confusion of statute, judicial decision, and legal fiction" (Porter 1965, 277). Economic power was thus co-ordinated by lawyers, in conjunction with the technical and administrative sector of the Canadian economy and the directors of financial institutions. For Porter (1965, 276), the interrelationship of these sectors served to consolidate economic power.

Porter (1965, 278) also addresses the links between lawyers, elite economic interests, and political life, noting that elite lawyers were often directly linked with either the Liberal or Conservative parties of the day; some had served as members of parliament or held some other political office. According to Porter (1965, 391–92), lawyers played a "prominent role" in the Canadian political system and had done so at the federal cabinet level since Confederation. Porter (1965, 392) concludes that the increased influence of lawyering represented "a further narrowing in the occupational background of the political directorate."

Gender and Stratification: Law Schools and Lawyering

In the nineteenth century, the practice of law in Canada was the exclusive province of men. Backhouse (1991, 293–94) observes that no women served as magistrates, coroners, or judges during most of the nineteenth century in Canada. The first woman who was called to the bar—Clara Brett Martin, in 1897—was also the "first woman admitted to the profession of law in the British Commonwealth" (Backhouse 1991, 293). Salvos of ridicule and derision were commonly directed at nineteenth century North American women who sought admission to legal practice or otherwise challenged the "naturalness" of law as a gentleman's profession.

Law schools in North America have seen a dramatic increase in the proportion of female to male students. Of all graduates of American law schools in 1980, about 30 percent were women (Seager and Olson 1986, section 23). Hagan (1989, 835) notes that in Western nations, between 30 and 40 percent of students enrolled in law schools in the 1980s were women. This contrasts with a figure of less than 10 percent a decade earlier. In Canada, women make up approximately half of the student population in law schools. Boyle (1986, 97) notes, however, that even though women are clearly in evidence in contemporary law schools in Canada, there is a tendency to instruct law students "as if women do not matter."

Law schools in Canada have traditionally played a key role in legal training, since, almost without exception, those who wish to practise law must graduate from a university baccalaureate program in Canada (Gall 1983, 153). In the early 1980s there were very few part-time programs and no night programs available for those wishing to obtain a law degree (Gall 1983, 153). It has been pointed out that the dominant structure of university education is not well-suited to many women applicants, particularly single mothers. In general, women, more than men, are enrolled in part-time undergraduate studies in Canadian universities, and part-time students are at a "disadvantage" because they are considered for fewer sources of support, in the form of scholarships, bursaries, and fellowships, than full-time students (Dagg and Thompson 1988, 7). Historically, there have also been serious obstacles to women of colour entering the legal profession. The first black woman was admitted to the Ontario bar in 1960; and it was not until 1976 that a Native woman graduated from a Canadian law school (Backhouse 1991, 325–26).

The teaching of feminist jurisprudence in Canadian law schools has received increased attention in recent years. Although the mandate of legal education goes well beyond ensuring competency among prospective lawyers, it may, in fact, be reproducing sexist patterns of socialization. These patterns are perhaps most visible in the legacy of hiring practices at Canadian law schools. Women constitute only nineteen percent of law faculty across Canada (Makin 1989, A1). Moreover, the teaching of feminist theory and jurisprudence in Canadian law schools has become a very controversial area. In 1986, Sheila MacIntyre, a law professor at Queen's University, issued a memorandum to all members of the Queen's Law School outlining the disruptions and other forms of resistance by students and faculty toward a feminist perspective in legal training. In direct contrast to the ethos of collegiality among university faculty, the author referred to patterns of isolation, hostility, and discreditation of feminist discourse within law faculties. MacIntyre's memorandum directly addressed gender bias in law schools and the importance of teaching methods that dealt with actual relations of social inequality. The situation at Queen's University has been linked with a general backlash against feminism and the entrenched resistance to critical teaching,[1] particularly in the area of feminist jurisprudence:

> Law school will reinforce the inequality of women until more feminists are hired. As long as there are only a few, they are easy targets for abuse, and can come to believe that their problems are personal rather than institutional (Dagg and Thompson 1988, 71).

In 1988, many people protested the decision not to appoint Professor Mary Jean Mossman as dean of Osgoode Hall Law School (Makin 1989). In their study of the professoriate, administration, and student body of Canadian universities, Dagg and Thompson (1988, 60–65) document a substantial gap between the rhetoric favouring an end to discriminatory hiring practices among university administrations, and the actual implementation of such policies as gender-neutral language and curricula or affirmative hiring practices. The authors also note that feminists who are openly involved in feminist praxis risk losing tenure and jeopardizing their chances for promotion within the professoriate (Dagg and Thompson 1988, 72–73). The structure of peer review in promotion and tenure decisions can have a chilling effect on academic expression and community service. Dagg and Thompson (1988, 73) note that women are hired for nearly two-thirds of lecturer positions, whereas 93 percent of tenured full professors are men. The net effect of a male-dominated structure that is often hostile to explicit feminist teaching and research is to "jeopardize the career of young scholars who are committed to any but mainstream, conservative ideals" (Dagg and Thompson 1988, 73). Women "have a far more difficult task" in winning promotion than do men in all areas: engineering, health professions, social sciences, humanities, and education, for example (Dagg and Thompson 1988, 72).

Christine Boyle, a well-regarded and established law professor, describes the atmosphere of intimidation confronting women who wish to incorporate feminist materials into the law school curriculum (or other curricula): "The message is obvious—keep quiet and try to make the fact that you are a woman as inconspicuous as possible. I think more than twice about raising feminist issues in a classroom where there is a danger that I will be accused of incompetence, have my class disrupted by people to whom freedom of speech means their freedom to attack me through pornography, and have to work in a setting in which I cannot post a notice without it being ripped down or defaced" (Boyle 1986, 111). Concern over misogyny in university teaching has, however, resulted in changes that attempt to include feminist content in law schools. Boyle (1986, 106-7) provides several examples of implicit and explicit references to feminist materials in formal teaching situations as well as in more practical situations, such as legal aid clinics, where students must deal with the problems experienced by poor women clients.

Hagan (1989) explores the irony that, while lawyers espouse a doctrine of equal treatment within democratic societies, there are significant differences between male and female lawyers with respect to annual income and other factors. Building on earlier studies that documented substantial disparities in income between male and female lawyers—including Adam and Baer's (1984) research on Ontario lawyers—Hagan (1989) provides a comprehensive examination of a sample of practising lawyers in Toronto. According to the study, male lawyers reported an average income (before taxes) of $86 756, while female lawyers earned $44 210 on average (Hagan 1989, 838). Hagan also discovered that, while increases in specialization status for male lawyers resulted in substantial increments of income, "the comparable gain for women is small and nonsignificant" (Hagan 1989, 846). It was also noted that income varied dramatically with the kind of firm or employer. Male lawyers in managerial or supervisory positions in medium to large firms earned $84 000 on average, while male partners in small firms averaged $53 000. At the lower end of occupational mobility, substantial differences were observed for female lawyers. Hagan (1989, 847) puts it succinctly: "Women suffer most financially at the bottom of the mobility ladder, while men benefit most at the top." He concludes by noting that, while many women lawyers are earning substantially higher incomes than they would in less powerful work settings, these women are also experiencing greater *disparities* in earnings within the legal profession than they would in many other settings (Hagan 1989, 849–50).

In another study of class structure and the Toronto legal profession, Hagan, Huxter, and Parker (1988, 9) report a tendency for women lawyers to be situated in "a legal working class." Even though this tendency toward stratification between women and men in the profession may reflect the relatively recent increase in the number of women in law schools and legal practice, Hagan, Huxter, and Parker (1988, 31) note that women are "significantly underrepresented" in more prestigious jobs such as management and supervisory positions, as well as in the role of small employer. Hagan, Huxter, and Parker (1988, 31) conclude that, at present, "women are about twice as likely as men to be found in this combined 'underclass'."

Hagan, Huxter, and Parker (1988, 36) also bring forward the importance of class factors in their finding that Jewish lawyers were underrepresented in the capitalist class category of lawyers; that is, lawyers who participated directly in law firm decisions, and who had two or more levels of subordinates over whom they had sanctioning or task powers. The capitalist class lawyers worked in firms with 30 or more lawyers on staff. Specifically, less than 1 percent of Jewish lawyers in their sample fell into this category, compared with 8.4 percent of Anglo-Saxon lawyers. This finding from a Toronto-based study corresponds with other studies documenting the underrepresentation of Jewish lawyers in elite firms in New York, Chicago, and Detroit (Hagan, Huxter, and Parker 1988, 36).

Hagan, Huxter, and Parker (1988, 51–52) acknowledge the complexity of these dynamics and traditional patterns of inequality along lines of gender and ethnicity. On the one hand, they assert that legal practice in Toronto continues to be dominated by older, white Anglo-Saxon males who have trained at the larger law schools, such as Osgoode Hall Law School and the University of Toronto Law School. On the other, they point to increased access to positions of power within the legal profession, for both women lawyers and Jewish lawyers. Nevertheless, recent research suggests that women continue to face difficulties in gaining their share of partnerships in the legal profession (see Hagan et al. 1991) and still constitute only a small percentage of professional bar associations (see Brockman, forthcoming).

Lawyering and Legal Socialization

As law has developed in scope and intensity in modern times, the legal profession has also increased in numbers and diversity of work. Lawyers are often depicted as a monolithic interest group, with essentially similar training, income, work situations, and beliefs. The ideal of a homogeneous community of lawyers does not jibe with the very real stratification that exists within the modern legal profession. In practice, legal practitioners are subject to rivalry and competition from other lawyers; there are variations in the nature of their work (from general practice to highly specialized legal firms); and there are substantial differences in income and prestige, from relatively low-paid lawyers to "elite" lawyers (Cotterrell 1984, 195).

A number of sociological studies have confirmed discrepancies and contradictions between lawyers' idealized roles, and the roles they actually take on in advising clients, and in litigation. On the one hand, they are united in their dedication to clients (and the wider community) and their commitment to principles of justice; on the other hand, this dedication can easily be undermined by a variety of factors, including sheer economic necessity (Cotterrell 1984, 197), pressures of time, political factors, and so forth. Kidder (1983, 131–32) uses the American situation to illustrate the shortfall of consumer protection law (that is, its limited implementation and effectiveness) and the structural reasons affecting lawyers' unwillingness to use existing consumer protection laws. Despite the passage of the Magnuson-Moss Warranty Act in 1975, research in Wisconsin established that many lawyers were unaware of the Act two years after its passage. Moreover, there was often little monetary inducement for lawyers to become familiar with the provisions of this Act or to engage in time-consuming litigation on behalf of consumers. Kidder (1983, 131) indicates that, under such circumstances, lawyers are likely to take on the role of *mediators* rather than initiate courtroom proceedings. The end result is often either a reluctance to become involved in consumer complaints or a very compromised legal approach that emphasizes mediation (Kidder 1983, 131).

Louthan (1979, 84) emphasizes the limits inherent in lawyers' practices. Legal socialization can result in a style of lawyering that is conservative. Pivotal to many decisions regarding public policy and the private sector, the "legal style" characteristically sets formal limits to how issues are framed and how resolutions are formulated. Louthan (1979, 87) is, however, aware of challenges to this conservative style of lawyering. He discusses the emergence of so-called "soft law" curricula including environmental law, Native people and justice, and poverty law. He cautions, however, that environmental law is constrained by a host of "legal niceties" and "legal technicalities," among them the courts' willingness to permit acceptable levels of polluting and the barriers to obtaining "standing" in such matters of public law (Louthan 1979, 90–91; see also Chapter Nine).

SUMMARY

This chapter has examined the nature of law schools, legal practice, and judicial decision-making within the area of sociolegal studies. A number of critical studies adhere to the liberal ideal of altruistically-minded lawyering and the impartial nature of judicial reasoning and judgements. We have noted the complexities of this issue: the variations among professional associations and the differences in the nature of legal practice in various jurisdictions.

The growth of critical legal studies has fostered renewed interest in ways of altering such structures as the curriculum of law schools and the composition of the law faculty so as to include those who have been expressly or tacitly excluded, especially women and racial minorities. This critical approach has generated considerable opposition, but has also led to initiatives such as inquiries into employment equity programs and provision for access to law school for groups who would otherwise be disadvantaged (for example, encouraging Micmacs and blacks to apply to Dalhousie Law School). The legal profession and the judiciary, no less than the structure of law itself, are beset by contradictions between legal operations and the realization of justice.

STUDY QUESTIONS

❏   Liberal scholars may welcome the increased involvement of women in the legal profession in Canada. Review the structural barriers that have traditionally faced women aspiring to legal practice. What structural factors might impede women in completing law school, or in establishing a career in law?

❏   The judiciary is, according to liberal-pluralist theory, an independent body that resolves competing claims or charges in a neutral, fair manner. Discuss the more critical premise that judges are in effect key players in maintaining unequal power relations in law and society.

NOTE

1. Pfohl (1980, 254–55) stresses the importance of critical pedagogies. Exposure to such teaching is seen as allowing students to resist practices that perpetuate various social injustices as well as affording them the opportunity to develop alternatives to the existing social order.

REFERENCES

Adam, B., and D. Baer (1984) "The Social Mobility of Women and Men in the Ontario Legal Profession." *Canadian Review of Sociology and Anthropology* 21 (1): 22–46.

Backhouse, C. (1991) *Petticoats and Prejudice: Women and Law in Nineteenth-Century Canada*. Toronto: The Women's Press.

Boyle, C. (1986) "Teaching Law As If Women Really Mattered, or, What About the Washrooms?" *Canadian Journal of Women and the Law* 2: 96–112.

Brindle, D. (1991) "Prison Psychiatric Care Crisis." *The Guardian* (Manchester), December 10: 1.

Brockman, J. (forthcoming) "'Resistance by the Club' to the Feminization of the Legal Profession." *Canadian Journal of Law and Society*.

Brockman, J., and C. McEwen (1990) "Self-Regulation in the Legal Profession: Funnel In, Funnel Out, or Funnel Away?" *Canadian Journal of Law and Society* 5: 1–46.

Cotterrell, R. (1984) *The Sociology of Law: An Introduction*. London: Butterworths.

Dagg, A., and P. Thompson (1988) *MisEducation: Women and Canadian Universities*. Toronto: Ontario Institute for Studies in Education.

Fennell, P. (1980) "Solicitors, Their Markets, and Their 'Ignorant Public': The Crisis of the Professional Ideal." In *Essays in Law and Society*, edited by Z. Bankowski and G. Mungham, 7–26. London: Routledge and Kegan Paul.

Flood, J. (1991) "Doing Business: The Management of Uncertainty in Lawyers' Work." *Law and Society Review* 25 (1): 41–71.

Galanter, M. (1983) "Mega-Law and Mega-Lawyering in the Contemporary United States." In *The Sociology of the Professions: Lawyers, Doctors and Others*, edited by R. Dingwall and P. Lewis, 152–76. London: Macmillan.

Gall, G. (1983) *The Canadian Legal System* (2nd edition). Toronto: Carswell.

Hagan, J. (1985) "The Corporate Advantage: A Study of the Involvement of Corporate and Individual Victims in a Criminal-Justice System." In *The New Criminologies in Canada: State, Crime, and Control*, edited by T. Fleming, 112–31. Toronto: Oxford University Press.

——— (1989) "The Gender Stratification of Income Inequality Among Lawyers." *Social Forces* 68 (3): 835–55.

Hagan, J., M. Huxter, and P. Parker (1988) "Class Structure and Legal Practice: Inequality and Mobility Among Toronto Lawyers." *Law and Society Review* 22 (1): 9–55.

Hagan, J., M. Zatz, B. Arnold, and F. Kay (1991) "Cultural Capital, Gender, and the Structural Transformation of Legal Practice." *Law and Society Review* 25 (2): 239–62.

Kidder, R. (1983) *Connecting Law and Society: An Introduction to Research and Theory*. Englewood Cliffs, New Jersey: Prentice-Hall.

Louthan, W. (1979) *The Politics of Justice: A Study in Law, Social Science, and Public Policy*. London: Kennikat Press.

McCormick, P., and I. Greene (1990) *Judges and Judging*. Toronto: James Lorimer.

Makin, K. (1989) "Feminist Content in Courses Stirs Debate at Law Schools." *The Globe and Mail* (December 26): A1–A2.

Mandel, M. (1989) *The Charter of Rights and the Legalization of Politics in Canada*. Toronto: Wall and Thompson.

Martin, R. (1986) "The Judges and the Charter." In *The Social Basis of Law: Readings in the Sociology of Law*, edited by S. Brickey and E. Comack, 207–24. Toronto: Garamond Press.

Neubauer, D. (1988) *America's Courts and the Criminal Justice System* (3rd edition). Pacific Grove: Brooks/Cole Publishing Co.

Olsen, D. (1980) *The State Elite*. Toronto: McClelland and Stewart.

O'Malley, P. (1988) "Law Making in Canada: Capitalism and Legislation in a Democratic State." *Canadian Journal of Law and Society* 3: 53–85.

Peay, J. (1989) *Tribunals on Trial: A Study of Decision-Making Under the Mental Health Act 1983*. Oxford: Clarendon Press.

Pfohl, S. (1980) "Teaching Critical Criminology: The Ethical Issues." In *Radical Criminology*, edited by J. Inciardi, 245–56. Beverly Hills: Sage Publications.

Porter, J. (1965) *The Vertical Mosaic: An Analysis of Social Class and Power in Canada*. Toronto: University of Toronto Press.

Razack, S. (1991) *Canadian Feminism and the Law: The Women's Legal Education and Action Fund and the Pursuit of Equality*. Toronto: Second Story Press.

Seager, J., and A. Olson (1986) *Women in the World*. London: Pluto Press.

Spohn, C. (1990) "The Sentencing Decisions of Black and White Judges: Expected and Unexpected Similarities." *Law and Society Review* 24 (5): 1197–1216.

Wylie, W. (1983) "Instruments of Commerce and Authority: The Civil Courts in Upper Canada 1789–1812." In *Essays in the History of Canadian Law*, edited by D. Flaherty, 3–48. Toronto: The Osgoode Society.

Zander, M. (1980) *The Law-Making Process*. London: Weidenfeld and Nicolson.

CHAPTER EIGHT

The Criminal Sanction in Canada

Even when a criminal act is certainly harmful to society, it is not true that the amount of harm that it does is regularly related to the intensity of the repression which it calls forth. In the penal law of the most civilized people, murder is universally regarded as the greatest of crimes. However, an economic crisis, a stock-market crash, even a failure, can disorganize the social body more severely than an isolated homicide.

(Emile Durkheim, *The Division of Labour in Society*)

INTRODUCTION

The power of the criminal law is conventionally viewed as a public resource. As noted in Chapter Two, Durkheim presented repressive law (including what is now seen as the criminal sanction) as indispensable to societal functioning. In contrast to private law—in which specific actors may negotiate or litigate such issues as property rights, torts, and the like—criminal law is the quintessential exercise of state power, executed in the public interest. Criminal law was not always cast in this public light. Beattie (1986) outlines how criminal charges in England were for many years brought by private parties, and prosecution followed similarly private lines. In modern Western countries, however, the evolution of criminal law has meant (1) a tremendous increase in the number of laws, charges, institutions, and officials entrusted with the police, the courts, and the edifice of corrections; and (2) a shift from privately initiated prosecution to a public bureaucracy of state officials.

Many writers have challenged the conventional definition of criminal law as a neutral, public resource. In general terms, they have argued that the application of criminal sanctions has been class-biased. This means that a variety of acts that cause substantial injury or other damage may be removed from criminal law altogether if such injurious acts are linked with powerful capitalist interests. Historically, this meant that powerful persons were virtually immune from criminal charges. Chambliss (1982, 169) contends that criminal law in European societies has historically been applied against the working class and other relatively powerless groups. For example, police and prosecutors are frequently reluctant to lay criminal charges (such as criminal negligence) against employers when workers are injured or killed in the workplace (Reasons, Ross, and Paterson 1981; Glasbeek and Rowland 1986). Another example of class bias is the use of regulatory law against large firms for anti-trust violations (Smandych 1991) or for extensive polluting practices (Schrecker 1989). The reluctance to use criminal sanctions against these more "respectable" actors contrasts with the widespread use of prison—or criminal charges in general—for people who are more publicly visible and less powerful. This has led to the juxtaposition of "suite crime" (corporate crime, which is largely immune from criminal sanctions) and "street crime" (Goff and Reasons 1978). Street criminals are subject to greater public and police surveillance and have fewer resources to contest criminal charges.

For some groups, the use of criminal law can become much more of a certainty. As discussed in Chapter Five, Native people face higher probability of arrest, conviction, and incarceration than the average citizen. Native people have been much more likely to be incarcerated for public drunkenness, for example (Hagan 1976), and both male and female Native people are overrepresented in many prisons across the country (LaPrairie 1987). In 1991, a speaker at the Women and Law conference in Vancouver stated that a spate of suicides by Native women at the federal prison for women in Kingston underscored the discrimination this group experiences. Removed from their communities, they faced not only racism and sexism, but profound isolation.

Significantly, critical theorists have pointed out that, while the use of the criminal sanction against women warrants attention, changing control tactics affecting women have permeated the wider society, as social control becomes "less visible, and more effective" (Davis and Faith 1987, 173). The authors outline how poverty has become "feminized" in the United States, with men's incomes (on average) exceeding incomes for women. Despite a dominant ideology that celebrates women's political, economic, and social gains, Davis and Faith (1987, 175) point out that the majority of jobs women take are insufficient to support their families above the poverty line. Other researchers support this insight into the links between patriarchy, gender, and social inequality. Carlen (1988, 4–5) reports that, in England and Wales, lower-class women have, for decades, been more likely to be incarcerated than middle-class women. Furthermore, poor women from ethnic minorities are more likely to be imprisoned. Carlen (1988, 4) estimates that the proportion of women from ethnic minorities who have been imprisoned is four times the proportion of other adult women in the wider society.

Significantly, much of this work on the sociology of law and gender has emphasized how various legal and cultural practices bolster a patriarchal ideology. Davis and Faith (1987, 176–84) point out that pornography, sexual assault, and prostitution are some of the factors that undermine egalitarian relations between men and women. Specifically, misogynist portrayals of violence against women in mass media are criticized for their "reaffirmation" of men's control over women. The authors also challenge various widely-held beliefs about sexual assault, including the minor nature of sexual assault, the disreputable status of women who are assaulted, and a "no-means-yes" denial by men of women's resistance to unwanted sex (Davis and Faith 1987, 176–79). The authors also suggest that female prostitutes face discrimination from police authorities, especially women of colour, who are most likely to be arrested and sentenced to prison (Davis and Faith 1987, 183). Criticisms of the 1984 Report of the Badgley Committee[1] emphasize the patriarchal structure of our institutions in relation to child sexual abuse. Lowman (1985, 513) interprets the Committee's approach as incomplete, inasmuch as it treats child sexual abuse as an individual problem, and pays insufficient attention to the structural forces underlying sexual abuse of children. The Report is also criticized for failing to put such problems in a context of gender (i.e., most known offenders are male) or to discuss the patriarchal aspects of the supposedly benevolent state intervention in the lives of youth. Efforts to toughen prostitution laws have thus often been criticized, both for ignoring the structural factors that lead to prostitution and the sex trade generally, and for the palpable failure of many recent attempts to better regulate prostitutes (Larsen, forthcoming).

MURDER, CRIMINAL LAW, AND THE DEATH PENALTY

Murder is at the centre of public controversy over criminal penalties, including the abolition or restoration of the death penalty. Many scholars have confirmed that, while certain crimes are often associated with "the crime problem," especially crimes of violence, the staple of criminal law is the defence of private property. Nevertheless, in media accounts and popular writing, murder remains an object of intense controversy.

Neil Boyd (1988) provides a critical account of murder in Canada. He outlines several aspects of the phenomenon of murder, including the doubling of the homicide rate between 1966 and 1975 (Boyd 1988, 4). He notes that, while some other countries have a higher rate of homicide—approximately four times greater for the United States than Canada—other countries such as Japan and Britain have approximately one-half the rate of murder as Canada (Boyd 1988, 4). Brantingham and Brantingham (1984, 132–33) report that, while homicide was a "rare" crime in Canada, there was a 121 percent increase in the criminal homicide rate between 1962 and 1975.

Even though North America has witnessed an increase in the rate of violent crime, including homicides, Boyd (1988) suggests that the character of these crimes has not changed markedly. In stark contrast to the sensational media images of serial murders or contract killings (in which the killing is premeditated), Boyd (1988, 9) concludes that murder in Canada is primarily unplanned and is prompted by a series of causes: alcohol or other drug use, domestic conflicts, and poverty: "Most murderers are basically ordinary people in socially and economically desperate circumstances. They were fuelled by alcohol or other drugs, and killed family and friends, usually over money or sexual betrayal" (Boyd 1988, 9).

Boyd is not only concerned with the particulars of murder cases—he also addresses social policy for murderers. In keeping with other researchers (Fattah 1972; Hagan 1991, 219), Boyd (1988) argues that there is no established general deterrence function associated with the death penalty. Moreover, the use of lengthy sentences—especially the minimum 25-year sentence for those convicted of first-degree murder—has not proved to be effective in deterring others from homicide or in rehabilitating offenders.

The nature of murder—and of violent crimes in general—is reviewed by Archer and Gartner in their award-winning book, *Violence and Crime in Cross-National Perspective* (1984). Using official measures to produce a Comparative Crime Data File on 110 nations, the authors provide valuable insight into how the nature of violent crimes has changed over time. Archer and Gartner (1984) provide evidence that, despite the popular notion linking high murder rates with cities, there is no convincing historical proof that murder rates have risen as cities grew in size. Reviewing four studies of Buffalo, Boston, and Philadelphia from the 1850s to the 1950s, Archer and Gartner (1984, 100) note that these cities experienced a "consistent decline" not only in murder rates but in rates of other serious crimes as well. A variety of other studies of national rates of murder in Australia, India, France, Germany, Sweden, and England confirm that homicide rates did not automatically increase as major cities increased in size (Archer and Gartner 1984, 101).

A corollary to these findings is that rural areas—often conceived as low-crime areas—reveal quite high rates of homicide. Archer and Gartner (1984, 103) note that suburban and rural areas in America have higher homicide rates than small cities, and approximately the same rates as those in cities of 50 000 to 100 000 residents. The most important conclusion of the authors' longitudinal study of U.S. cities between 1926 and 1970 is that large cities had consistently higher rates of homicide than the national average for any given year (Archer and Gartner 1984, 108–9).

Social scientists have also explored the merits of the capital punishment debate in Canada and elsewhere. Boyd (1988) provides a clear argument against reinstatement of the death penalty in Canada. Other scholars have used the capital punishment debate to reconsider the value of the death penalty in terms of legal ideologies and social control. Archer and Gartner (1984, 120) note that sentiment in favour of the death penalty has increased in the United States in recent decades. They attribute this phenomenon to the rising crime rate, especially the homicide rate, which has increased dramatically since the mid-1960s (Archer and Gartner 1984, 120). Brantingham and Brantingham (1984, 132) also refer to a significant increase in violent crime in Canada since the 1960s. Between 1962 and 1975, for example, the rate for attempted murder increased by 460 percent; the rate for rape increased by 161 percent. The authors add that, while the rates of violent crime tapered off in the 1970s, they began to increase toward the end of the decade: "The 1980 rates for these crimes were the highest ever recorded" (Brantingham and Brantingham 1984, 132).

Many scholars criticize the argument that capital punishment is an effective deterrent to potential criminals. Research that attempts to show a positive relationship between the death penalty and crime deterrence has been criticized for serious methodological weaknesses (see Archer and Gartner 1984, 125). There is general agreement that the homicide rate does not change dramatically (either increase or decrease) whether the death penalty is abolished or restored (Archer and Gartner 1984, 129). Cross-national studies of fourteen countries that have abolished the death penalty indicate that there is "little change" in the homicide rate in the short term after abolition (Archer and Gartner 1984, 132). In fact, these countries generally experienced decreased, rather than increased, rates of homicide (Archer and Gartner 1984, 136).

Comack (1990) takes a critical look at the implications of the capital punishment debate in Canada. She notes that, despite a history of Conservative party support for the death penalty, the capital punishment debate in 1987 was structured in such a way as to defuse a "political crisis" facing the Conservative federal government (Comack 1990, 88–89). Thus, even though the government avoided reinstatement, the debate itself served to successfully manage the law-and-order issues that confronted the Canadian state. Even though the result—the rejection of the reinstatement of the death penalty through a free vote in the House of Commons—appears to be a victory for liberalism, Comack (1990, 94) suggests that such stellar displays of compassion obscure less visible political strategies, especially cutbacks in health and social services and increases in more repressive areas, such as criminal justice.

CORPORATE CRIME AND CRIMINAL SANCTIONS

Studies of the criminal law and criminal sanctions have broadened in scope in the past generation. Growing attention has been paid to the ways in which criminal laws are constructed and applied, with particular attention focused on the relative immunity of corporations and their employees from criminal prosecution. This new emphasis calls into question earlier formulations of the social contract and the social consensus that governs laws.

In Canada, it is well-established that the Criminal Code has been enforced selectively. Brannigan (1984, 109) reviews Canadian studies of criminal sanctioning and concludes that the "slant" of laws produces a higher rate of conviction—and relatively severe sentencing patterns—for lower-class

Canadians. He adds that the ideology of excusing illegal behaviour by corporations as merely "poor business practices" creates an imbalance in the application of criminal law. Goff and Reasons (1978) offer a critique of the excessive use of the criminal sanction against victimless crimes such as prostitution, gambling, and illicit drug use. They argue that these crimes should be decriminalized, whereas many corporate activities should be brought within the framework of criminal law. Goff and Reasons (1978, 14) note that large corporations, with their enormous concentration of resources and power, have little public accountability. Legislation that ostensibly would govern these corporations—including the first anti-combines legislation, passed in 1899— was weakened by the failure to permanently establish a federal enforcement agency to counteract illegal combines activity (Goff and Reasons 1978, 47). In more modern times, Goff and Reasons (1978, 59) observe that only a limited number of decisions were made against Canada's largest corporations between 1952 and 1972, and that there had been an overall reduction in the number of decisions against these corporations between 1966 and 1972.

In the United States, Edwin Sutherland's classic study, *White Collar Crime* (1949), documents extensive patterns of illegal and unethical conduct on the part of corporations. While more recent studies appear to present illegal and unethical conduct as part and parcel of American business practices,[2] Chambliss (1982) provides a detailed account of corruption at all levels of American society, establishing a clear link between the ostensibly neutral systems of justice and politics and a wide variety of criminal activities. Chambliss (1982, 180) concludes that collusion and corruption are "as much a part of corporate business as they are a part of crime networks everywhere." The explanation for such collaborations among government officials and criminal networks stems from the profitability and efficiency such a network produces.[3] Chambliss contends that crime networks linking "legitimate" businesses and government to such illegal activities as drug trafficking and gambling are evident not only in the United States but throughout Europe and other continents (Chambliss 1982, 183–89).

Glazer (1987, 201–3) notes that *whistleblowers*—people who publicly criticize their employers, such as police forces, industrial firms, and so forth—are often subject to retaliation from their superiors. Promotions may be denied them, or they may be fired; blacklisting practices may eliminate future employment once they are identified as disloyal to the employing organization.

The use of regulatory and criminal laws to combat corporate crime is seen by many observers to be ineffective. Coleman (1989, 168–69) notes that some government agencies have improved their resources for investigating and prosecuting certain kinds of crimes and offences; however, in many cases, these agencies are simply understaffed. Interestingly, there appears to be a tendency to lay charges against "minor occupational offenders," while large-scale efforts involving complex, costly, and uncertain litigation may be disbanded (Coleman 1989, 169). Even when cases are brought before the courts, it is commonplace for American judges to accept *nolo contendere* ("no contest") pleas by defendants, which tend to reduce the stigma associated with the offence. The general finding is that white-collar criminals receive more lenient sentences than other criminals but some studies indicate mixed findings with respect to occupational status and criminal sentencing for white-collar crimes (see Coleman 1989, 171–72). It is important to bear in mind that few corporate crime cases even reach the point of criminal sentencing. A study in Wisconsin reported that of all sanctions for corporate crimes, only about 4 percent involved criminal proceedings. And for corporate executives who were convicted, "62.5 percent received probation, 21.4 percent had their sentences suspended, and only about one in four (28.6 percent) received short jail sentences" (Coleman 1989, 173).

Although criminal sanctions against white-collar criminals have proved ineffective, there are other options for prosecuting corporate offenders. These options include the civil suit, brought forward by individual victims, or the class-action suit, initiated by persons who share an identical or similar grievance. Coleman (1989, 170–71) outlines several obstacles to realizing these suits, including the considerable delays associated with some suits, recent restrictions that inhibit the impact of class-action suits, and some companies' reliance on technical declarations of bankruptcy to evade liability for dangerous products or working conditions. Coleman adds that while there have been considerable judgements brought against some corporations, civil actions "seldom result in just compensation for all the victims of a dangerous product" (Coleman 1989, 171).

The dreary record of successful prosecutions for corporate criminals has generated considerable interest in new forms of regulation. Some observers favour the use of the criminal sanction against corporate illegality that poses a serious threat to public safety or property. Others recommend a more regulatory approach, one that would not pose excessive restrictions on what Frank and Lombness (1988, 91) call the "good apples," that is, organizations that comply with regulations.

ENVIRONMENTAL CRIME

> *So you cut all the tall trees down*
> *You poisoned the sky and the sea*
> *You've taken what's good from the ground*
> *But you've left precious little for me*
> *You remember the flood and the fall*
> *We remember the light on the hill*
> *There should be enough for us all*
> *But the dollar is driving us still*

(Midnight Oil, "River Runs Red," Sprint Music, 1989)

One way to approach the topic of corporate power is by examining the application of environmental law. This is an area that clearly affects all people worldwide. The Science Council of Canada has stated that freshwater pollution is among the most critical environmental issues for Canadians. The Council (1974, 34–35) singled out serious pollution problems in the Fraser Valley and Lower Mainland areas of British Columbia, as well as the extensive degradation of the Great Lakes and Gulf of Saint Lawrence areas in central and eastern Canada, which had "by far the biggest concentration of pollution problems." A central question in the environmental debate is whether law can serve as a pivotal force in resolving disparate economic and political interests. Much of the available literature—some of which is discussed below—takes a pessimistic outlook on the supposedly neutral role of lawmaking and law enforcement as idealized by some liberal pluralists.

Many of the concepts we have become familiar with—equality before the law, mystification, and the predominance of special, powerful interests over the general interest—resurface in analyses of environmental laws. The area of environmental law would appear to be of particular interest to the body politic, given the scale of environmental damage in highly developed and developing countries. It is noteworthy that some comprehensive assessments of contemporary ecological damage indicate that earlier periods were hardly a golden age of pristine practices. The World Commission on Environment and Development (1989, 242–43) credits municipal-level innovations for reducing certain kinds of damage in urban areas. More generally, the Commission concludes that air quality in "most urban areas" has improved relative to earlier situations in such major centres as London, Paris, and other large cities.[4]

Caputo et al. (1989, 161) contrast growing concern over environmental pollution with earlier standards in Canada. They note, for example, that at the turn of the twentieth century, tidal disposal of sewage was a common practice in municipalities in Nova Scotia. Many others have noted the growing ideological emphasis on technological innovations and burgeoning industrial growth in Canada and worldwide. This developmental ethos was not accompanied by a concern for environmental issues. Caputo et al. (1989, 161) review several major environmental catastrophes of recent years: the nuclear accidents at Three Mile Island and Chernobyl; mercury poisoning in Minimata, Japan and on the Grassy Narrows Reserve (northern Ontario); the leak of poisonous gas from Union Carbide's plant at Bhopal, India (see also Bhullar 1990); and the *Exxon Valdez* oil spill off the coast of Alaska in 1989.[5] It is ironic that despite greater publicity surrounding environmental protection, "governments seem to be unable or unwilling to force polluters to stop their destructive practices" (Caputo et al. 1989, 161).

Once again, the modern controversy over environmental damage must be seen in historical perspective. The network of government officials and key officials in corporations has emerged, over time, as a private resource, in which many decisions are made behind closed doors. This has often been noted with respect to the polluting practices of pulp and paper mills in British Columbia, for example, and to the decision in the 1920s by General Motors and other corporations to promote the use of fossil fuels rather than electricity for public and private transport (see Caputo et al. 1989, 162).

The work of Ted Schrecker is a major contribution to understanding the political and economic context associated with environmental law. In one essay, Schrecker (1989) discusses the *de facto* right of industry to place residues in the natural environment. This practice facilitates production inasmuch as it allows producers to pass on pollution-related costs to "society as a whole," instead of eroding profits (Schrecker 1989, 173).

Schrecker (1989, 173) states that, despite earlier common-law protections, there is no established right, in modern times, for people exposed to air pollution to be compensated for related injuries. Schrecker thus develops an argument against the usefulness of law, as it stands, in providing recourse for palpable damages.

There is, however, a dialectical element in the creation of such contemporary legislation as environmental laws: while profitability is a key factor in regulating (or failing to regulate) environmental pollution, both the private sector and government ministries must also take other considerations into account (Schrecker 1989, 174). Government legitimacy and the legitimacy of the private sector clearly rest on taking action, or at least the appearance of taking action. Nevertheless, many researchers point to the narrow scope of current government legislation concerning pollution. For example, Schrecker (1989, 174) states that only five groups of substances are listed under the purview of the Environmental Contaminants Act. Schrecker (1989, 175) adds that provincial legislation is further restricted by its limits on acceptable concentrations of substances (e.g., parts per trillion for dioxin emissions from pulp and paper mills) rather than on total emissions into waterways. He notes that, in Ontario, the development of pollution-related standards

> has historically taken place mainly through the control order process, which is . . .
> secret. Parties outside the charmed industry-government circle . . . are typically
> involved only at the final stage: public meetings where audiences are treated to a
> defence of a negotiated position previously agreed to by government and the firm
> in question (Schrecker 1989, 176).[6]

Schrecker (1989, 183) concludes that business interests are "uniquely important" in setting public policy limits.

McLaren (1984) provides a different interpretation of the nature of environmental regulation in his discussion of industrial and commercial development in nineteenth century Ontario. He discusses the case of Antoine Ratté, a small businessman who operated a rowboat rental business on the banks of the Ottawa River. For eighteen years, the river area had been fouled by the dis-

charge of the lumber mills about a kilometre upriver. Ratté protested this pollution, alleging that the detritus interfered with his boat operations and generally
befouled the area with noxious odours and, occasionally, gas explosions.

Ratté eventually launched an action for damages in 1885, but his action was
dismissed. The details of the case need not be recounted here, but essentially the
court held that as a riparian owner, Ratté could not claim rights in the water or
subsoil, as there had been no legal transfer to him; since his property fronted a
water lot, not the river as such, he could not claim riparian rights. Ratté persisted
with legal action, successfully appealing the initial decision; after a total of seven
appeals (six by the defendants), Ratté finally received damages in 1892.

McLaren uses this case study to address the evolution of regulatory mechanisms in Canada. He notes that in the last decade of the nineteenth century,
several regulatory and administrative mechanisms were established, which
served to mediate economic development in Canada (McLaren 1984, 257).
McLaren suggests that these new mechanisms reflected a growing concern
over the negative impact of unfettered industrial and commercial growth.

Parallel to this growing sensitivity on the part of politicians and civil servants was the emergence of a greater public awareness of the unfortunate
consequences of economic growth. It was no longer safe to assume that the
environment could forever receive humanity's waste products and assimilate
them without permanent injury (McLaren 1984, 255–56).

In environmental law and government regulatory policy, we can see the serious contradictions between the spirit of the law (and its claims of progress in
eliminating or minimizing various forms of pollution) and the net effect of continuing pollution in Canada. A renewed awareness of how economic power is
translated into legal advantage undermines the argument of law as an arena of
conflict, where various groups petition on a more or less equal footing for restrictions or approval with respect to development. As in the area of corporate crime,
the environmental movement has taken a critical look at regulatory bodies and
their failure to redress environmental accidents. Many critics suggest that not
only is current legal regulation inadequate for dealing with the scale of damage
to the environment, but short-term gains can be eliminated very easily. Webb
(1990, 220), while conceding that courts do serve to limit and guide bureaucratic
action with respect to pollution control, provides a note of caution:

> Often . . . there is very little that can be done in law to make the bureaucrat's posi-
> tion more tolerable: political willpower, for example, can disappear with a change
> in governing party or a downturn in the economy, and no amount of legislation
> can guard against its disappearance.

With respect to water management, other observers have noted that the current
fragmentation of government functions and poorly-coordinated approaches
have greatly hindered efforts to improve the quality of Canada's water supply.
For some, the government's ad hoc approach is "completely untenable" (Foster
and Sewell 1981, 95).

Webb (1988, 24–33) identifies several difficulties with current legislation pertaining to pollution control. In her report to the Law Reform Commission of Canada, she noted that some of the legislation was simply "unrealistic," and if enforced, some industries would not be able to operate and obey the relevant law. Such oversimplified legislation would thus need to be refined in order to give greater guidance to those at risk of pollution-related charges. Webb (1988, 24–33) notes that some jurisdictions have expanded their repertoire of sanctions, going beyond fines or jail terms, and using such options as forcing polluters to compensate victims, publicizing offences, and passing on investigative costs from government authorities to polluters. Webb (1988, 32) recognizes, however, that Canadian courts have "rarely imposed" the full range of penalties against industrial polluters.

Environmental justice is a growing area within the sociology of law. It has fostered the growth of radical approaches to environmental damage, such as "deep ecology," in which a new ethic of environmental consumerism is developed against the dominant ethic of pleasure, acquisition, and private interests. This new emphasis has attracted interest from the political right, with many free-market proponents exploring how economic factors might be taken into account in reassessing environmental protection (see Block 1989). From this conservative outlook, private economic interests and the public interest are not completely opposed. Ethicists have also explored traditional and evolving frameworks of justice, with some arguing for international cooperation on a global level to regulate energy consumption, and thereby reverse environmental damage. Wenz (1988, 340–43) argues that, since industrialized nations tend to benefit more from current patterns of energy consumption and wealth than do poorer nations, a greater burden would be placed on these more advantaged nations and on the relatively affluent citizens within them. The point remains that environmental damage, even when repeated and severe, has traditionally been seen as a regulatory problem, not as a crime per se.

CRIMINAL JUSTICE AND SOCIAL ORDERING

Traditional approaches in criminology placed considerable emphasis on the study of criminals as individuals, or on the social context in which crime occurred. More recently, there has been a far greater appreciation among critical scholars of the *political* context of the application of criminal law. Accordingly, emphasis has shifted from the study of criminals as such, to the workings of the state and other disciplinary institutions, especially with respect to how the modern state and related institutions extend their control over people (see Lowman, Menzies, and Palys 1987).

The liberal-pluralist assumption that the criminal law works not only to punish criminals, but to provide strong safeguards for the sake of accused people—

the presumption of innocence, due process of law—has been challenged by many scholars concerned with how the state secures compliance and social order. Ericson and Baranek (1982, 1986) present original findings on the status of defendants before criminal law. Their work, *The Ordering of Justice: A Study of Accused Persons as Dependants in the Criminal Justice Process* (1982),[7] focuses on a catchment area outside of Toronto. The authors used participant-observation techniques, documentary analysis, and interviews to understand the dynamics of the criminal justice process for a group of defendants. Their work challenges the premise of legal authority derived from an authentic social consensus about law. It is also critical of the applicability of liberal, formal safeguards within the legal structure, especially with respect to defendants' rights. Ericson and Baranek (1982) trace the social transformation of the accused person (the defendant, with legal rights and integrity) into a dependant, who has very limited power when enmeshed in the criminal justice bureaucracy.

The authors bring forward four major themes with respect to the ordering process. First, the premise that personal and interpersonal conflicts become "state property" (Ericson and Baranek 1986, 41) is crucial. This proprietary action represents a "foreclosing" of choices and decisions by the accused person. Whether innocent or guilty, once charged with an offence, the accused person is typically able to resolve the charge by turning his or her fate over to several legal actors. In Canada, these are the Crown prosecutor, defence attorneys, judges, and others linked with the formal legal process for criminal cases. Second, individuality—the hallmark of liberal-democratic ideology—is substantially undermined in this ordering process. Individual decisions—such as entering a plea of guilty or not guilty—reflect "submission to pressure from others and to structural arrangements" (Ericson and Baranek 1986, 42). A third theme is the way in which the individual accused often rationalizes his or her submission as just. The elements of mercy and majesty (see Hay 1975 and Chapter Three of this book) are used to elicit fear and relief in the defendant and thereby to secure a sense of legitimacy for the criminal justice system. Ericson and Baranek (1986, 43) put this as follows:

> We find that on the whole the accused expresses satisfaction with the process, and especially with the sentencing outcome and the judge who pronounces it. His satisfaction results from the impact of his appearance in court: regardless of what took place up to that point, the order and aura of the court serves its mystical function and makes the accused a true believer.

The fourth theme—reform—is discussed extensively by the authors. The structuring of individual dependency on authorities is set in the wider context of the social order and how social relations are "re-ordered" by state agents. Ericson and Baranek (1986) are sceptical of the promises of reformers: diversion from the formal court process and changing legal rules to the advantage of the accused are noted, then critiqued in light of expanding governmental authority in Canada. State discretion, which translates as state power, remains largely intact, a fact illustrated by the considerable powers of official discretion even in jurisdictions that seem to have removed such discretion by the use of "fixed penalties" for criminal offences (Ericson and Baranek 1986, 44–46).

Ericson (1983) reverses the notion of law's power to reform social arrangements: in effect, legal initiatives and powers really act so as to re-form existing structures of legal and social inequality. The author thus discounts the ideal of a criminal-law-enforcement apparatus that is being reformed (i.e., improved, made more responsive and democratic). The stated concerns for social equality and social justice are thus often not translated into emancipatory practices by state officials. The Canadian Charter of Rights and Freedoms is singled out by Ericson (1983, 2) as a legal initiative whose "public character" ostensibly is to promote greater equality for Canadians, but whose "social character"—the actions of legislators and other officials—generally has the opposite effect.

The Charter appears as a legal initiative that is imposed on citizens, not a power that was developed from substantial consultation with citizens. Despite this distance between the public and the Charter, proponents of the Charter present it as "a radical enhancement of democracy" (Ericson 1983, 11). Ericson notes, however, that the Charter has, in fact, added to the considerable discretionary powers of state authorities. Thus, illiberal governments are able to embrace high-sounding enactments while using repressive measures against their citizens. Ericson (1983, 20–21) illustrates this paradox by citing how the United Nations Charter of Human Rights has been adopted by totalitarian nations (South Africa and Argentina, for example); in Canada, the passing of the Protection of Privacy Act gave legitimacy to police invasions of citizens' privacy, almost invariably with judicial authorization for requests to wiretap or otherwise monitor private activities of citizens.

The symbolic power of legal ideology works to reinforce the image of a political system that safeguards a "reasonably equal balance" between state powers and citizens' rights (Ericson 1983, 3). Law also strengthens the legitimacy of a control culture, in which police forces are respected and obeyed by much of the public. This image of a decent society, moving toward greater degrees of decency and social equality, is belied by increases in such structured inequalities as homelessness, unemployment, and social isolation (Ericson 1983, 7–9).

In contrast to liberal-democratic ideologies of law, which emphasize the value of citizens' pressure groups in altering legal arrangements, more critical approaches have recognized the power of state agents in deflecting or co-opting grass-roots initiatives. McMahon and Ericson (1987, 38) document how state agents intervene in a variety of ways so as to "convert the property of the outside reform group into its instrumental value for the state." The instance they refer to is the attempt to establish an effective civilian review body of the

Toronto police force. McMahon and Ericson (1987) trace the mobilization of protests against two events: the 1979 shooting death of Albert Johnson, who had emigrated from Jamaica to Toronto; and the wide-scale police raid of gay bathhouses in Toronto in 1981. The authors point out that, despite a variety of associations lobbying against police use of deadly force and interference in the lives of gay citizens, the initial protests against police powers were transformed by authorities in the police commission and other official agencies into a more co-operative arrangement between state officials and citizens. Opportunities to openly criticize state agendas are limited by various structures, including the practice of appointing officials to the police commission and the use of closed-door meetings, which limit public scrutiny or commentary (McMahon and Ericson 1987, 56–57). Such gatekeeping measures, in conjunction with processes that marginalize radical critics of policing procedures (and less visible minorities, such as gay activists), thus provide for concrete accountability to other state officials, with nominal accountability to the citizenry at large. Ironically, attempts to reform the police may be followed by a "solidification" of police and state control (McMahon and Ericson 1987, 65).

Taylor (1981) has argued for alternate solutions to crime than those forwarded by the political right (among them, right-wing criminologists). Using England and Canada as examples, Taylor (1980, 1981) challenges the conservative ideology that crime stems from a lack of discipline, and that law-and-order powers must be increased to instil "social discipline." Taylor (1981, 210–12) points to how social antagonisms and inequality are, in fact, social products, and how, without a genuine "community of interest" for citizens, the right-wing agenda of greater police powers, more severe prison sentences, the death penalty, and incapacitation of offenders will continue as social policy. Taylor (1981, 210) notes that crime rates have likely increased in the past decade, including crimes that threaten women and people of colour (predatory crimes, racist attacks by white supremacists, and so forth). Taylor's work coincides with other arguments for socialist transformation of the alienating political and economic arrangements in Britain (see, for example, Benn 1980). Significantly, such work combines a critical, theoretical outlook on the capitalist state and society with practical changes to the objectives and structure of social institutions such as work, law, and political life. For groups that have traditionally been managed by the state—people of colour, renters, women, welfare recipients—Taylor envisions a community-based approach that would strengthen them, not only in terms of criminal law, but of social justice:

> Such an enfranchising, for example, of women's organizations in relation to local police committees, would significantly transform the character and function of particular aspects of the police and the *local* state (Taylor 1981, 205; italics in original).

THE PENAL SANCTION IN CANADA

The wry observation that "the rich get richer, the poor get prison" (Reiman 1989) underscores the general theme in the sociology of criminal law: inequalities in society are often translated into incarceration of those who are economically disadvantaged. Reiman's work deals with the now familiar theme of how powerful interest groups, who have been implicated in causing severe harm to health and the environment, are virtually exempt from criminal prosecution. He also documents the overrepresentation of economically marginal people in U.S. prisons. Gosselin (1982) uses Marxist-based theory to reassess the evolution of the prison in Canada. He challenges the orthodox view of the prison as a necessary last resort in defence of public safety. For Gosselin (1982, 17), the prison is part of a wider pattern of the "repressive apparatus of the state" in Canada.

At the inception of the prison institution, prior to Confederation, prison regimes were very harsh, with corporal punishment and other sanctions given for a variety of breaches of prison regulations (Gosselin 1982, 72). The first penitentiary—Kingston Penitentiary—was still under construction when its first prisoners were admitted in 1835 (Gosselin 1982, 71). In 1873, a second penal institution—the St. Vincent de Paul Penitentiary—was established in Quebec. Gosselin reviews the expansion in the number of penal institutions, noting that, in over a century of experimentation with the prison system, this system has been adapted "to the ever-expanding needs of the capitalist system which gives it life" (Gosselin 1982, 81).

Culhane (1985) has written extensively about prisoners' rights in Canada and elsewhere, and has translated her concerns into social action. Culhane (1985, 57–58) notes how National Prison Justice Day—August 10 of each year—has been observed by many Canadian prisoners and their supporters since its inception in 1976. Culhane's work appreciates the different form of prisoners' struggles against the rather monolithic and unresponsive apparatus of prison bureaucracy and the justice system in general.

Sociological factors also come into play in the discussion of the legal realities facing many prisoners. There has been a longstanding critique of the ways in which legal resources and safeguards have not been extended to prisoners, as evidenced by the practice of granting them privileges rather than extending them rights. It has also been noted that prison conditions are often not corrected, and even such practices as placing prisoners in punitive or administrative segregation (i.e., solitary confinement) are largely under the discretionary control of prison authorities, with little external review (Jackson 1983). Critics also charge that prison officials give a greater priority to prison security—including prevention of escapes—than to life-saving measures (Burtch and Ericson, 1979).

Many modern studies of crime control have called into question not only agents' practices, such as arrest, prosecution, and sentencing, but also the wider context of social control. Ericson, Baranek, and Chan (1987, 1989), for example, have written a number of critical works on how the media are used to create an overarching ideology that re-establishes political authority. At the same time, Ericson (1991, 242) is sensitive to contradictions in media coverage of crime, law, and justice. He notes that the mass media are more pluralistic than some writers allow: "While mass communications are hierarchial and structured by power, so that particular institutions, people, topics, and formats predominate, they still provide an appreciably open terrain for struggles for justice."

Ericson is certainly not alone in exploring possibilities for making institutions such as law and media more responsive to struggles for justice. Sargent (1989, 60–61), for example, discusses corporate crime and law, concluding that the traditional hegemony of the legal system is being challenged, and to some extent influenced, by consumer groups and many other groups seeking to transform law. Herman and Chomsky (1988, 306) portray the American mass-media network as serving to induce conformist beliefs and behaviours that are largely congruent with the needs of the privileged and powerful. The authors conclude that, with this media network, the state has succeeded in inculcating conformity and deference in Americans without resorting to sheer repression or other kinds of coercion. They acknowledge that this is not a total system, inasmuch as media have at times served other interests than state propaganda. Mathiesen (1987, 71) notes that modern media have served to present communications in a way that essentially preserves or extends "the power of groups which are already in power." He notes, however, that future media may provide a more interactive potential between the telecast information and the viewer. Mathiesen (1987, 75) stresses that political struggles against media messages that promote deference and subordination involve the creation of "alternative communication networks." Nevertheless, Mathiesen is well aware of the danger of co-optation through the media. Ericson, Baranek, and Chan (1987, 358–59) note that journalists, among other media workers, must establish some degree of legitimacy with their readerships and sources.

SUMMARY

The idealistic image of criminal law as reflecting a clear consensus of morality and social defence has been eclipsed by more critical approaches to criminal sanctioning. These approaches focus on the power relations among various groups—along lines of gender, race, and social class—and how the use of criminal law maintains these relations.

The renewed interest in crime as an index of social conflict is paramount among the recent developments in criminology. Marxist-based criminology, for example, documents the economic factors that underly patterns of crime control in capitalist societies. There has also been a shift in scholarly interest away from studies of criminals and deviants as problems in their own right toward a more critical assessment of criminal justice officials and other state agents. The power of media construction of what constitutes "dangerousness" has also been challenged, with many writers critiquing mass-media constructions of crime and authority, and some offering alternative approaches. Concurrent with these developments, a number of critical theories derived from feminism and ecological concerns have redirected scholarly interest away from narrow interpretations of Criminal Code sanctions to more general approaches to punitive measures.

Scholarly opinion, not surprisingly, is divided on the topic of the criminal sanction. Some favour extensions of state powers in the interests of order and justice; others are extremely sceptical of the political agenda of crime control agencies and their potential for reform from within or from outside pressures. The example of corporate crime seems to evoke mixed opinions, perhaps corresponding to the mixed evidence on state regulation of the private sector. Cullen, Maakestad, and Cavender (1987) suggest that many actions—civil actions, for example, as well as government-initiated regulatory actions—serve a largely symbolic purpose. Thus, they find some importance in the symbolic movement against corporate illegalities. Even with the legacy of leniency toward these offences, Cullen, Maakestad, and Cavender (1987, 27) detect a popular movement that is more aware of the effects of white-collar crime and motivated to redirect legal actions that had previously been tolerated or excused by legal officials and many members of the public.

STUDY QUESTIONS

❑ Discuss the phenomenon of murder, with particular attention to how murder is socially defined. Discuss Boyd's (1988) premise that such social definitions serve to apply severe sanctions (such as long-term imprisonment) to a relatively powerless group of marginalized persons.

❑ Review the debate over criminalization of certain corporate wrongdoings, including environmental pollution. How do legal ideology and government practice serve to excuse or tolerate what might be seen as "crimes"? In what ways is legal policy *dialectical*, that is, reflecting contradictions in society and in the legal apparatus?

❑ What regulations are in place with respect to environmental protection in Ontario? What strategies are used in "resisting regulation" (Schrecker 1989, 178–83)? How might Schrecker's analysis of these regulations be applied in your locality?

❑ The mass media are clearly one of the more important sources of information in modern societies. Critically assess the ways in which media representations of crime and law-breaking generally are portrayed (or distorted) by media sources. To what extent do media programs contribute to social ordering?

NOTES

1. This committee was officially known as the Committee on Sexual Offences Against Children and Youth. The Report was based on approximately three years of research (Lowman 1985, 508).

2. Blumberg (1989) provides a detailed account of illegal, or simply dishonest, dealings in all sectors of the American marketplace. These include automobile sales and servicing, retailing, the restaurant business, and advertising. Blumberg (1989, Chapter 10) concludes that "honest businesses," while not a complete rarity, are unusual in this marketplace.

3. Chambliss (1982, 180–81) contends that criminal activity on a large scale is "good business," and that under a capitalist economic system, with its emphasis on private property and economic exchanges, such crime networks are inevitable.

4. The Commission (1989, 242) states that public opinion played a crucial role in generating initiatives to improve air quality, purity of drinking water, and the disposal of toxic wastes. The Commission (1989, 242) remarks that physical conditions "have improved steadily during the past century, and this trend continues, although the pace varies between and within cities."

5. See also the discussion by Brannigan (1984, 121–22) concerning the devastating effects of mercury poisoning in Minimata, Japan, and also in the Dryden area of northern Ontario. Both instances occurred in the 1970s.

6. There is a parallel here with Ericson and Baranek's (1982) account of the *dependency* of weaker actors on official decisions and the *secrecy* that characterizes many aspects of the criminal justice process. See also Sarat and Felstiner's (1986) analysis of the client's disadvantaged position in matters of family law in Chapter Nine.

7. *The Ordering of Justice: A Study of Accused Persons as Dependants in the Criminal Justice Process* received the 1982 John Porter Award, under the auspices of the Canadian Sociology and Anthropology Association. The John Porter Award honours the year's most outstanding book in Canadian sociology.

REFERENCES

Archer, D., and R. Gartner (1984) *Violence and Crime in Cross-National Perspective*. New Haven: Yale University Press.

Beattie, J. (1986) *Crime and the Courts in England, 1660–1800*. Princeton: Princeton University Press.

Benn, T. (1980) *Arguments for Socialism*. Harmondsworth: Penguin.

Bhullar, B. (1990) "Union Carbide and the Bhopal Disaster: A Case Study in the Causes of Corporate Crime." In *Studies in Corporate Crime*, edited by R. Gordon, 123–51. Burnaby, British Columbia: School of Criminology, Simon Fraser University.

Block, W., ed. (1989) *Economics and the Environment: A Reconciliation*. Vancouver: Fraser Institute.

Blumberg, A. (1989) *The Predatory Society: Deception in the American Marketplace*. New York: Oxford University Press.

Boyd, N. (1988) *The Last Dance: Murder in Canada*. Toronto: Prentice-Hall.

Brannigan, A. (1984) *Crimes, Courts, and Corrections: An Introduction to Crime and Social Control in Canada*. Toronto: Holt, Rinehart and Winston.

Brantingham, P., and P. Brantingham (1984) *Patterns in Crime*. New York: Macmillan.

Burtch, B., and R. Ericson (1979) *The Silent System: An Inquiry into Prisoners Who Suicide*. Toronto: Centre of Criminology.

Caputo, T., M. Kennedy, C. Reasons, and A. Brannigan, eds. (1989) *Law and Society: A Critical Perspective*. Toronto: Harcourt Brace Jovanovich.

Carlen, P. (1988) *Women, Crime and Poverty*. Milton Keynes: Open University Press.

Chambliss, W. (1982) *On the Take: From Petty Crooks to Presidents*. Bloomington: Indiana University Press.

Coleman, J. (1989) *The Criminal Elite: The Sociology of White Collar Crime*. New York: St. Martin's Press.

Comack, E. (1990) "Law and Order Issues in the Canadian Context: The Case of Capital Punishment." *Social Justice* 17 (1): 70–97.

Culhane, C. (1985) *Still Barred from Prison: Social Injustice in Canada*. Montreal: Black Rose Books.

Cullen, F., W. Maakestad, and G. Cavender (1987) *Corporate Crime Under Attack: The Ford Pinto Case and Beyond*. Cincinnati: Anderson Publishing Company.

Davis, N., and K. Faith (1987) "Women and the State: Changing Models of Social Control." In *Transcarceration: Essays in the Sociology of Social Control*, edited by J. Lowman, R. Menzies, and T. Palys, 170–87. London: Gower Books.

Ericson, R. (1983) "The Constitution of Legal Inequality." John Porter Memorial Address. Ottawa: Carleton University Press.

——— (1991) "Mass Media, Crime, Law, and Justice: An Institutional Approach." *British Journal of Criminology* 31 (3): 219–49.

Ericson, R., and P. Baranek (1982) *The Ordering of Justice: A Study of Accused Persons as Dependants in the Criminal Justice Process*. Toronto: University of Toronto Press.

——— (1986) "The Reordering of Justice." In *The Social Dimensions of Law*, edited by N. Boyd, 41–65. Toronto: Prentice-Hall.

Ericson, R., P. Baranek, and J. Chan (1987) *Visualizing Deviance: A Study of News Organization*. Toronto: University of Toronto Press.

——— (1989) *Negotiating Control: A Study of News Sources*. Toronto: University of Toronto Press.

Fattah, E. (1972) *A Study of the Deterrent Effect of Capital Punishment with Special Reference to the Canadian Situation*. Ottawa: Information Canada.

Foster, H., and W. Sewell (1981) *Water: The Emerging Crisis in Canada*. Toronto: Canadian Institute for Economic Policy.

Frank, N., and M. Lombness (1988) *Controlling Corporate Illegality: The Regulatory Justice System*. Cincinnati: Anderson Publishing Company.

Glasbeek, H., and S. Rowland (1986) "Are Injuring and Killing in the Workplace Crimes?" In *The Social Dimensions of Law*, edited by N. Boyd, 66–85. Toronto: Prentice-Hall.

Glazer, M. (1987) "Whistleblowers." In *Corporate and Governmental Deviance: Problems of Organizational Behavior in Contemporary Society*, edited by M. Ermann and R. Lundman, 187–208. Oxford: Oxford University Press.

Goff, C., and C. Reasons (1978) *Corporate Crime in Canada: A Critical Analysis of Anti-Combines Legislation*. Toronto: Prentice-Hall.

Gosselin, L. (1982) *Prisons in Canada*. Montreal: Black Rose Books.

Hagan, J. (1976) "Locking up the Indians: A Case for Law Reform." *Canadian Forum* 55 (658): 16–18.

——— (1991) *The Disreputable Pleasures: Crime and Deviance in Canada* (3rd edition). Toronto: McGraw-Hill Ryerson.

Hay, D. (1975) "Property, Authority and the Criminal Law." In *Albion's Fatal Tree: Crime and Society in Eighteenth Century England*, edited by D. Hay, P. Linebaugh, J. Rule, E.P. Thompson, and C. Winslow, 17–63. New York: Pantheon Books.

Herman, E., and N. Chomsky (1988) *Manufacturing Consent: The Political Economy of the Mass Media*. New York: Pantheon Books.

Jackson, M. (1983) *Prisoners of Isolation: Solitary Confinement in Canada*. Toronto: University of Toronto Press.

LaPrairie, C. (1987) "Native Women and Crime in Canada: A Theoretical Model." In *Too Few to Count: Canadian Women in Conflict with the Law*, edited by E. Adelberg and C. Currie, 103–12. Vancouver: Press Gang.

Larsen, E. (forthcoming) "It's Time to Acknowledge the Inevitable and Revise Canada's Prostitution Laws." *Policy Options*.

Lowman, J. (1985) "Child Saving, Legal Panaceas, and the Individualization of Family Problems: Some Comments on the Findings and Recommendations of the Badgley Report." *Canadian Journal of Family Law* 4 (4): 508–14.

Lowman, J., R. Menzies, and T. Palys, eds. (1987) *Transcarceration: Essays in the Sociology of Social Control*. London: Gower Books.

McLaren, J. (1984) "The Tribulations of Antoine Ratté: A Case Study of the Environmental Regulation of the Canadian Lumbering Industry in the Nineteenth Century." *University of New Brunswick Law Journal* 33: 203–59.

McMahon, M., and R. Ericson (1987) "Reforming the Police and Policing Reform." In *State Control: Criminal Justice Politics in Canada*, edited by R. Ratner and J. McMullan, 38–68. Vancouver: University of British Columbia Press.

Mathiesen, T. (1987) "The Eagle and the Sun: On Panoptical Systems and Mass Media in Modern Society." In *Transcarceration: Essays in the Sociology of Social Control*, edited by J. Lowman, R. Menzies, and T. Palys, 59–75. London: Gower Books.

Reasons, C., L. Ross, and C. Paterson (1981) *Assault on the Worker: Occupational Health and Safety in Canada*. Toronto: Butterworths.

Reiman, J. (1989) *The Rich Get Richer and the Poor Get Prison*. New York: John Wiley & Sons.

Sargent, N. (1989) "Law, Ideology, and Corporate Crime: A Critique of Instrumentalism." *Canadian Journal of Law and Society* 4: 39–75.

Schrecker, T. (1989) "The Political Context and Content of Environmental Law." In *Law and Society: A Critical Perspective*, edited by T. Caputo, M. Kennedy, C. Reasons, and A. Brannigan, 173–204. Toronto: Harcourt Brace Jovanovich.

Science Council of Canada (1974) "The Quality of Natural Environment." In *Protecting the Environment: Issues and Choices—Canadian Perspectives*, edited by O. Dwivendi, 21–37. Toronto: Copp Clark.

Smandych, R. (1991) "The Origins of Canadian Anti-Combines Legislation, 1890–1910." In *The Social Basis of Law: Critical Readings in the Sociology of Law*, edited by E. Comack and S. Brickey, 35–47. Toronto: Garamond Press.

Sutherland, E. (1949) *White Collar Crime*. New York: Dryden Press.

Taylor, I. (1980) "The Law and Order Issue in the British General Election and Canadian Federal Election of 1979: Crime, Population and the State." *Canadian Journal of Sociology* 5 (3): 285–311.

———— (1981) *Law and Order: Arguments for Socialism*. London: Macmillan.

Webb, K. (1988) *Pollution Control in Canada: The Regulatory Approach in the 1980s*. Ottawa: Law Reform Commission of Canada.

———— (1990) "Between Rocks and Hard Places: Bureaucrats, Law and Pollution Control." In *Managing Leviathan: Environmental Politics and the Administrative State*, edited by R. Paehlke and D. Torgenson, 201–27. Peterborough, Ontario: Broadview Press.

Wenz, P. (1988) *Environmental Justice*. Albany: State University of New York.

World Commission on Environment and Population (1989) *Our Common Future*. Oxford: Oxford University Press.

CHAPTER NINE

Reproduction and Law: Midwifery, Abortion, and Family Law Reform

INTRODUCTION

This chapter addresses three topics connected with earlier discussions of feminist jurisprudence, the politics of criminal law, and the nature of family law. The three topics—the modern midwifery movement in Canada, the debate over legal provisions for therapeutic abortion, and the limits of family law reform in Canada—illustrate how political and social movements seek to influence existing laws and public opinion, and how laws that influence women directly emerge from, and may be altered by, particular cultures and legal struggles. Yet at the same time, it seems that legal reform is often forestalled, or implemented in ways that restrict women's access to reproductive care, therapeutic abortion, or an adequate context for child-rearing after separation. This chapter thus brings us directly into a discussion of the limits of law, as well as the extent to which particular groups are denied full participation in the social contract.

A central theme of this chapter is the way in which the Canadian legal structure has been used to translate law into power and to secure social order in a variety of spheres: the family, the economy, and the regulation of such private decisions as reproduction. Beginning with the midwifery movement's efforts to legalize midwifery practice in Canada, we will see how the politics underlying law and social policies suggest the difficulties that certain interest groups face in challenging existing legislation and services. The following discussion also outlines various contradictions in legal policies, including the difficult process by which marginalized groups seek to gain a more legitimate status in law. The first instance discussed is the legal status of midwives in Canada and the efforts of the contemporary midwives' movement to establish midwifery services. The discussion of midwifery serves as one model of how a social movement can succeed or be co-opted in its objectives.

MIDWIFERY AND LAW

The word "midwife" comes from the Old English *mid-wyfe*, which, in the context of childbirth attendance, refers to a woman who assists other women in childbirth. In virtually every country in the world, midwives attend women in labour and at various stages of pregnancy or following childbirth. Midwives help to deliver the majority of children in the world (Kitzinger 1988). But while the midwife remains an important person in most cultures—known in Mexico as *la partera* (companion) and in France as *sage femme* (wise woman)—in Canada, the existence of midwives is not as well known. It is not unusual for people to venture that midwives are no longer active in Canada, having been replaced by medical and nursing professionals.

In the 1970s, lay midwives—also known as community midwives, and in earlier times, as granny midwives—became active in attending women throughout pregnancy and at delivery. This movement was linked with the resurgence of community-oriented midwifery practice in North America. Medical procedures such as Caesarean section, forceps delivery, induction of birth, and the unnecessary use of medication and fetal monitoring were seen as unjustifiable interference with the normal progress of labour (Arms 1977). As part of a movement to humanize obstetrics and to allow for birthing situations tailored to women's needs, midwives have lobbied for legal recognition, autonomy, and respect for their distinctive status. Midwifery controlled by other professions—most notably, physicians or nurses—would, for these advocates, be midwifery in name only.

The "midwifery challenge" (Kitzinger 1988) has been met with a mixture of support and resistance. This situation has led to the current state of uncertainty surrounding midwifery. Repressive law (such as prosecution of midwives for criminal negligence) and other state measures (such as coroner's inquests) have been ineffective in redressing this state of uncertainty. Midwives seek to assert their own autonomous status as experts in the management of normal obstetrics, separate from obstetrical nursing, general practice, and specialty obstetrics. Midwives seek self-regulation through a college of midwives and believe in greater recognition of parental rights in birth and continuity of care for expectant mothers through pregnancy, labour, delivery, and into the postpartum period.

Among all industrialized nations, Canada is the only one that has not legally recognized midwifery. Largely replaced by physicians and nurses, midwives in Canada and the United States were discouraged from attending births. Childbirth was increasingly defined as a medical event, properly supervised by medical practitioners in hospital settings. This ideology of medical control was reinforced by legislation restricting or prohibiting other forms of birth attendance. Laws were enacted to prohibit the practice of midwifery in Canada (Burtch 1988b). Jordan (1980, 96–97) notes that many American states outlawed midwifery, and midwifery became isolated from theoretical and clinical training in birth:

> In Europe, scientific advances became incorporated into the repertoire of mid-wives' techniques. In the United States, on the other hand, no systematic attempts were made to upgrade the profession through training. Midwives were increasingly seen as ignorant and dirty. Childbirth passed into the medical realm, and midwifery suffered a decline that is only beginning to be reversed.

Restrictive laws and ideologies surrounding birth established medicalized birth as a desirable norm that was in the interests of birthing women and the public at large. As midwives became less prominent, the work of obstetrical and maternity-care nurses was limited. The sphere of practice for nurses was circumscribed, with male physicians now "presiding" over birth. Gaskin (1988, 42), referring to the American context, sees a great irony in this situation.

> By the 1920s, the United States had founded a truly novel custom: that of sanctioning men to make the rules and supply the knowledge for an intimately physical process that they never experienced. Lost totally to the general public was the idea that a woman could be trained to safely attend another woman in labour.

Significantly, as midwifery was being eclipsed in twentieth century Canada, primary attendance was not transferred to female physicians. Despite the role of the Ontario Medical College for Women (closed in 1906) and the subsequent establishment of the Women's College, female physicians were a rarity. Buckley (1979, 128–29) reviews this process, noting that, in 1911, only 2.7 percent of physicians in Canada were women; this percentage fell to 1.8 percent in 1921.

Medical control of obstetrics led to a cultural transformation of birth. Attempts to connect the tradition of birth as a neighbourly and community-oriented event saw the formation of the Victorian Order of Nurses (VON) in 1897. Mason (1988, 107–8) depicts the VON as a movement that "threatened the doctors' prospects for hegemony over birth" more directly than other efforts to preserve the traditional, neighbour-oriented birth culture. Mason (1988, 108) notes that the VON initiative to provide training to lay midwives generated "virtually unanimous" opposition by the medical profession. The end result was a lessening of the nursing role envisioned by VON proponents, such that VO nurses were primarily seen in the role of assistants to physicians (Mason 1988, 109).

The medicalization of birth thus involved the transformation of women into receptive clients or assistants to physicians. Men were primarily responsible for decisions surrounding birth and the knowledge base of obstetrics. Women were no longer active in understanding and influencing their own well-being. In childbirth, this meant that many women were constrained in their experience of giving birth.[1] One woman describes her experiences of childbirth in Canada in the 1950s:

> I had my first baby in the mid-50s and it was very impersonal and very terrifying. You went to the hospital and your husband just dropped you off. He wasn't allowed to come into the case room or the delivery room. You went into the delivery room and you were with strangers. You didn't know anybody. I think the most terrifying part for me was delivering when you were laying on your back. Your legs were strapped in stirrups, and then he strapped your hands down, so you were completely strapped down and that's how you delivered. Just before the baby was born, they put you under again and when you woke up this is when you were told if it was a boy or a girl, and then you never saw your child again, usually until the next day . . . It was lonely, very lonely . . . I found all three births a terrifying experience for me" (Gerrie White, quoted in *Midwifery and the Law* 1991).

White contrasts her own experiences with the birth of her first granddaughter, who was delivered at a home birth in Vancouver in 1976. She describes the birth as "a very loving experience," much different from the way women were delivered a generation before. Significantly, although White had raised three children she had never experienced delivery, due to the 1950s practice of forceps delivery with the mother unconscious. For a generation of women, birth had become very much a medical event.

These first-hand experiences of birth support the argument that births need not be routinely controlled so that women giving birth and their supporters are excluded or strictly supervised by medical and nursing staff. Indeed, recent changes in childbirth procedures have been characterized by a general effort to humanize obstetrics, including the growing practice of women establishing birth plans to set out their expectations of birth, rooming-in of mothers and newborns, as well as greater access to the birth for partners and relatives (see Wagner 1985, 94–96).

Proponents of midwifery comment that approximately 80 percent of births worldwide are attended by midwives (Kitzinger 1988). Those countries in which midwifery is an established practice report the lowest rates of infant and maternal mortality and the lowest instance of surgical intervention in childbirth. A growing scientific literature has been cited in defence of the competency of qualified midwives who work in systems where midwifery is respected and legal (Wagner 1985). In Canada, despite the lack of scientifically rigorous evaluations of midwifery practice or of home births, a variety of exploratory studies have challenged the assumptions that home births or midwifery attendance are inherently more hazardous than other arrangements (Burtch 1988a; Tyson 1990; Walker, Pullen, and Shinyei 1986).

The resurgence of midwifery in Canada and the United States has nevertheless generated considerable resistance. Canadian midwives seeking legal recognition and acceptance within the health system have, to date, not succeeded in establishing the requirements of a distinct profession: control over their work, a self-regulating body to establish standards of care and "disciplinary" measures, legal protection, and specialized research and education forums. In the United States, there has been some acceptance of *nurse-midwifery*, in which midwifery is established as a subspecialty of nursing (Varney 1983). In Canada, there have been attempts to place midwives within the compass of provincial nursing bodies. On the other hand, there has also been pressure to establish midwifery as a distinct profession, with multiple routes of entry to practice. These multiple routes would include nursing training, yet would also allow for direct entry to midwifery training and certification.

In British Columbia, community midwives are still liable to prosecution under the provincial Medical Practitioners Act for illegally practising midwifery (ironically, under this Act, physicians were granted the power to act as a midwife, while midwives were not). Conflicts thus emerged between orthodox birth attendants—primarily general practitioners, obstetricians, and obstetrical nurses working on labour and delivery wards in provincial hospitals—and the midwives, who sought alternatives to hospital-based, medically supervised childbirth. These conflicts developed most dramatically when the midwives were placed in legal jeopardy. This entailed the threat of prosecution under criminal and quasi-criminal[2] law. Midwives could be charged with criminal negligence causing death (or injury) if a mishap occurred in a home birth situation. They could also be charged with practising medicine without a licence—for example, under the B.C. Medical Practitioners Act—if a complaint was registered.

Burtch (1988b) sets out three main points concerning the legal status of midwives. First, the state is pivotal in determining this status (Burtch 1988b, 313). The state is responsible for enacting and enforcing legislation governing birth attendance; moreover, provision of childbirth services—medical insurance plans, hospital services, and so forth—is largely administered through provincial or federal bureaucracies or agencies that depend on government payments for their operations.

Second, pregnancy has been seen as a medical model, although it is not inherently a disease state (Burtch 1988b, 314). Thus, pregnancy and the course of delivery tend to be viewed as pathological, or potentially pathological, states that require medical supervision and control. The midwifery movement counters this medical model image, arguing that the patient (or client) can take a more active, more informed role during her pregnancy, and that midwifery training is best suited for normal pregnancies and deliveries.

Third, there has been renewed interest in the role of economic and political factors in structuring health care. Doyal (1981) emphasizes the political economy of health care, in which health is treated as a commodity, and profit becomes a consideration in the formation of maternity and infant services. A hierarchy is perpetuated within medical and nursing spheres, such that nurses are less influential and less rewarded than physicians. And in contrast to the liberal ideal of equal treatment for all people, social class, gender, and race remain important variables in the composition of health care services. Law thus operates in a dialectical way, embedding "real rights" for individuals, but within a dominant ideology of medical and state control (Burtch 1988b, 314).

The Safety of Home Birth in Canada

Midwives tend to be flexible in their practices. Most have experience acting as a labour coach for women giving birth in hospital. For community midwives in Canada, home birth is a source of income and gives them more autonomy in attending to the mother in labour and birth. What makes midwives unique is their willingness to respect their clients' wishes. This quality is very reassuring for women, whether they wish to birth in hospital or at home.

The home birth controversy is especially pertinent in Canada, since community midwives tend to be the only practitioners who attend births at home, raising questions about safety (Burtch 1988a, 361–62). Burtch notes that there have been mixed findings concerning the safety of home birth. In countries where home birth is, or has been, an established part of maternity services, there is evidence that home births do not result in higher rates of infant (or maternal) mortality. Before proceeding, we must take a number of variables into account: the competency of the midwives, the presence or absence of guidelines for screening clients (that is, referring them to other services if they are "at risk"), the provision of emergency back-up services if the pregnancy becomes complicated, and general factors such as diet, sanitation, and income.

The issue of safety, and how this issue has been used to support or denounce midwifery practice, is addressed in a study of attempted home births, primarily in British Columbia and Ontario, from the late 1970s to 1986. The study also explores issues other than infant mortality.[3] Burtch (1987a, 1987b) reviewed over 1000 attempted home births in these provinces.[4] The results of this exploratory study were interpreted as supporting earlier research that midwives could attend home births without jeopardizing the safety of mothers or fetuses at term (see also Burtch 1988a). In keeping with other studies from the United States and several European countries, it was found that in terms of birth outcomes (deaths and injuries), there is no statistical evidence that midwives are less competent than other practitioners. Furthermore, as set out below, there was evidence that community midwives' work was completed with lower levels of intervention and morbidity.

One of the dilemmas confronting the midwifery movement is the danger of its being co-opted by the dominant medical and nursing professions. If midwifery remains on the margin, as an occupation without legal status, its clientele will be limited, and midwives may face serious legal jeopardy if there is injury or death in the course of a midwife-attended childbirth. Nevertheless, if midwives are integrated into the health care system, it has been argued that they may no longer be able to provide the same level of intimate, noninterventionist service to women. As we will discover in the following sections, a variety of court and other official inquiries have provided encouragement to those seeking legalized, self-directed midwifery in Canada.

Coroners' Inquests and Inquiries in Ontario

The viability of midwifery practice has not been a staple concern of the media or of government health care priorities in Canada. Midwifery does, however, receive prominent attention when a home birth attended by a midwife results in the death of an infant. Often, a coroner's inquest[5] may be held to determine the cause of death and the circumstances surrounding the birth.

Many of the recommendations resulting from coroner's juries in Ontario have advocated the establishment of midwifery as a separate profession, with specific guidelines for midwifery practice. These recommendations are largely similar to those outlined in the 1987 *Report of the Task Force on the Implementation of Midwifery in Ontario*. We will review five Ontario coroner's jury reports in this section. In the following section, we will compare these recommendations with available coroner's inquiries and inquests in British Columbia.

Inquest into the Death of Jean Ritz.   The first coroner's inquest that we will examine was convened on May 19, 1982, after the death of Jean Ritz. The cause of death was attributed to anoxia, due to an abnormal function of the placenta. This was caused by an infection that was "introduced into the uterine cavity as a result of rupture of the amniotic membrane." Since the infant was stillborn, the focus of the inquest was on the quality of care necessary to prevent such complications. The jury made two recommendations, each dealing with standards, education, and awareness:

1. The College of Physicians and Surgeons of Ontario and the College of Nurses of Ontario together should set up standards for and establish a program of study in midwifery leading to a licence to practise midwifery in the province of Ontario.

2. Literature should be made available on home and hospital births.

The first recommendation—concerning education, standards, and licensing—was made in the context of international guidelines for birth attendance. Professional experience and regulation were thus important in framing a system of midwifery in Ontario. At the same time, the second recommendation recognized that expectant parents should be able to make an informed choice with regard to possible sites for birth (in hospital or in the home). In general, the jury's recommendations, brief as they are, signalled a need to respect the plurality of choices in birth and to establish standards of care so that future complications and deaths are avoided or minimized.

Inquest into the Death of Simon Steell.   The coroner's jury findings on July 12–13, 1982, in the inquest into the death of Simon Steell, also favoured the regulation of midwifery. It was found that the infant died of accidental asphyxia *in utero* during a home delivery attended by two birth coaches and a family physician. The recommendations resulting from this inquest dealt with the role of midwifery, regulatory mechanisms, and the role of physicians in home births. Six recommendations were made:

1. The College of Physicians and Surgeons should establish minimum standards for procedures and equipment for home births. Uniform standards should be developed and published for use by physicians attending home births.

2. Complete written records should be kept by the physician throughout the entire course of pregnancy, including the events of labour and delivery in the home. This recommendation arose from the fact that no documentation had been made in this particular case, and there was no clinical record for review.

3. Because of the risk of unforeseen complications that may arise, monitoring of maternal and fetal status should be done regularly throughout the entire course of labour and delivery. This was felt to be a necessary precaution, since changes in the fetal heart rate may go undetected by those in attendance. Frequent monitoring in the second stage of labour was recommended.

4. The Province of Ontario should establish a training and accreditation program for birth coaches. This recommendation is to ensure an adequate level of care for home births.

5. In cases where fetal death or morbidity occur, the placenta should be retained for pathological examination. If the placenta is retained, further examination into the cause of death may help prevent such deaths in the future.

6. A study should be done to investigate the practicality of establishing home birth neonatal trauma teams. Such teams would be similar to the "flying squads" in England and Holland, which are called in to assist with home birth complications.

The recommendations of the 1982 Steell inquest supported the practice of midwifery, while establishing the role of the physician in home births and the need to standardize physicians' responsibilities.

Inquest into the Death of Daniel McLaughlin-Harris.   This Toronto inquest made an extensive review of the events leading to the infant's death. The jury concluded that the death could have been avoided if the mother had been transported to hospital sooner. The jury also cited the infant's low birth weight, the age of the mother, and the strictures on transportation from Toronto Island to the city as cofactors in the infant's death. While the jury seemed to find fault in this attempted home birth, the recommendations advocate the regulation and professionalization of midwifery, not its eradication. The jury made fifteen recommendations:

1. Midwifery should be legalized in Ontario, with strict penalties for the "non-obeyance" of such legislation.

2. The midwifery profession must be recognized and incorporated as an integral part of the Ontario health care system.

3. Midwifery as a profession should have a governing body to control and discipline midwife activity. The jury recommended a two-phase plan: under phase one, midwives should be governed as a specialty within the College of Nurses of Ontario; under phase two, after a five-year organizational and planning period, a new college should be established, called the College of Midwives of Ontario.

4. Standards of conduct should be established by the governing body for midwives, in accordance with internationally recognized standards and practices.

5. The international standard of midwifery training set down by the International Federation of Obstetricians and Gynaecologists and the International Confederation of Midwives should be followed. The recommendation further specified that the institution to train midwives should have a status equivalent to that of Ryerson Polytechnical Institute of Toronto.

6. Before licensing, each midwife must pass a comprehensive written and/or oral board exam. The exam should be administered by the governing body for midwives.

7. Malpractice insurance should be compulsory for any midwife practising in Ontario.

8. The legislation legalizing midwifery should include a clause allowing licensing of existing qualified midwives.

9. Since parents' freedom of choice cannot be controlled, parents should be educated about birth options, and be able to judge the risks and benefits of particular options. Health practitioners should not be censured for attend-

ing or being involved in a home birth. Finally, the provincial College of Physicians and Surgeons should establish safety standards for home births.

10. Licensed midwives should be given admitting privileges and standing in hospital maternity wards.

11. Midwifery services should be covered, at least in part, by the Ontario Health Insurance Plan (OHIP) to make it accessible to Ontario residents, regardless of socio-economic status.

12. Birthing centres should be established. The centres should be attached to hospitals to allow ready transfer to emergency services.

13. Emergency vehicles—police, fire, ambulance—should update or augment existing resuscitation equipment to provide better care for infants and newborns.

14. The governing body of midwives should specify standard equipment to be used by midwives in home birth situations.

15. The Ministry of Health should continue to support the Extended Role Nurse Program at McMaster University, as well as other programs aimed at improving maternity care services in Ontario.

More comprehensive in its recommendations than the previous two inquests, the McLaughlin-Harris inquest showed a favourable outlook toward pluralistic maternity care. Note, however, that the recommendations tended to place midwifery within a legalistic, regulatory framework in which midwives were not completely autonomous. The requirement of malpractice insurance, for example, corresponds with a formally rational administrative system, in which expectant mothers would have rights (to sue midwives) and an insurance fund would be accessible to protect midwives.

Inquest into the Death of Kevin Woods.   This inquest convened between November 19 and 24, 1986. It had been established that the infant died of hypoxic-ischemic encephalopathy two days after birth. The mother desired a home birth, but was transferred to hospital by the attending midwife when complications became evident. At the hospital, attendants monitored the fetal heart rate. The jury noted that monitoring could have been more frequent, that there were difficulties inserting the intravenous needle, and that the fetal heart strip was not available. Shortly after birth, the baby was diagnosed as having severe brain injuries. Life support was discontinued two days after birth. The coroner's jury, considering the available evidence and testimony, made eight recommendations:

1. All prenatal information, such as the midwife's report, should be included in the hospital admission record.

2. Hospital protocol for labour and delivery rooms should be reviewed and updated annually by obstetric teams. The fetal heart rate should be taken after every contraction, or every five minutes (at a minimum), in the delivery room.

3. Patient refusal of any treatment, including fetal heart monitoring, should be charted.

4. Use of fetal heart monitoring and uterine contraction monitoring should be as continuous as possible.

5. An electronic fetal heart monitor should be available in the delivery room.

6. The pediatrician on call should be within a fifteen minute travel radius.

7. Ongoing educational upgrading on new procedures should be provided to the obstetric team. This would include upgrading on reading of monitor strips, set-up of intravenous needles, and procedures for resuscitation and stimulation of newborns.

8. Chart recording should be as detailed as possible, especially during the second stage of labour.

The jury report makes little mention of midwives, aside from the recommendation that their reports be included in the admission record. The facts of this case confirm that certain hospital procedures may also require upgrading.

Inquest into the Death of Elisha Leenhouts.   In contrast to the circumstances surrounding the death of the infant Kevin Woods, the inquest into the death of Elisha Leenhouts on July 7, 1987, indicated that this baby died at a midwife-attended home birth. Although the post-mortem revealed that the infant died of respiratory failure, caused by a total collapse of the right lung, it was suggested that the baby would have had a 50 percent chance of survival had the birth occurred in hospital. It was also suggested that if an ultrasound examination had been performed earlier in the pregnancy, the malformation would have been detected, thereby alerting caregivers to the risk. The coroner's jury provided six recommendations:

1. Birthing centres should be advocated for all hospitals in Ontario.

2. Hospitals in Ontario should be more receptive to the wishes of parents in the birthing process. Home-style settings should be provided.

3. The Ministry of Health should educate the public on homecare services, public health services and available facilities.

4. Parents should inform a physician if they plan a home birth.

5. Legislation should be enacted that would require an expectant mother planning a home birth to submit to an ultrasound examination and any other available medical investigatory techniques deemed necessary by a physician.

6. Legislation should be enacted so that babies born in a home setting are examined by a licensed medical practitioner within two to four hours after birth.

The recommendations from these five inquests generally indicated support for a more established, formal system of midwifery in Ontario. While some findings are critical of certain midwifery practices, there are also criticisms of hospital procedures and services. Attention is paid not only to the role of midwives, but also to the roles of physicians and nurses in home and hospital-based births. A recurring theme of these recommendations is the value of legalizing midwifery and providing specialized training in accordance with international guidelines. The inquests stressed the importance of public education about the risks and benefits of various birthing settings. Home birth was generally seen as a viable option, but one that required greater monitoring and co-ordination within the health care system. The dual and complementary roles of physicians and midwives were emphasized. While the juries promoted the formal establishment of midwifery in Ontario, they also recognized that there are situations in which hospitals are better equipped to handle complicated deliveries. The facts presented in the McLaughlin-Harris and Woods inquests, however, underscore the reality that infants may die regardless of the place of birth.

Coroner's Inquests and Inquiries in British Columbia

The midwifery movement in British Columbia has addressed the need for a separate, more autonomous status for the practising midwife. The movement itself differs over such issues as the site of birth—e.g., hospital-based midwifery, domiciliary (home birth) midwifery, or alternative birthing centres—and optimal training for midwives (under the auspices of schools of nursing, for example, or provision of "direct entry" of students into distinct midwifery schools). Differences of opinion are, however, most dramatic in discussions of the prosecution of midwives.[6]

Referring to the office of the chief coroner to investigate circumstances pertaining to infant deaths is an alternative to the adversarial and guilt-oriented context of criminal prosecution. In British Columbia, midwifery practice has traditionally been reviewed through the coroner's office. Again, the general thrust of inquest recommendations has been the need to establish clearer guidelines for midwifery practice. Attention has also been drawn to specific features of hospital care in cases where mothers and infants are transferred there for complications of labour or delivery.

On June 30, 1988, the coroner's jury investigating the death of a newborn, Alexandra Bellingrath, recommended that "midwives . . . should be legalized and given autonomous professional status when dealing with low-risk obstetrics." The jury also recommended that hospital staff "be receptive" to telephone calls from midwives who are about to transfer mothers to hospital. Of the jury recommendations, Kaufman (1989, 2) concludes that recognition of midwifery received clear and unequivocal support.

One of the limitations of coroner's inquests is that their recommendations and conclusions are drawn from a single case and not from the practices of midwives as a group. Kaufman (1989, 2) warns that, while the result of the Bellingrath inquest in B.C. was seen as positive by many midwives, recommendations based on one situation could also have been unfavourable. She adds that inquests are expensive and "inherently reactive" as a means of provoking a political solution to health-related problems. She urges those concerned with health policies to take a more active stance in health promotion, and adds that, on the basis of logic, midwives should fare well.

Professional Support and Resistance

It is commonplace to pit an emerging group against more established health professions. In the case of midwifery, however, there are differences of opinion within the medical establishment. Midwives themselves differ with respect to the nature of their practice, qualifications, and so forth (Benoit 1988). In some cases, there is fairly strong support within the medical community for implementing midwifery services. Even so, most medical and nursing associations express concern over the home birth option. A Statement on Midwifery approved by the Society of Obstetricians and Gynaecologists of Canada noted that there was "a large amount of work to do" before midwifery could be established in Canada. Nevertheless, the Society recognized that "certified, licensed midwives play a major role in provision of services to pregnant women in most western countries" (SOGC 1986, 1). The Statement referred to "a widely recognized exodus" of physicians—both general practitioners and specialists in obstetrics and gynecology—from obstetrical care in Canada. The Society expressed concern over proper standards of training and practice for midwives in Canada. The SOGC (1986, 4) is also on record as disapproving of home births. Birth attendance, other than that in accredited institutions such as hospitals or birthing centres, should be discouraged:

> The issue of home births is often confused with the introduction of midwifery. The Society of Obstetricians and Gynaecologists of Canada believes that these are two (2) entirely different issues. Our Society wishes to re-emphasize its policy that "*Ideally all deliveries should occur in an accredited hospital maternal unit.*

We strongly disapprove of home births as not being in the best interest of either mothers or infants. Any free standing childbirth centre should have a physical and organizational attachment to an existing accredited maternity centre. Introduction of nurse midwifery or midwifery does not alter this policy" (SOGC 1986, 4, emphasis in original).

Professional views on midwifery appear to be divided. Some point to a split in opinion among physicians over the value of midwifery. One obstetrician recalls the results of a survey of B.C. doctors:

> It is my feeling, from talking to a lot of family physicians across the province, that you are probably looking at a 50-50 balance. Fifty percent would be in support of some kind of midwifery . . . either working with them in the office, or in the hospital, or in a referral pattern. Another 50 percent would be either uneasy, or strictly opposed . . . When I was involved in the Executive of the B.C. Medical Association section of Obstetricians and Gynaecologists, I at some stage sent out questionnaires to the obstetricians and gynaecologists in this province who were practising obstetrics. At the time, 75 percent were in support of some type of midwifery in this province (Bernd Wittmann, quoted in *Midwifery and the Law* project 1991).

A statement in the *Canadian Medical Association Journal* provided little support for autonomous midwifery services in Canada. The statement followed a reformist line, suggesting that high-quality obstetrical care could be provided by existing personnel. Specifically, nurses could undertake greater responsibility in obstetrical care, but under the direction of physicians (Baker 1989, 24).

The Registered Nurses' Association of B.C. (RNABC) has also considered the possibility of implementing midwifery as an established health profession. In its Position Statement on Midwifery, the RNABC (1987) supported nurse-midwifery as an extension of nursing practice. The Statement also indicated that qualified nurse-midwives could participate in care during pregnancy, labour, and delivery (and presumably in the postpartum period). The 1987 Statement endorsed the sentiment of the Western Nurse-Midwives' Association that the health care system in Canada is not able to support home births, specifically, "back-up support services for emergencies" (RNABC 1987). It is especially significant that the RNABC Board of Directors continues to envision only nurse-midwifery as a health profession:

> RNABC recognizes that there are non-nurse midwives in British Columbia who have been formally educated and certified in other countries. However, the Association is not convinced that the non-nurse midwife is a viable concept in the British Columbia health care system at this time. RNABC does not therefore support the concept of midwifery as an autonomous and self-regulating health discipline . . . RNABC is strongly opposed to the practice of midwifery by unqualified and unregulated persons who have neither the necessary education nor legal authority to practice in the midwife role (RNABC 1987).

This "middle position" (Cutshall 1987) on midwifery has not been set in stone, however. Although the RNABC Board has twice established a position more conservative than that recommended by two special committees struck to consider issues in midwifery, it is also on record as wishing to promote further discussion among its membership. As it stands, however, the RNABC official position lends no support whatsoever to autonomous midwifery practice, including out-of-hospital deliveries or deliveries by community midwives.

The status of midwives hinges in part on the perceived need for professional birth attendants. In Ontario and Quebec, which have the highest proportion of obstetricians to population, fewer than half of births are attended by family physicians (Anderson 1986, 12). As family physicians become less prominent in labour and delivery, the case for midwifery services rests on the need for specialized care (for uncomplicated labours and deliveries) and especially the need for rapport and continuity of care between birth attendant and mother.

It is clear that most community midwives—active or "retired"—do not favour the implementation of midwifery being controlled by nursing associations. The midwifery movement now stresses co-operation among various health professions that preserves the integrity of autonomous midwifery practice.[7] The concept of nurse-midwifery is, for some experts, a curiosity. Flint (1986) argues for a rethinking of midwife training, noting that, while direct entry to midwifery practice is possible in the United Kingdom, most midwives have been trained as nurses first. Flint (1986) believes that nursing training should *not* be a prerequisite for midwifery education.[8]

In Canada, many midwives see the concept of nurse-midwifery as compromising the special relationship between client and midwife. Placing midwives under the supervision of physicians, and within the compass of nursing, would artificially restrict midwives' skills. Assimilating midwifery within the conventional structures of the obstetrical team within hospitals would also undermine continuity of care for expectant mothers. In her background paper for the Canadian Parliament, Baker (1989, 24–25) makes a strong argument against a compromised status for midwives: midwives would be more restricted if they were regulated by provincial colleges of nursing; moreover, without co-operation between physicians and midwives, "legalization and regulation would not be meaningful" (Baker 1989, 24).

Legalized Midwifery

A common goal for midwives actively involved in the Midwifery Task Force of B.C. and the Midwives' Association of B.C. is legalized, autonomous midwifery. Few midwives are willing to continue practice without an assurance that the law will not be invoked against them. Criminal prosecution, coroner's investigations, or prosecution for practising medicine without a licence are everpresent threats for community midwives. Recent events underline the seriousness of these threats. In the mid-1980s in Vancouver, B.C., following an infant's death after an attempted home birth, two midwives—Gloria LeMay and Mary Sullivan—were found guilty of criminal negligence causing death. The conviction was appealed and the appellants were found guilty on a new charge of criminal negligence causing bodily harm (to the mother), a charge which had been substituted for the original one. In 1991, six years after the first conviction, the Supreme Court of Canada acquitted both midwives. This was in keeping with the general trend in Canada, which was to acquit mid-wives facing formal charges under criminal or quasi-criminal law. Other midwives have been subject to coroner's inquests or inquiries, and in at least one case in B.C, criminal prosecution was seriously considered, following an infant death. In Alberta, in 1990, a longstanding community midwife, Noreen Walker, was charged with practising medicine without a license, even though the delivery was successful, and no complaint was registered by the parents (Jimenez 1990). On June 5, 1991, a trial judge directed an acquittal without calling for defence witnesses (Moysa and Aikenhead 1991).

Much of the literature concerning midwifery considers parental choice in childbirth as complementary to professional concerns over standards of care. Well-informed parents should be able to choose from a variety of birth options that do not compromise their health or that of their children. For many, the existing law in Canada does not adequately recognize the issue of parental rights in childbirth. Peter Leask, a Vancouver-based lawyer with extensive involvement in midwifery litigation and the midwifery issue generally, favours a legal model that parallels European systems. He holds that Canadian laws governing midwives could follow European laws that respect parental choice in birth, and that protect midwives who honour parents' choices.

The obstetrical system in the Netherlands is frequently held up as an exam-ple of a legal system that promotes parental choices in birth while enjoying a record of maternal and infant safety. Anderson (1986, 13–14) attributes the success of the Dutch system to three factors: the establishment of highly-trained midwives as "primary caregivers," clear guidelines for referral of clients seeking home births, and thorough postpartum care by maternity-aid nurses. This system of referral, training, and care, combined with a culture that promotes birthing choices, contrasts with the poorly integrated legal interven-tions that have characterized midwifery trials and inquiries in Canada. These interventions have, to date, posed considerable costs to midwives, and ignore the many recommendations for the establishment and promotion of midwifery.

As a result of these legal interventions, many midwives have ceased to attend home births. Only a handful of the women who were attending home births in the Lower Mainland of B.C. in the early 1980s have maintained their practices. Even established community midwives have discontinued their prac-tice. Legal representation can amount to several years' worth of income for midwives, who are not well-paid to begin with.

The lack of legal recognition for midwives has had a chilling effect on the recruitment of new midwives. This means that, unlike other, more recognized, professionals—nurses and physicians, for example—there are no new cohorts of midwives being produced regularly in Canada. The "trials of labour" also serve to drain the limited funds of groups such as the Midwives' Association of B.C. Funds that were raised in support of midwifery practice and education are thus diverted into legal spheres (Burtch 1987a). This "legalization of politics" (Mandel 1989) poses considerable costs for midwives and also deflects legal discourse away from issues such as parental choice and the ways in which midwifery services might be integrated into Canadian health care.

Midwives have lobbied for the power to regulate the conduct of their profession, as is the case with other professions, such as medicine, nursing, and law. Establishing a self-regulated college would allow midwives to set up guidelines for safe management of labour and birth and, where needed, to review particular instances where such management is in question. Not all midwives favour such a proposal, since they fear they would likely be controlled to some extent by provincial health officials. Midwives have also expressed concern over the ways in which midwifery practice might be restricted, as guidelines became more conservative, and penalties (fines, suspensions, loss of licence) became established within such a college.

DeVries (1985) examines how the violation of regulatory law by American midwives raises serious questions about the value of legal regulation of practice. He cites examples in which lay midwives have been arrested and required to post substantial bonds, among other forms of disciplinary action (DeVries 1985, 119–20). The value of self-regulation, for DeVries, is not entirely positive. Once subject to a licensing law, midwives' practices are not reviewed by peers alone, but by "a legal code that defines acceptable and unacceptable behavior" (DeVries 1985, 120). In situations where midwives are not subject to regulatory laws, there are several factors that can operate in their favour. These include (1) the rarity of charges being brought by clients against midwives and the reluctance of clients to testify against midwives; (2) the generation of positive publicity concerning alternative birth practices and other information favourable to midwives; (3) the mobilization of financial and other support from other midwives; and (4) a tradition of "hesitancy on the part of the courts to penalize unlicensed midwives" (DeVries 1985, 121).

Discipline of licensed midwives is another matter. Once licensed, midwives are subject to the scrutiny of medical personnel. In two cases in Arizona, midwives were either suspended from practice or had their licence revoked. One case involved assistance at a diagnosed breech birth; the other, a decision to let the parents grieve over the baby's death (when fetal heart tones could not be detected), instead of requesting medical assistance immediately. Both actions were in violation of the law regulating midwifery practice in Arizona. In that state, midwives are not only subject to complaints by physicians about conduct that may be inappropriate or illegal; they are also integrated into a health network, in which they must provide "detailed reports" to the state department of health services, which can be reviewed at any time. DeVries draws special attention to the lack of media coverage of the Arizona cases. Significantly, "midwife organizations and alternative birth groups did not rally to the support of the accused" (DeVries 1985, 131).

DeVries's work highlights the dilemma of using state law to regulate parental choices and midwifery practice. While the use of repressive law, such as criminal prosecution, has traditionally not resulted in conviction of unlicensed midwives, legal costs are invariably high, and the adversarial nature of such actions can widen the gulf between midwives and physicians. On the other hand, DeVries (1985, 136–37) indicates that, where licensing is established, midwives subject to legal codes face loss of the right to practise as a midwife and possibly loss or suspension of a nursing license. As such, the once-blurred legal status of midwives practising outside the system is sharpened by legalization, but in a manner that retains an edge of punitiveness. Gaskin (1988, 56) reinforces DeVries's argument, noting that restrictions on certain practices—for example, midwives being prohibited from administering drugs to stop hemorrhaging—may lead midwives to conceal certain aspects of birth care.

It has also been pointed out that legalization in itself does not guarantee adequate midwifery services. Midwifery can be established—certainly—but it can also be whittled away or removed. Gaskin (1988, 56) cites the case of a Florida law allowing direct-entry midwifery. The law was passed following years of lobbying by the Florida Midwives' Association; however, a counter-lobby by Florida physicians served to reverse the direct-entry law. Midwives who had completed direct-entry training could continue practising, but for other aspirants, "the door was closed" (Gaskin 1988, 56). Even in European countries where midwifery is well-established, recent policies have led to fragmented care in obstetrics. This fragmentation clearly undermines the continuity of care that midwives prize. Wagner (1985, 94) notes that the role of the midwife as an advocate for women is undermined by greater recourse to technology (machine-minding), rising rates of Caesarean section, and other measures that weaken the "close personal social support" traditionally provided by midwives.

Midwifery and Law: Summary

The reappearance of community-based, independent midwifery practice in Canada in the mid-1970s challenged the medicalization of childbirth. As a countercultural movement in Canada and elsewhere, midwifery offered an alternative to hospital-based, professionally directed management of birth. The appropriation of childbirth by the (predominantly male) medical profession and the cultural definition of women as incapable of managing birth were strongly contested in theory and practice by midwives. Reversing the opinion that they are anachronistic, midwives have argued that their work is highly skilled, and that they play a sensitive role in the birthing process (Flint 1987). The struggle they face reflects not only the modern takeover of obstetrics by medical and nursing specialists, but the legacy of repression of alternative healers in Europe and North America, including midwives and herbalists (Ben-Yehuda 1980; Ehrenreich and English 1973).

There are several contradictions in the situation for Canadian midwives today. On the one hand, midwifery receives wide support on the international level. The Triennial International Congress of Midwifery will be held in Vancouver in 1993, the first time that the congress has been convened in Canada. On the other hand, prosecution of midwives continues. In B.C., only a few community midwives continue to practise, and the midwifery project at Vancouver's Grace Hospital has not been expanded to match requests for midwifery attendance. The midwifery debate in Canada may well culminate in a co-opted version of midwifery, which would constrain the autonomous character of midwifery as it was in the 1970s and 1980s. These constraints include mandatory insurance liability coverage, conservative guidelines of practice, no clear commitment to respecting out-of-hospital births, and the requirement that physicians supervise midwives during labour and delivery.

Midwifery practice in Canada has largely been arrested through (1) failure to implement midwifery services, despite recommendations from numerous quarters, and (2) use of repressive laws to prosecute midwives under criminal or quasi-criminal law, or to subject midwives to the costly procedures of inquiries or inquests. In the short term, the objectives of the midwifery movement have been undermined through limited government support, sensationalized media accounts of untoward births, a pervasive ideology of physician dominance in childbirth, and the chilling effects of legal interventions. Midwifery trials reflect deep contradictions in the construction of women's power (as workers and mothers), and the power of criminal and quasi-criminal laws in securing social ordering.

The reappearance of community-based, independent midwifery practice in British Columbia in 1975 has been followed by a series of events that have transformed the nature of the original midwifery movement. Begun as a collective initiative with a primary emphasis on mother and infant safety, the midwifery movement sought to support women who were seeking to give birth outside of the traditional hospital setting and without recourse to unnecessary medical interventions. The politics of midwifery as a countercultural movement were articulated in Raven Lang's *Birth Book* and Ina May Gaskin's *Spiritual Midwifery*, and in a wider set of practices and writings surrounding women's health care (Gaskin 1988, 52–54).

Despite the many legal setbacks that have stalled the growth of midwifery in Canada, there have been many positive developments that have strengthened the solidarity of Canadian midwives. Securing the 1993 International Congress of Midwifery in Vancouver was a major coup. Another accomplishment is the development of the Vancouver-based Midwifery School. Now accredited with the Washington State Department of Health, the school has graduated 28 students and established several preceptorships (clinical placements) internationally. Another important development is the growing effort of midwives to establish coalitions among themselves. The *realpolitik* of professional resistance as well as limited resources among pro-midwifery groups has led to broader alliances among activist groups. In British Columbia, for example, the Midwives' Association of B.C. has established working relationships with the Western Nurse-Midwives' Association, the Midwifery Task Force, the Midwives' Association of North America, and the International Confederation of Midwives, and has also maintained contact with provincial government representatives (e.g., Ministry of Health), the Registered Nurses' Association of B.C., and the British Columbia Medical Association, among others. Gaskin (1988, 59–60) notes a growing interest in midwifery among U.S. women, and adds that the most effective strategy for associations favourable to midwifery is to enter into "coalitions." Gaskin cites the Midwives' Alliance of North America (MANA) as one example of the solidarity that exists among different kinds of midwives. This solidarity holds the promise of extending the values and benefits of midwifery to society at large.[9]

There have been, nevertheless, several discouraging setbacks for midwifery. Many founding midwives are no longer practising. The B.C. School of Midwifery has ceased operation, due to limited enrolments, which, in turn, were linked with the lack of a legal status for trained midwives in the province. There are also continuing financial pressures involved in the legal defence of those midwives facing inquiries or, more rarely, criminal prosecution.

Although there is resistance to full implementation of midwifery care in many Canadian jurisdictions, the recommendations of international associations lend considerable support to the movement for qualified midwifery services. The International Confederation of Midwives, for example, has supported the implementation of midwifery in Canada to the point of designating Vancouver as the site for the 1993 Trienniel International Congress of Midwifery, as already mentioned. The World Health Organization has plainly favoured the recognition and development of midwifery: "The training of professional midwives or birth attendants should be promoted. Care during normal pregnancy and birth, and following birth, should be the duty of this profession" (World Health Organization 1987).

The developments in midwifery advocacy and practices underline the importance of human agency in shaping culture as well as government policies and the outlooks of the health professions. As the conflicting evidence is weighed, it is clear that there are no convincing arguments against the implementation of midwifery services as part of Canadian social policy. Opponents of midwifery seem to keep midwives in the backcourt by means of expensive litigation and fallacious arguments concerning women's preferences in childbirth and the costs of establishing midwifery training and practices. Midwives are moving to the fore-court, however, and now have international support, a growing research base,[10] and a history of promoting safe, pluralistic birth attendance.

The political will of government officials, legislators, and the medical and nursing professions is likely to be decisive in determining the future of mid-wifery in Canada. As Carol Smart (1989) has cautioned, it is crucial that we recognize that new forms of legal control may create substantial gaps between what women seek by way of freedoms, and what is offered to them in policies.

ABORTION AND LAW

The abortion debate in Canada has been extremely contentious and shows no sign of abating. At the extremes, interest groups have argued for pro-life or pro-choice social policies, sometimes relabelling each other as anti-choice and anti-life. In this battle, reproductive rights have been established and then dis-mantled, with no clear direction for the development of legal and social issues surrounding abortion. Public opinion studies in Canada have shown no clear majority of people favouring either a complete ban on access to therapeutic abortion or, at the other extreme, abortion "on demand," that is, as an unfet-tered personal right of every woman. It has been noted that religious denomination is often correlated with outlook on abortion. Hartnagel, Creechan, and Silverman (1985, 415) report that Catholics and "more funda-mental Protestants" are most opposed to legalization of abortion, whereas those with no religious affiliation, along with Jews, Unitarians, and atheists, are the most liberal with respect to abortion. The author found that, while members of dominant status groups—e.g., older, male, well-educated, affluent, and of British ancestry—were more likely to have a liberal outlook on abortion law, other variables such as church attendance and religiosity were necessary in explaining abortion approval or disapproval (Hartnagel, Creechan, and Silverman 1985, 417 & 423; see also Clarke 1987).

The right to abortion involves struggles by women to gain access not only to abortion for unwanted pregnancies but also to contraceptive information and devices. In 1969, the use of contraceptive devices became legal in Canada, and abortion was permissible under certain conditions. The decision to grant and perform a therapeutic abortion rested with therapeutic abortion committees composed of physicians, and with those physicians who were willing to per-form the operation.

Historically, reproduction has been aligned with political power. Different interests vied for influence over contraception and abortion policy in Canada during the nineteenth and twentieth centuries. For example, some socialists encouraged the use of contraceptive devices to emancipate women from the demands of large families, while others opposed contraception, believing that a socialist society could support large families (McLaren and McLaren 1986, 140–41). Consider also the *revanche des berceaux* ("revenge of the cradle" in Quebec, in which French-Canadians maintained a majority of the population in New France, then Quebec, through a high birth rate), and fears of "race suicide" (whereby the numbers of the dominant culture shrink in the face of a decline in birth rate and of an increase in immigration) in Canada, Britain, and the United States (see McLaren and McLaren 1986, 17). The following excerpt from Roch Carrier's novel *Heartbreaks along the Road* (1987, 146) illustrates some of the concern surrounding the changing attitudes toward reproduction:

> Far away, in the cities, life was no longer as the good Lord had made it, no longer good as it had been in the olden days. People no longer believed in religion's holy truths; they wanted to change their wife or husband like a shirt; children were no longer a blessing but a trial; many pregnant women were ashamed of their bellies, as if they were an infirmity; women refused to obey their men; now they were refusing to let themselves be seeded, and what is a field without seed? Children no longer obeyed their parents and parents no longer even wanted to be obeyed ....

Civil disobedience was evident in Canada, with Dr. Henry Morgentaler and his supporters involved in the establishment of abortion clinics in Quebec, Ontario, and elsewhere. His legal battles included a prison sentence, and a series of appeals to the Supreme Court of Canada. In January 1988, in *Morgentaler et al.*, the Supreme Court of Canada struck down a statute in the Criminal Code that legalized abortion in accredited hospitals, provided that it was certified—by committees of doctors—that pregnancy endangered a woman's life, or physical or mental health.

In another case, in the summer of 1989, the Quebec Court of Appeal upheld an injunction on behalf of Jean-Guy Tremblay that prohibited his ex-girlfriend, Chantal Daigle, from getting an abortion. This injunction, which would have strengthened efforts by males to veto women's reproductive choices (see Gavigan 1986), was not upheld. By the time the Court of Appeal decided against the injunction, however, Daigle had defied the injunction, having had an abortion in the United States even before the Court's decision was handed down. Currently, Canada is still without an abortion law, since a recent proposal for an amended law failed to gain majority approval by the Canadian Senate. Moreover, old problems have resurfaced, such as regional disparities in women's access to abortion, and unwillingness of some medical and nursing staff to assist in abortion procedures (see Gavigan 1987, 276–77).

Gavigan: Contradictions in Abortion Law

Gavigan (1986) examines the contradictory nature of the criminal law and abortion policy in Canada. Although she is sensitive to the myriad ways in which women have been discriminated against in law, she does not accept the perspective that sees laws as simply reflecting the interests of men; law may, indeed, afford some protections for women. For example, Canadian legislation has been interpreted to deny biological fathers a veto right in a legal abortion. Gavigan also argues that, while women remain "substantively unequal," they have achieved a measure of formal equality (Gavigan 1987, 266–67). The achievement of formal equality for women in this century is not a hollow victory: it reflects ongoing struggles by women, not merely concessions from the dominant classes or the goodwill evolving from a maturing society. Gavigan (1987, 268) notes that because women can no longer be portrayed as mere property, or "objects of exchange," they have various rights—among them the right to vote, to hold public office, and to own property. As such, women are now "legal subjects," and are able to form strategies to create a "radical restructuring" of society and gender relations (Gavigan 1987, 264).

Gavigan notes, however, that there have been general efforts to limit women's access to legal abortion (Gavigan 1987, 276–77). These efforts stem from the constituencies that are legally able to restrict women's access to abortion, including government officials and medical practitioners. Under Canadian constitutional arrangements, the administration of health care falls within provincial jurisdictions. Thus, despite the observation that not all Canadian women enjoy ready access to hospitals (or clinics) with accredited therapeutic abortion committees, or other provisions for therapeutic abortions, most hospitals do not offer such services (Gavigan 1987, 270–77). Medical practitioners, under the previous liberalized abortion policies, could recommend or reject a woman's request for a therapeutic abortion. Thus, the power to decide whether or not to continue a pregnancy rested not with women but with government agencies and medical practitioners. Building on the feminist critique of formal protections for women, Gavigan (1986, 117) notes that the intersection of law and medicine, while inhibiting men's prerogatives (specifically, claims for veto power over abortion decisions), has reproduced "the subordinate position of women."

Davis (1987, 373) refers to a "crisis" with respect to women's freedom to obtain therapeutic abortions. What appears to have been a liberalization of American abortion law has been recast in the form of continued constraints on women's options in reproduction. Like Gavigan, Davis believes that control over abortion has been transferred from police authorities to physicians, resulting in a new form of state power over women: "A stronger alliance now exists between state and medical groups with certain negative implications for women's autonomy" (Davis 1987, 373). Davis's approach, in keeping with other critical theoretical approaches, challenges the validity of liberal-consensus theory. Conflicts such as the abortion debate are seen as emerging not from widely shared customs or general features of social harmony, but rather from struggles for dominance among opposing groups. Law, like social relations generally, assumes an essential position in power relations, especially with respect to social inequalities and social domination (Davis 1987, 373–74).

An example of this struggle among groups is the criminalization of abortion in the United States. Davis (1987, 376–77) notes that prior to the 1870s, abortion was "a relatively common practice," with approximately one abortion per five to six live births between 1840 and 1870. The criminalization of abortion was linked with movements protesting against vice (including abortion and obscenity). One such movement was led by Anthony Comstock, described by Davis (1987, 394) as "an American morals crusader," in the late nineteenth and early twentieth centuries. Another factor in the decreased use of abortion was the declining birth rate, especially among American-born, white Protestants. Davis (1987, 378) adds that there was also concern over patient deaths following abortion attempts; significantly, the American Medical Association began to lobby against the "evil" of abortion. Davis (1987, 378) thus places the changes in abortion law in a social context, contending that outlawing abortions served to promote an ideology of feminine domesticity (placing women as full-time mothers and homemakers) and to allay fears of a decrease in white, Protestant citizens.

Davis describes later changes in abortion law, including decriminalization policies in many American states in the 1960s and 1970s, and the landmark Supreme Court decision in Roe v. Wade in 1973. Gavigan (1987, 280) notes that this ruling "held that the constitutionally protected right to privacy extended to freedom in decisions regarding abortion." Furthermore, state legislation limiting women's rights in this regard had to be based on "compelling state interest." Gavigan (1987, 280) notes that very shortly after the decision, state legislatures implemented laws restricting women's choices, including waiting periods prior to abortion, cuts in medicaid funds, and enactment of various processes surrounding spousal or parental consent and notification. Davis (1987, 385) refers to nearly 200 abortion bills brought forward within four months of the 1973 Roe decision. She notes that, while many bills raised issues of safeguarding women's health, other aspects, such as protection of hospitals that did not permit abortions and bans on second-trimester abortions in clinics, were essentially "hostile to women's reproductive rights" (Davis 1987, 385). As was the case in Canada, physicians became more prominent, serving as gatekeepers in approving or denying abortion requests. This situation thus empowered medical interests, while "severely diluting" (Davis 1987, 383) women's power to decide whether or not to terminate pregnancies. The fragmented nature of state policies, extensive litigation on a case-by-case basis, and contradictory approaches to women's integrity in abortion choices resulted in a "crazy-quilt pattern" (Davis 1987, 383), in which women's access to an abortion varied considerably from state to state, and likely within particular states.

Similar findings were made with respect to abortion practices in Canada. The Report of the Committee on the Operation of the Abortion Law (Canada 1977, 238–40) commented on variations in consent requirements pertaining to the age of the woman requesting the abortion. The Committee (Canada 1977, 140–41) also noted "sharp regional disparities" in women's access to abortion, due in part to a lack of (then necessary) therapeutic abortion committees in many hospitals, and compounded by physicians' decisions not to perform therapeutic abortions. The Committee (Canada 1977, 140–41) found that nearly half of the obstetrician-gynecologists surveyed did not perform abortions. The net effect was that, despite the formal procedures then in effect under the Criminal Code, "obtaining therapeutic abortion is in practice illusory for many Canadian women" (Canada 1977, 140–41). Nevertheless, since the *Roe* decision, the net effect has been that more low-cost, safe therapeutic abortions were permitted than at any time prior to the Supreme Court ruling (Davis 1987, 387).

Eisenstein (1988, 186–87) observes that the United States Supreme Court has confirmed its 1973 abortion ruling in more recent times. In a 1986 case *(Thornburgh v. American College of Obstetricians and Gynaecologists)*, the Court did uphold a Pennsylvania law that would have interfered with women seeking abortions (Eisenstein 1988, 186–87). Eisenstein notes that the Court was divided on this case—the ruling was 5 to 4—but that the result was an affirmation of the privacy doctrine. Eisenstein adds that, while the privacy doctrine has been useful strategically in preserving some degree of reproductive autonomy for women, the overall effect of such rulings is to obscure "the political nature of the private realm" of sexuality (Eisenstein 1988, 187).

Davis (1987, 391) contends that abortion laws and policies have served to consolidate the "medicalization" of abortion, allowing more for the convenience and empowerment of professional objectives than for the convenience of women. MacKinnon (1987, 101) concludes that in the United States, "every ounce of control that women won out of this legalization has gone directly into the hands of men—husbands, doctors, or fathers—or is now in the process of attempts to reclaim it through regulation." She adds that abortion reforms have been recast as a "private privilege" rather than a "public right." In this process, she notes that a strong measure of oppression concerning women's sexuality remains intact—an everyday pervasive power in which the political and personal spheres are inseparable.

Access to abortion is a central issue in the North American debate. Such provisions as enabling physicians or hospitals to refuse abortions helped to undermine access to abortions. Davis (1987, 392) notes that in 1981, two-thirds of counties in the United States had no one to provide abortions to women. Moreover, low-income women were rendered particularly dependent due to underfunding of abortion services and subsequent amendments that have centred on fetal rights.

In the wake of *Roe*, Davis (1987, 393–94) concludes that the feminist goal of using abortion rights as a point of departure for securing a wider range of "social, political, and economic rights" has been substantially undermined. The end result of this situation is to alienate women thorough legalization of abortion, a process that does not redress social class divisions in the United States or substantially enhance women's rights as citizens. This alienating process has been especially severe for welfare-dependent women. Thus, far from transcending earlier patriarchial forms of women's dependency, the abortion initiative has been blunted in practice. Currently, the state has promoted medical constructs of pregnancy

> by effectively isolating the woman in her reproductive decision, or making it contingent on a willing physician. Abortion reform yields, not a revolutionary entity and way of life, but a depoliticized consumer product which serves to primarily benefit middle and upper-middle class women and their medical providers (Davis 1987, 395).

The abortion debate remains vital, with considerable lobbying for legal change—to restrict, eliminate, or broaden access to abortion—and difficulties faced by "both sides" of this divisive issue. It is important to recognize, however, that despite variations in services and in governing laws, many feminist writers see a logic—a "continuity"—within these diverse practices. Eisenstein (1988, 18–19) observes that relations of power surrounding reproduction (among other areas) retain a coherence. This includes ways in which male bodies maintain a "gendered privilege," and inequalities between women and men are partly reinforced by the agency of the state.

It is important to keep in mind that abortion law, and social policies surrounding abortion, vary considerably across jurisdictions. On the basis of her comparative study of legal systems in Europe and the United States, Glendon (1989) describes the American approach as unique and extreme. Specifically, in the United States, there is virtually no regulation of abortion until the fetus is between 24 and 28 weeks old. This contrasts with the situation in other countries, in which such regulation usually begins at 10 to 12 weeks' gestation. Furthermore, the U.S. context was striking inasmuch as other options, such as childrearing, are not well-supported by public policy programs. The polarized outlook on abortion (pro-life vs. pro-choice) was not as evident in European countries, where a compromise between access to abortion and the sanctity of life was the norm (Glendon 1989, 473).

FAMILY LAW REFORM

Family law is concerned with the rights and responsibilities associated with marriage, childrearing, separation, and divorce. The following section pursues the major theme of this book—the social context of law and the link between the living law and the law in action—in a discussion of the politics of marriage and the legal processes following marital breakup. This section provides examples of a macrosocial approach to legal reform and uses a feminist interpretation of jurisprudence (Morton 1988). This macrosocial approach goes far beyond particular cases in family law and concentrates on wider patterns of stratification, patriarchy, and ideology and how these patterns influence legal processes. Reference is also made to sociological work that is based on qualitative research, specifically, studies of lawyer-client interactions that use participant observation and tape recording (Sarat and Felstiner 1986). We will also review exploratory research on child support provisions and attitudes toward state intervention in family issues in British Columbia (Burtch, Pitcher-LaPrairie, and Wachtel 1980, 1985).

The application of family law principles has generated tremendous controversy within the legal profession and with respect to social policy generally. For some advocates of a liberal approach, marriage and family law should serve to mediate conflicting interests between estranged spouses so as to achieve a resolution for all parties. This process could involve reconciliation—in which the spouses agree to sort out their differences and continue living together—or mediated settlements—in which court services (or related services) enable the ex-spouses to resolve such issues as child custody, child support, and division of assets and property. In cases where parties cannot resolve their differences, a settlement may be imposed by the court. This is perhaps most dramatic in cases in which both parties seek child custody.

The description of marriage and family law as a means of resolving family or spousal conflicts is often presented in a liberal framework. That is, law is seen as above the interests of any one party and as acting in a fair, impartial manner in the interests of justice. Many feminist scholars challenge this liberal-pluralist concept. They point to the patriarchal basis of marriage laws and the ways in which modern legal processes place women at a disadvantage. As we will show in the following section, it is often argued that, despite the liberalization of family law (for example, easier access to divorce) and general concessions to women, marriage law and family law serve in many respects to consolidate the power of men over women, economically, socially, and politically.

Morton: "Dividing the Wealth, Sharing the Poverty"

Morton (1988) assesses the reform of family law in Ontario. Her assessment strengthens the view that legal reforms often conform to power relations, and that results of such reforms often perpetuate legal and economic inequalities. A series of "ideological shifts" in the 1970s resulted in increased attention to family law as a specialty in legal practice and, more fundamentally, to the appropriateness of measures to regulate family obligations after separation. Morton (1988, 258) notes that the Ontario Law Commission, in its 1975 discussion of family obligations, sought to equalize the "formal rights and responsibilities" of men and women. This included the equal opportunity for women to compete in the economic marketplace. She argues that the opposition of women and dependent children remains altered, but "unimproved" (Morton 1988, 254). Specifically, with the ideological shift away from women's dependency on men—signalled by the formal right to collect spousal support (alimony)—and a presumption that women ought to become self-supporting after marital separation, women were disadvantaged in some very important respects. Wives were not, in principle, entitled to spousal support, and in the minority of cases where alimony was allowed, it was set only for a limited period. Declaring husbands and wives as equal, independent legal entities obscured the substantive inequalities evident between men and women.

Morton provides a strong argument that women remain disadvantaged through their attention to domestic matters and discriminated against in the waged work force. This disadvantaged position is structurally rooted in a complex mix of capitalism and patriarchy. The weaker position of women is often intensified after marital dissolution, for "the female spouse is likely to have a more poorly paid job and also to bear the primary responsibility for childcare costs" (Morton 1988, 261).

Morton's analysis is set against the liberal ideal of gradual improvement through law. She regards law as an area of conflict that reflects struggles of class and gender. Specifically, modern law reflects a predominantly male perspective, and feminist jurisprudence is developed to understand the material interests of women and dependent children. The strengths of Morton's arguments include her clear illustrations of specific legal reforms in Ontario, her appreciation of the ways in which legal reforms designed to benefit and protect all parties can be turned to an advantage for estranged husbands/fathers, and the meshing of her discussion with those of other feminist theorists to reinforce scepticism of the benevolent and ostensibly nonpartisan nature of legal regulation of the family.

There are, however, a number of concerns about Morton's approach as well as about other kinds of research on parenting obligations and contributions after separation. First, Morton focuses squarely on "the material interests of women (and their dependent children)" (Morton 1988, 254). The word "their" obscures paternal obligations or concerns and establishes mothers as essentially exclusive caretakers of dependent children. This approach bypasses the possibility that not all men benefit materially from family law and overlooks instances in which men may act as co-parents (or primary parents). Seel (1987, 129) provides an alternative perspective that takes fathering seriously:

> It is not until they become fathers that most men experience sexism directly; that is, prejudice against them simply on grounds of their sex. But once a man embarks on fatherhood for the first time he will be lucky to escape it. Firstly, there is institutional prejudice: in the antenatal clinic where he may be matronized, in the labour room where he may be treated as an irrelevance, and in the postnatal ward where he may be treated as an inconvenience . . . (Seel 1987, 129).

Seel (1987, 129) adds that "the exclusiveness of the phrase *mothers and their children* is not just a slip of the pen" (italics in original). Support for greater involvement of fathers in child-rearing is evident in other forms; for example, a recently-issued poster by the Ottawa organization Brotherpeace ("Men breaking silence to end men's violence") lists men's domestic responsibilities, such as sharing housework and involving themselves in the care of children. Such initiatives have been dismissed by some writers, as if men facing sexism are either seriously deluded, or so rare that serious analysis is beside the point.

Another criticism of Morton's analysis is her lack of attention to how social power and parenting responsibilities vary across social class, time, and culture. There is evidence, for example, that unemployed men in England not infrequently undertake housework that would traditionally be seen as "women's work." Attention to these nuances would provide a more complete picture of the topic without necessarily undermining Morton's critique of law and gender relations.

Morton's perceptive and articulate portrayal of a feminist jurisprudence of contemporary family law also fails to offer a practical direction for gender relations. In large part, it demystifies idealized notions of family law, rather than exploring future directions and possibilities for men, women, and children.

Finally, the motif of women left to their own devices after marital dissolution appears overly static. Morton's analysis does not satisfactorily take into account alternative situations, such as remarriage, support other than through the estranged spouse, career progress for some women, or other variables. This is not to suggest that an unjustifiably optimistic approach is warranted; nevertheless, Morton's interpretation does not completely avoid the danger of stereotyping women as victims.

That said, there is ample evidence for the general conclusion that women, despite their status as formal legal subjects, are often not well-served by existing family law and other resources after marital separation and divorce. Freeman (1984, 2–3), for example, attacks complacent myths of the dramatic improvement in women's situations. Using studies from the United Kingdom and the United States, he concludes that the norm is for mothers and dependent children to suffer more than ex-husbands (and, where applicable, their new spouses). Freeman (1984, 2–3) also notes that many women are forced onto social security following marital breakup.

Sarat and Felstiner:
"Law and Strategy in the Divorce Lawyer's Office"

In a study by Sarat and Felstiner (1986), 115 lawyer-client conferences were observed and tape-recorded in Massachusetts and California. The researchers complemented this methodology by attending court and mediation sessions and conducting extended interviews with lawyers and clients. Sarat and Felstiner's ethnographic account of lawyer-client interactions is almost unique; there are few empirical research studies of the interactions between divorce strategies and legal dynamics.

The authors identified three important themes in lawyer-client discourse:

1. general characterization of legal system and its key actors

2. advantages and disadvantages of negotiation or trial as legal strategies

3. "legal construction of the client"

The research largely confirmed the disadvantage that many clients face in the restructuring of divorce actions by legal experts. The authors state: "What lawyers say to their clients is not necessarily derived from statutes, rules, and cases and does not involve a literal translation of legal doctrine, nor could the legal system as it is presented in the lawyer's office be understood by clients from untutored observation" (Sarat and Felstiner 1986, 94). Thus, knowledge of legal terminology and legal strategies is very limited for most clients. Many writers have noted that the specialized terminology used by lawyers means that law and legal processes are often "impenetrable," even for well-educated laypersons (Sarat and Felstiner 1986, 103). One example in this study is the issuing of a restraining order against a wife. The order appeared to have been issued incorrectly, contrary to the formalist ideal of procedures in a rational legal system (Sarat and Felstiner 1986, 100). Although the order had been issued incorrectly, her lawyer informed the woman that her rights were not protected by law. Specifically, she now had no right to inspect property of which she owned 50 percent, as set out by community property doctrine in her state. The point is that for practical purposes, this lawyer recommended that the woman should not bother correcting the court's error, and should move on to settle the divorce case. Thus, the image of the legal system from the lawyer's perspective is cynical and realistic (Sarat and Felstiner 1986, 108)—a perspective that runs the risk of undermining the legal ideology of fairness and justice.

Lawyers often try to persuade their clients to seek negotiated settlements rather than litigation. The structure of these lawyer-client interactions is such that the lawyers are more powerful in striking deals. Clients, for the most part, are limited to initial instructions and "after-the-fact" ratifications (Sarat and Felstiner 1986, 110). This study is useful inasmuch as it challenges the notion that many family lawyers are oriented to adversarial divorce proceedings. It also raises concerns over the notion that conciliation activities offer advantages to clients. Gerard (1984, 288–91) points to the need for greater integration of conciliation services, as well as the importance of equal power relationships, with the mediator taking a neutral role in the discussions.

Marriage Preparation, Separation, and Divorce

Burtch, Pitcher-LaPrairie, and Wachtel (1985) provide an exploratory study of public perceptions of law. Their article focuses on public attitudes toward marriage law, separation, and divorce and uses in-depth interviews with 93 B.C. residents, chosen through "snowball" sampling. Bear in mind that this is not a random sample. Significant splits of opinion become evident as issues become more specific. Thus, the points of consensus in this exploratory sample were far from complete.

The results of the study showed that the most acceptable strategy for people contemplating marriage was marriage preparation. Nevertheless, few respondents favoured mandatory courses. Marriage preparation could be offered under various auspices, including state, private charities, private services, and religious instruction. Women were more likely than men to endorse these preparatory courses, especially women with three or more children.

The strategy of a marriage contract was not as acceptable overall. Some saw it as a "realistic" beginning to marriage; others saw it as undermining romantic union, or as ineffective in anticipating future difficulties and their resolution.

Trial marriage (cohabitation) was the least favoured strategy, especially among housewives and church-affiliated respondents. Trial marriages elicited considerable ambivalence, but there was a general concern about the possibility of uncommitted partners. Only childless respondents were more favourable than unfavourable to trial marriages.

Virtually all respondents favoured a one-year separation period for ex-partners who were unable to reconcile their differences. Few were content with the three-year guideline in place in 1980. Still, many took the issue of separation seriously, as the following excerpt indicates. One respondent, who was uncomfortable with a one-year separation policy commented: "If it's just a straight walkout, I think yes, there should be a three-year waiting period. I mean, a marriage isn't a joke so you can't go writing papers off saying 'I'm hitched, ditched, and switched'" (Burtch, Pitcher-LaPrairie, and Wachtel 1985, 381). Respondents often referred to the limited utility of formal legal solutions, especially time delays and other inconveniences, as well as difficulties with receiving court-ordered maintenance (see Burtch, Pitcher-LaPrairie, and Wachtel 1980). A liberal-pluralist ideology was commonly noted: "The State's best role was that of fostering mature consideration, extending services while allowing pluralistic choice" (Burtch, Pitcher-LaPrairie, and Wachtel 1985, 382). As noted throughout this book, however, liberal principles are often difficult to translate into concrete situations of equality. In this respect, and despite the general liberalization of divorce procedures, it is best to appreciate the historical moral messages underlying marriage and divorce law. Backhouse (1991, 198–99) found that few nineteenth century women in Canada were encouraged to consider a divorce action. Women were exhorted to preserve the original marriage and to endure a situation that frequently involved serious physical abuse. Women were often unable, for economic and geographic reasons, to avail themselves of legal protection. Backhouse (1991, 198) concludes:

> The law's perspective on marriage was patriarchal and hierarchical, with a double standard that treated female adultery more seriously than male adultery built into the legal framework, in some cases expressly and in others implicitly through the pleadings of lawyers and the decisions of judges.

The authors noted the relative absence of a radical feminist argument in the sample (Burtch, Pitcher-LaPrairie, and Wachtel 1985, 383). Instead, a liberal-pluralist ideology was foremost for people interviewed. The State should provide a variety of services, and protect individual choices in beginning or terminating a marriage (Burtch, Pitcher-LaPrairie, and Wachtel 1985, 382).

SUMMARY

The importance of feminist studies on reproductive rights and the politics of family relations has been well-established in recent research and theorizing. The dynamics of the midwifery movement offer an example of the mixed results in which feminist theories are actualized: some Canadian jurisdictions are likely to legalize midwifery in the very near future (as Ontario did in November 1991), while others apparently do not wish to explore the issue seriously at this time. This variability in concrete results is also reflected in the fragmented nature of abortion services across Canada and the ambivalent nature of Canadian law concerning this controversial area.

The three general areas discussed in this chapter—childbirth options, abortion, and family law—provide considerable support for a major theme in this book: the gap between legal ideals and actual implementation of rights. This implementation becomes complex and controversial. There have been efforts by the courts to provide a more considered approach to child custody, such that estranged parents might agree to co-parent their children. Ideally, this would provide more continuity for children and both parents, and may result in a more cordial divorce. Feminists have quickly countered, however, that efforts to reach joint custody can be used strategically to undermine the power of the primary parent (most often, the mother), and to impose a parenting arrangement that serves neither the children nor the mother. At another level, there are ongoing problems for many women in receiving adequate child support, a situation that can pose substantial hardships after separation. Finally, lest we become complacent with formal legal victories in areas of reproductive choice or in family law, it is important to note that these victories can be undone. There is growing evidence of a backlash against feminism (Menzies and Chunn 1991, 63–67)—for example, trivializing expressions of violence against women (Ahluwalia 1991, 56). Laws can be reversed, or policies established that undermine the spirit of formal legal equality. The issue remains whether legal advances in these areas will be consolidated or weakened in future.

STUDY QUESTIONS

❑   The status of Canadian midwives illustrates how social conflicts reach into the legal sphere. Summarize the key argument for and against the legalization of midwifery in the Canadian provinces. How has the course of legal cases affected the status of midwives?

❑   Mary Morton (1988) observes of family law reform in Ontario that, while women's status has been altered through legal enactments and changing policies, it is essentially unimproved. How does Morton assess the prospects of developing a feminist jurisprudence? According to Morton, what "material interests" of women and children are not taken into account, or are not properly assessed, by family law?

❑   The feminist critique of patriarchy may include reference to how women are "objectified," that is, their essence and individuality reduced to the status of an object. Discuss whether or not Morton (1988) tends to objectify or distort the status of husbands and fathers.

NOTES

1. In the traditional birth culture in Canada, women used a variety of birthing positions, before the lithotomy position (in stirrups, with legs abducted) became virtually mandatory in modernized obstetrics. "Most women tried to walk around and keep to their activities as long as possible during the first part of their labour, and squatting seems to have been common during the pushing stage" (Mason 1988, 102).

2. A quasi-criminal offence is an offence to which a penalty is attached. Quasi-criminal offences are found in other federal and provincial statutes, but not in the Criminal Code.

3. Maternal mortality is quite rare in childbirth in North America. In developing countries, however, maternal deaths related to childbirth may be much more common. It has been estimated that 99 percent of maternal deaths worldwide occur in developing countries, and that many of these deaths are preventable. The International Confederation of Midwives has launched a worldwide "safe motherhood" initiative, seeking to reduce maternal mortality by 50 percent by the turn of the century.

4. A handful of these attempted home births occurred in Saskatchewan. In the doctoral dissertation (Burtch 1987b), the majority of cases were drawn from B.C., followed by Ontario, and then Saskatchewan.

5. A coroner's inquest involves a jury, consisting of six people drawn from the community. Jury members are not mandated to make any determinations concerning the legal responsibility of a person (or persons) involved in the death. The jury may,

however, "make recommendations directed to the avoidance of death in similar circumstances" (Section 25(3), B.C. Coroner's Act).

6. *Regina v. Sullivan and Lemay.* In 1987, two B.C. midwives were convicted of criminal negligence causing harm. On appeal, the initial conviction of criminal negligence causing death was quashed. The midwives were convicted of criminal negligence causing bodily harm (to the mother). On appeal to the Supreme Court of Canada, however, they were finally acquitted.

7. Anderson (1986, 12) reports that midwives' associations in British Columbia, Ontario, and Quebec favour legislation that ensures the autonomy of midwives. Legalization, which would place midwives in a dependent position beside physicians or nurses, has consistently been resisted.

8. Flint (1986) states that, while there may be advantages to adjunctive studies, midwifery stands as a discipline in its own right, and some elements of nursing training might be harmful in developing optimal care for mothers and newborns. Flint (1987) makes a strong statement for retaining midwifery as a community resource that is sensitive to the needs of women and infants.

9. Ehrenreich and English (cited in Edwards and Waldorf 1984, 195) conceive of a wider consciousness of birthing and childcare, such that these activities are not left to the responsibility of individual women, but recast as a "transcendent public priority."

10. The *Journal of Nurse-Midwifery* is one example of the current professional research on midwifery practice. Kitzinger (1988) provides a cross-cultural approach to midwives' work. See also collections of recent advances in research by midwives (Robinson and Thomson 1991).

REFERENCES

Ahluwalia, S. (1991) "Currents in British Feminist Thought: The Study of Male Violence." In *New Directions in Critical Criminology*, edited by B. MacLean and D. Milovanovic, 55–62. Vancouver: The Collective Press.

Anderson, C. (1986) "Midwifery and the Family Physician." *Canadian Family Physician* 32: 11–15.

Arms, S. (1977) *Immaculate Deception: A New Look at Women and Childbirth in America.* New York: Bantam Books.

Backhouse, C. (1991) *Petticoats and Prejudice: Women and Law in Nineteenth-Century Canada.* Toronto: The Women's Press.

Baker, M. (1989) "Midwifery: A New Status." Background Paper for the Library of Parliament (BP-217E). Ottawa: Research Branch, Library of Parliament.

Benoit, C. (1988) "Traditional Midwifery Practice: The Limits of Occupational Autonomy." *Canadian Review of Sociology and Anthropology* 26 (4): 633–49.

Ben-Yehuda, N. (1980) "The European Witch-Craze of the 14th to 17th Centuries: A Sociologist's Perspective." *American Journal of Sociology* 86: 1–31.

Buckley, S. (1979) "Ladies or Midwives? Efforts to Reduce Infant and Maternal Mortality." In *A Not Unreasonable Claim: Women and Reform in Canada, 1880s–1920s*, edited by L. Kealey, 131–49. Toronto: The Women's Press.

Burtch, B. (1987a) "Community Midwives and State Measures: The New Midwifery in British Columbia." *Contemporary Crises* 10 (4): 399–420.

—— (1987b) "Midwifery Practice and State Regulation: A Sociological Perspective." Ph.D. dissertation, University of British Columbia.

—— (1988a) "Midwives and the State: The New Midwifery in Canada." In *Gender and Society: Creating a Canadian Women's Sociology*, edited by A. McLaren, 349–71. Toronto: Copp Clark Pitman.

—— (1988b) "Promoting Midwifery, Prosecuting Midwives: The State and the Midwifery Movement in Canada." In *Sociology of Health Care in Canada*, edited by B.S. Bolaria and H. Dickenson, 313–27. Toronto: Harcourt Brace Jovanovich.

Burtch, B., C. Pitcher-LaPrairie, and A. Wachtel (1980) "Issues in the Determination and Enforcement of Child Support Orders." *Canadian Journal of Family Law* 3 (1): 5–26.

—— (1985) "Marriage Preparation, Separation, Conciliation, and Divorce: Findings from the Public Images of Law Study." *Canadian Journal of Family Law* 4 (4): 369–84.

Canada (1977) *Report of the Committee on the Operation of the Abortion Law*. Ottawa: Supply and Services Canada.

Carrier, R. (1987) *Heartbreaks along the Road*. Translated by Sheila Fischman. Toronto: House of Anansi Press.

Clarke, A. (1987) "Moral Protest, Status Defence and the Anti-Abortion Campaign." *British Journal of Sociology* 38 (2): 235–53.

Cutshall, P. (1987) "Midwifery Revisited." *RNABC News* (July/August): 23.

Davis, N. (1987) "Abortion and Legal Policy." *Contemporary Crises* 10: 373–97.

DeVries, R. (1985) *Regulating Birth: Midwives, Medicine, and the Law*. Philadelphia: Temple University Press.

Doyal, L., with I. Pennell (1981) *The Political Economy of Health*. Boston: South End Press.

Edwards, M., and M. Waldorf (1984) *Reclaiming Birth: History and Heroines of American Childbirth Reform*. Trumansberg, N.Y.: The Crossing Press.

Ehrenreich, B., and D. English (1973) *Witches, Midwives and Healers*. Old Westbury, N.Y.: The Feminist Press.

Eisenstein, Z. (1988) *The Female Body and the Law*. Berkeley: University of California Press.

Flint, C. (1986) "Should Midwives Train as Florists?" *Nursing Times* (February 12).

—— (1987) *Sensitive Midwifery*. London: Heinemann.

Freeman, D. (1984) "Introduction: Rethinking Family Law." In *State, Law, and the Family: Critical Perspectives*, edited by D. Freeman, 1–6. London: Tavistock.

Gaskin, I. (1988) "Midwifery Re-invented." In *The Midwife Challenge*, edited by S. Kitzinger, 42–60. London: Pandora Books.

Gavigan, S. (1986) "Women, Law and Patriarchial Relations: Perspectives in the Sociology of Law." In *The Social Dimensions of Law*, edited by N. Boyd, 101–24. Toronto: Prentice-Hall.

—— (1987) "Women and Abortion in Canada: What's Law Got to Do With It?" In *Feminism and Political Economy: Women's Work, Women's Struggles*, edited by H. Maroney and M. Luxton, 263–84. Toronto: Methuen.

Glendon, M. (1989) "On Abortion and Divorce in the Western World." In *A World of Ideas*, edited by B. Flowers, 470–83. New York: Doubleday.

Hartnagel, T., J. Creechan, and R. Silverman (1985) "Public Opinion and the Legalization of Abortion." *Canadian Review of Sociology and Anthropology* 22 (3): 411–30.

Jimenez, M. (1990) "Midwife Must Stand Trial, Judge Decides." *The Globe and Mail* (November 10).

Jordan, B. (1980) *Birth in Four Cultures: A Crosscultural Investigation of Childbirth in Yucatan, Holland, Sweden and the United States.* Montreal: Eden Press/Women's Publications.

Kaufman, K. (1989) "Midwifery on Trial." *The Midwifery Task Force Journal* 2 (1): 1–2.

Kitzinger, S., ed. (1988) *The Midwife Challenge.* London: Pandora Books.

MacKinnon, C. (1987) *Feminism Unmodified: Discourses on Life and Law.* Cambridge: Harvard University Press.

McLaren, A., and A. McLaren (1986) *The Bedroom and the State: The Changing Practices and Policies of Contraception and Abortion in Canada, 1880–1980.* Toronto: McClelland and Stewart.

Mandel, M.(1989) *The Charter of Rights and the Legalization of Politics in Canada.* Toronto: Wall and Thompson.

Mason, J. (1988) "Midwifery in Canada." In *The Midwife Challenge,* edited by S. Kitzinger, 99–129. London: Pandora Books.

Menzies, R., and D. Chunn (1991) "Kicking Against the Pricks: The Dilemmas of Feminist Teaching in Criminology." In *New Directions in Critical Criminology,* edited by B. MacLean and D. Milovanovic, 63–70. Vancouver: The Collective Press.

Midwifery and the Law (1991) Educational videotape. Directed by Keet Neville and Michael Doherty and produced by Brian Burtch. Simon Fraser University (Continuing Studies) and the Knowledge Network. 30 minutes.

Morgentaler, Smoling and Scott v. The Queen (1988), 37 C.C.C. (3d) 449 (S.C.C.).

Morton, M. (1988) "Dividing the Wealth, Sharing the Poverty: The (Re)formation of 'Family' in Law in Ontario." *Canadian Review of Sociology and Anthropology* 25 (2): 254–75.

Moysa, M., and S. Aikenhead (1991) "Judge Finds Midwife Not Guilty of Illegally Practicing Medicine." *The Edmonton Journal* (June 6): 1.

Registered Nurses' Association of B.C. (RNABC) (1987) "Position Statement: Midwifery." *RNABC News* (July/August): 22.

Robinson, S., and A. Thomson, eds. (1991) *Midwives, Research and Childbirth: Volume II.* London: Chapman and Hall.

Sarat, A., and W. Felstiner (1986) "Law and Strategy in the Divorce Lawyer's Office." *Law and Society Review* 10 (1): 93–134.

Seel, R. (1987) *The Uncertain Father: Exploring Modern Fatherhood.* Bath, England: Gateway Books.

Smart, C. (1989) *Feminism and the Power of Law.* London: Routledge and Kegan Paul.

Society of Obstetricians and Gynaecologists (SOGC) (1986) "SOGC Statement on Midwifery Approved at the Annual Business Meeting." *Update.* Typescript mimeo, 1–4.

Tyson, H. (1990) "A Study of 1,001 Home Births in Toronto, Canada." Paper presented at the International Congress of Midwifery, Kobe, Japan.

Varney, H. (1983) *Nurse-Midwifery.* London: Blackwell Scientific Publications.

Wagner, M. (1985) *Having a Baby in Europe.* Copenhagen: World Health Organization.

Walker, N., S. Pullen, and M. Shinyei (1986) "Birth Stats: Domiciliary Midwifery Report, 1980–1985." *Safe Alternatives in Childbirth.* Edmonton. (March/April) 3 (2): 5.

World Health Organization (1987) "Sixteen Recommendations from the World Health Organization." Reprinted in *California Association of Midwives Letter* (Summer): 9.

CHAPTER TEN

Current Directions in Sociolegal Studies

Equality is not the deepest thing, you know.

*I always thought that was just what it was. I thought it was
in their souls that people were equal.*

*You were mistaken; that is the last place where they are equal.
Equality before the law, equality of incomes—that is very well.
Equality guards life; it doesn't make it. It is medicine, not food.*

(C.S. Lewis, *That Hideous Strength*)

INTRODUCTION

This book has introduced a number of key concepts and studies in the sociology of law. This concluding chapter examines possibilities for changing the nature of law. Themes such as the limits of liberal ideology, critical practice in law, and methodological strategies for developing the field are discussed. As such, we move beyond a comparison of law in theory versus the "living law" to consider the possibilities for reforming or revolutionizing contemporary legal structures and legal processes.

As discussed in Chapter One, the roots of modern or postmodern movements[1] lie in earlier perspectives on the nature of legal and political authority. Classical works in the sociology of law have clearly outlined the important role of law in modernizing societies, and traced numerous contradictions between the ideal of legal authority as a legitimate arbiter of these conflicts and the reality of law as a powerful interest in its own right. The critics' challenge to legal formalism and legal positivism has been enhanced by a wide range of works on struggles by groups facing discrimination in law and society. These works stem from feminism and feminist critiques of jurisprudence (McDaniel 1991; Tomm and Hamilton 1988). Feminist groups, groups representing the needs of handicapped people, racial minorities, and aboriginal people, and peace and environmental groups collectively pose a strong challenge to traditional legal structures and to government policy generally (Young 1990).

Many modern efforts to transform (or reform) legal powers reveal a tendency toward activism among social scientists and legal scholars. Many would agree with the spirit of Roscoe Pound's interest in combining a *social control* perspective with pragmatism. Pound argued that legal scholars should not assume a strict detachment from issues of the day, and seek to act as if they were "legal monks" (Milovanovic 1988, 91). Pound also formulated a set of *jural postulates*:

1. no intentional harm to others

2. personal control over discoveries and acquisitions

3. good faith in contractual dealings

4. responsible control of potentially dangerous elements (Milovanovic 1988, 92)

While Pound has been criticized for not attending to structured inequalities in American justice and society, he nonetheless provides a critical approach to legal politics. He also maintains the importance of preserving legal authority. Pound described law as

> a highly specialized form of social control, carried on in accordance with a body of authoritative precepts, applied in a judicial and administrative process (Milovanovic 1988, 91).

As we consider the current directions in sociolegal studies, it is important to note that there are strong disagreements over the nature of law and the appropriate role of social scientists and legal scholars/practitioners. These disagreements emerge even within particular schools of thought. Legal realists, for example, show considerable differences of opinion and approach in their work. As noted in the chapter on feminism and law, there appears to be less emphasis on abstract analysis, and more attention to grounded work that investigates the actual results of decision-making (see Milovanovic 1988, 94).

The establishment of critical legal studies in recent decades reflects a growing interest in Marxist-based, feminist studies of law. Class, race, gender, and the perdurable concepts of discrimination, hegemony, and legal domination are at the forefront of critical legal studies. The critical legal studies approach, as it has matured, retains an interest in the role of legal ideology, including the process of *reification* (inflation of the law, thereby expanding its power of domination) and *hegemony* (use of ideology and other resources to secure the consent of oppressed people to the rule of an elite).

The critical legal studies approach offers not only a critique of significant disparities between legal ideals and law in practice, but also an analysis of how power is conveyed through socialization in law school. Power is seen as conveyed through patterns of dependency, hierarchy, and legal terminology

(Kelman 1987, 103). The approach also affords a viewpoint on contradictions in legal training: Kelman (1987, 184–85) observes that many law students appear receptive to progressive objectives, yet can also argue convincingly for "right-wing" economic policies, retaining some faith in the free market and propertied relations. One measure of changes in law school training will be the extent to which feminist jurisprudence and other equally progressive approaches are incorporated into curricula. These other approaches would include labour law (examining the dynamics of power between workers and owners) and critical approaches to anti-discrimination law and limits to affirmative action (see Milovanovic 1988, 103–5).

The critical legal studies approach also offers a careful look at the scale of devastation that can be brought to cultures in what are now seen as developing nations. Historical examples include the European influence in the South Seas in the eighteenth and nineteenth centuries (Moorehead 1974), culminating in the relocations and ruined economies of South Seas residents with the advent of nuclear testing. Closer to home, there is overwhelming evidence of genocidal and paternalistic policies by Euro-Canadians toward aboriginal peoples. The decimation of First Nations peoples, their forced removal onto reserves and into residential schools, and the imposition of western systems of criminal law all underscored these control-oriented policies (see York 1990).

This chapter reviews a few examples of works that fit with the more progressive, critical character of sociolegal studies. Mandel (1989) provides a critical look at the effects of the Charter of Rights and Freedoms, particularly its regressive character with respect to popular, democratic expressions. Brickey and Comack (1987) review instrumental Marxism vis-à-vis structural Marxism, with a view to reassessing the place of law in social transformation. Next, Elizabeth Comack (1988) disputes the ideal of "justice for all," based on the limited reforms in criminal law processes for battered women. Finally, Young (1990) examines the struggles of various social movements against oppression.

MANDEL: RULE OF
LAW AND CANADIAN POLITICS

Mandel, currently a professor of law at Osgoode Hall, provides a critical assessment of the Charter of Rights and Freedoms. Mandel (1989) notes that the enactment of the Charter generated various reactions from socialist and Marxist scholars. Mandel (1989) defines his own response as "negative."

Before addressing the implications of the Charter for Canadian politics, Mandel (1989) reviews the central debate between structural Marxists (exemplified by the late E.B. Pashukanis) and the English social historian E.P.

Thompson. Mandel (1989) relates how interest in Pashukanis's class writings on law and the state was revived along with a renewed interest in Marxist and socialist approaches to law. In particular, the legal precept of the *rule of law* was criticized. The rule of law rests on the realization of a legal sphere that is "autonomous and egalitarian." This idealized sphere was, according to its critics, nullified by the everyday oppression of the social relations of production under capitalism (Mandel 1989, 305). Mandel recaps the range of this critique, including the base-superstructure relationship and the less economically oriented approach that sees law as serving a legitimizing function under capitalism.

Mandel takes seriously the issue of the rule of law and whether or not the traditional *devaluation* (Mandel 1989, 306) of the rule of law is correct. One factor in such an assessment is the implementation of lawless, repressive policies under the Stalinist regime. These policies have been interpreted as a form of mass "terror." A second factor is the implication of devaluing the rule of law at a *theoretical* level, while acknowledging the importance of the rule of law as a *pragmatic* aspect of ongoing struggles about law (Mandel 1989, 306).

Mandel then moves to an appreciation of Thompson's classic work, *Whigs and Hunters* (1977). This book deals with the implementation of the Black Act in England in 1723, and especially the great number of offences that became capital offences. Clearly, the Black Act was a form of terror, one that established the importance of protecting private property. As a piece of "class legislation" (Thompson, cited in Mandel 1989, 306), however, the Black Act was not complete or all-powerful. Thompson outlines how the Black Act was resisted, undermined, and eventually repealed. Here, Thompson points out that the ideological power of law is contested, and that some concessions to interests other than the dominant class must be made. Otherwise, the legitimacy of law becomes fragile and possibly insupportable, except by repressive measures.

> We ought to expose the shams and inequities which may be concealed beneath this law. But the rule of law itself, the imposing of effective inhibitions upon power and the defence of the citizen from power's all-intrusive claims, seems to me to be an unqualified human good. To deny or belittle this good is, in this dangerous century when the resources and pretentions of power continue to enlarge, a desperate error of intellectual abstraction. More than this, it is a self-fulfilling error, which encourages us to give up the struggle against bad laws and class-bound procedures, and to disarm ourselves before power. It is to throw away a whole inheritance of struggle *about* law, and within the forms of law, whose continuity can never be fractured without bringing men and women into immediate danger (Thompson 1977, 266, emphasis in original).

The experience of repression is symbolized by the totalitarian regimes of Nazism and Stalinism in this century (see Mandel 1989, 307). Thus, despite the inequities of modern legal rule, Thompson still aligns himself with the democratic possibilities within the rule of law but not, as he humorously puts it, "the rule of the people by any old codger in a wig" (Mandel 1989, 308). Aware of the sham aspects of modern legal power, Thompson is nevertheless not prepared to abandon legality, with its protections and its possibilities for checking the absolute powers of the state or other sectors.

BRICKEY AND COMACK:
LAW AND SOCIAL TRANSFORMATION

Brickey and Comack (1987) make the valuable point that Marxist perspectives on law have tended to focus on a critique of Western legal systems. As such, the strategic use of law in promoting socialism has been underemphasized or, in some cases, disregarded altogether. There has nonetheless been stronger emphasis in critical legal scholarship on developing practical strategies for overturning oppression, including practical legal strategies. Brickey and Comack (1987) shift the focus from theorizing about law to considering the practical uses of law in the interests of social justice.

We have reviewed structural and instrumental Marxism earlier in this text. Brickey and Comack (1987, 98–99) outline several criticisms of the instrumentalist approach: the dubious link between class origins and political outlook; the emphasis on the economic base, with an unwarranted disregard for struggles at the superstructural level (i.e., the importance of "ideas"); and the importance of the capitalist state being legitimated by the ideology of fairness, justice, and equality. Brickey and Comack (1987, 98–99) add that attempts to see the law as instrumentally connected with a ruling class are unable to account for many forms of legislation that constrain capital accumulation. Such legislation includes "employment standards, human rights legislation, and workplace health and safety regulations" (Brickey and Comack 1987, 98).

The authors' discussion of structural Marxism (or neo-Marxism) builds on the rule of law as a political doctrine that legitimates and constrains political, economic, and social activities. The key point that formal equality does not reach into the stratified sphere of economics is well-taken (Brickey and Comack 1987, 100). Nevertheless, the state under capitalism is not entirely wedded to the interests of the dominant class, but mediates the conflicting interests of class, gender, race, age, and so forth, through its relative autonomy, which allows it to act semi-independently from any particular class.

Brickey and Comack voice their concern over the scepticism of structuralists regarding the value of law as "a vehicle for social transformation" (Brickey and Comack 1987, 101). The structuralist perspective is thus criticized for its failure to appreciate the influence of class consciousness, an influence that may curb state activities and the workings of the private sector.

Brickey and Comack (1987, 102–3) retain a critical outlook on law, recommending that it be recognized as only one means of effecting concrete social changes. The authors are uncomfortable with the lack of clarity surrounding the concept of "social transformation," and how it might be accomplished in the current day. Such an accomplishment would include engaging in legal struggles and struggles over rights, and accepting that, in the modern world of capitalist democracy, societies are "unavoidably legalistic" (Brickey and Comack 1987, 103). Law can thus be a fulcrum for progressive social movements. Brickey and Comack (1987, 103) caution that if legal struggles are not launched, current law-and-order campaigns may prevail in shaping law and social policies. They note that several groups are already active in formulating what they wish in terms of social justice: women, Native peoples, prisoners, and other "subordinated" groups (Brickey and Comack 1987, 103).

COMACK: BATTERED WOMEN AND SOCIAL JUSTICE

Once a taboo subject, only cryptically referred to in academic and popular literature, violence against women has recently come out into the open. It is now acknowledged that such violence is widespread, either as direct acts of injury or as threats against women (Stanko 1990). The study of "date rape" has likewise confirmed that such assaultive behaviour is far from rare.

One contentious area in the discussion of domestic violence has been the availability of legal defences for women who retaliate against their abusers, especially in cases of homicide of husbands or common-law husbands. Comack (1988) reviews two legal decisions concerning wife-battering in Manitoba, using these cases as a background for the wider issue of wife-battering and the concept of the "battered-wife syndrome" (see the earlier discussion in Chapter Four).

Comack (1988, 10–11) links the continuing phenomenon of wife assault with *structural* conditions that limit women's choices. Comack does not imply that all women are powerless or that the legal reaction is entirely unhelpful to all women who have been abused. Nevertheless, the play of male bias and misunderstanding remains central to Comack's analysis. It is also important to bear in mind that abused women often find that the police and prosecutors are far from effective in deterring batterers from injuring or harassing them.

Comack's work is clearly pertinent and informative and leads us to ask how her approach might be extended to account for violence by men against men. A wider approach to male violence and gender socialization is needed to trace and explain such variations in violent behaviour (see Boyd (1988) for a review of murder and social policy in Canada). Greater attention could be given to the overall victimization associated with violent crimes, for it appears that not only have Americans been exposed to a substantial increase in the likelihood that they will be assaulted, murdered, or sexually assaulted, but, as Davis and Stasz

(1990, 298) note, there are no indications that patterns of violence are ebbing. They add that this victimization is not spread evenly though American society: youths, and particularly black youths, are disproportionately victimized by violent crime.

Beyond assessments of victimization, an understanding of how physical abuse affects women could include legal strategies for victims of violence. Parallel to Comack's interest in the battered-wife syndrome as a legal defence, Goldberg-Ambrose (1989, 954–55) recommends that rape-trauma syndrome be employed in rape prosecutions. This emphasis on the physical and psychological impact of rape on the victim could be used to overcome conflicting testimonies or the cultural emphasis on women-blaming, in which women are held "responsible for controlling both sexes' sexuality" (Goldberg-Ambrose 1989, 954–55). Goldberg-Ambrose (1989, 954) concludes that such research could serve to reshape legal perceptions of the act of rape and its impact, and could thus hold the potential for transforming current legal practices surrounding rape.

YOUNG: ON JUSTICE AND
THE POLITICS OF DIFFERENCE

Much of the contemporary writing and research in the sociology of law emerges from a disenchantment with liberal ideals of harmony and shared interests. This disenchantment has given rise to new social movements that challenge existing premises and structures of law. These new social movements include the women's movement, gay liberation, and struggles by people of colour (including blacks, Hispanics, Native peoples) and disabled persons (Young 1990, 3). For Young (1990, 9), it is crucial to appreciate the diversity of these groups, rather than impose an artificial consensus as a guiding point for their aspirations and needs.

Young insists that the concept of *oppression* is crucial in any legal philosophy purporting to address these movements. Oppression takes several aspects: marginalization, exploitation, powerlessness, cultural imperialism (referring to the superiority or inferiority attributed to certain groups), and violence (Young 1990, 9). Young (1990, 179) thus cautions against using such overly general concepts as "the public": there is no homogeneous public, as many understand it, and efforts to establish this reified public in legal policy can be devastating for minorities. Young cites the "English-only" movement in the United States as a case in point—an example that also applies to the Canadian context, given the efforts to establish primacy of the English language or the French language in different provinces. Such one-dimensional approaches, embedded in law and social policy, would obscure linguistic differences in both countries. Another example of the inappropriatenesss of this concept of a universal public is available in studies of municipal politics in New England. Young (1990, 184) notes that, while all citizens are invited to participate in town meetings, some groups are underrepresented: disabled people, mothers, the elderly, racial minorities. At such meetings it is often "white middle-class men [who] assume authority more than others" (Young 1990, 184).

Young's emphasis on oppression leads her to make provocative statements about "right" and "wrong," an approach that raises as many questions as it answers. In the face of white male hegemony, for instance, she concludes that it is now improper to maintain or establish all-male clubs (thus excluding women), but all-women's associations are acceptable, and likely preferable. The point for Young (1990, 197) is to strategically combat oppression generated and "embedded" in social institutions:

> An all-male club of city officials and business people is wrong, for example, because it reinforces and augments networks of privilege among men that exist even in its absence. It is not wrong to found an all-women's professional association, on the other hand, to counteract the isolation and strains that many professional women experience as a result of being less than welcome minorities in their fields (Young 1990, 97).

This approach certainly places the abstract nature of much legal discourse over "rights" in a political context. Young's work thus takes seriously the embedded nature of privilege, and argues for wider mobilization of social movements concerned with social justice.

Another difficulty with Young's analysis is overgeneralization. Young (1990, 197) refers to the "priority of the point of view of white heterosexual men." Clearly, this generalization obscures differences among men, not only in opinions or values, but in social power. This tendency to group people is ironic, given Young's emphasis on diversity and struggling against stereotyping. The strength of her work, however, is her insight into how law, cultural practices, and state policies have often been implemented so as to exclude or silence various groups, and how it will take more than a liberal reshuffling of programs and opportunities to implement substantive change.

NEW DIRECTIONS IN THE SOCIOLOGY OF LAW

One of the most promising directions in sociological research on law has been the incorporation of rigorous qualitative and/or quantitative research in addressing legal issues. Hagan (1986, 57) favours a pluralistic approach to sociolegal research. As issues become more complex, and attention turns from formal legal rules to informal processes underlying legal decision-making, for instance, it becomes important to develop theories that are empirically grounded and attentive to less formal negotiations. These less formal processes include negotiated settlements via arbitration and mediation, and plea bargaining in criminal law (Hagan 1986, 48). Beyond this, Baar (1986, 60) proposes that quantitatively oriented research (e.g., statistical analyses) can and ought to be developed alongside more qualitative approaches.[2] The agenda for Canadian social science research on law, then, would emphasize law as process. Process theory[3] would be useful in tracing the nature of sociological developments in law, while maintaining a sensitivity to differences between various political cultures and structures, for example, between Canada and the United States. The literature thus takes on an *appreciative* quality that helps in an understanding of how legal policies often serve to tolerate social injustices.

Sociological research that combines theorizing with rigorous statistical analyses is a particularly promising approach to understanding legal issues. A recent example of this is Arnold's (1991) study of professional deviance among Ontario lawyers and disciplinary actions against them. Arnold (1991) provides a framework that examines why lawyers may become involved in unethical or illegal practices, and variations in sanctions for those in violation of professional standards of conduct.

Research of a more qualitative nature also helps us understand the power and limitations of law, dramatizing the gulf between legal rhetoric and legal practice. MacKinnon (1979, 192–93) uses the example of sexual harassment of working women to underline ways in which harassment has not been taken seriously, even when formal complaints have been made. For MacKinnon, sexual harassment is not merely inappropriate behaviour by an individual against employees or co-workers. Rather, it stems from and strengthens sexist values concerning women. It also places limits on women's position within the occupational structure. Sexual harassment

> singles out a gender-defined group, women, for special treatment in a way which adversely affects and burdens their status as employees. Sexual harassment limits women in a way men are not limited. It deprives them of opportunities that are available to male employees without sexual conditions. In so doing, it creates two employment standards: one for women that includes sexual requirements, one for men that does not.

MacKinnon (1979, 192) thus challenges the usefulness of assuming equality of the sexes before the law or in social life generally. She recommends adopting a "differences approach," one which appreciates gender (or race, class, or other extra-legal factors), since "most sexually harassed people are women" (MacKinnon 1979, 193; see also Ahluwalia 1991, 58–61; Boyle 1990; Young 1990).

The growth of coalitions is another new direction in the sociology of law. For example, specific interest groups have lobbied for greater access to abortion services, and in British Columbia and other provinces some of their efforts have been fostered by the work of provincial and national civil liberties associations (see Russell 1989). In this example, we see the potential for moving beyond traditional libertarian critiques of abuse of state authority to an appreciation of state measures that can be made more compatible with expressions of freedom (McKercher 1989, 245).

Simon and Lynch (1989) offer a number of suggestions concerning the development of research in the sociology of law. They report that such research has had a greater impact on criminal law policy than policies associated with civil law. They favour more venues for research on civil law in order to circulate recent research findings and to translate more of these findings into civil law areas. Even where solid sociolegal research is completed—for example, on the nature of the American legal profession—Simon and Lynch (1989, 835) comment that policy implications are not always sufficiently drawn. The social organization of professions such as law is interesting not only in its own right, but also in terms of how "non-elite" lawyers and legal services might be protected. This would seem especially pertinent as corporate power (and public-interest advocacy) continue to grow, and elements of what Galanter (1983) terms "mega-lawyering" become more prominent.

Another dimension to the sociology of law is the importance of restoring a greater sense of democracy at the community level. Some local organizations can reflect citizens' interests and possibly offset the interventionist, politically-motivated initiatives of more conservative political parties and governments (see Taylor 1981, 1983).

One final area is the value of legal protection for workers, along with other aspects of democratic politics, including expansion of individual liberties, strengthening of the democratic framework of politics, and consideration of the value of institutions like private property (see Fine 1984, 211–12).

STUDY QUESTIONS

❑ Outline three criticisms outlined by Brickey and Comack with respect to instrumental Marxism and three criticisms with respect to structural Marxism. How do these two critical approaches contrast with the dominant doctrine of the rule of law?

❑ What groups might successfully adopt the *collective* and *political* strategies recommended by Brickey and Comack (1987, 325–29)? What constraints are these groups likely to encounter in their legal struggles?

❑ The battered-wife syndrome, as discussed by Comack (1988), illustrates one aspect of criminal law: the use of psychological expert testimony in criminal trials. What concerns does Comack (1988, 9–10) voice with respect to the battered-wife syndrome, especially its use as a strategy for realizing justice for battered women? Do you agree with her emphasis on *structural* conditions affecting women, made concrete by their "lack of choice" (Comack 1988, 10)?

NOTES

1. Postmodern thinking is often directed against the dominant emphasis of the tradition of "Western reason" (see Young 1990, 3). As such, postmodern philosophical approaches avoid some of the doctrinaire politics and assumptions of liberal, conservative, and radical philosophy. Young (1990, 3) points out that postmodernism arises in part from a process of oversimplification, or "reductionism" in which there is greater emphasis on supposed similarities than on differences. See also MacKinnon (1979, 192–208) for a detailed argument *against* applying a doctrine of similarity in the context of sexual harassment of women employees. For MacKinnon, the nature of the harassing act, and its implications, are not equivalent for both sexes.

2. Baar (1986, 60) observes that, in studies of law, "quantitative data play a central role, and qualitative data become more important. Thus the most complex and illuminating picture of judicial decision making may come from the examination of a single case or related sets of cases."

3. Mohr states that process theory "tells a little story about how something comes about, but in order to qualify as a theoretical explanation of recurrent behaviour, the manner of the storytelling must conform to narrow specifications" (cited in Baar 1986, 62).

REFERENCES

Ahluwalia, S. (1991) "Currents in British Feminist Thought: The Study of Male Violence." In *New Directions in Critical Criminology*, edited by B. MacLean and D. Milovanovic, 55–62. Vancouver: The Collective Press.

Arnold, B. (1991) *A Life Course Dynamics Approach to Professional Deviance and Self-Regulation: The Case of Ontario Lawyers*. Unpublished Ph.D. thesis, Department of Sociology, University of Toronto.

Baar, C. (1986) "Using Process Theory to Explain Judicial Decision Making." *Canadian Journal of Law and Society* 1: 57–79.

Boyd, N. (1988) *The Last Dance: Murder in Canada*. Toronto: Prentice-Hall.

Boyle, C. (1990) "The Battered Wife Syndrome and Self-Defence: *Lavallee v. R.*" *Canadian Journal of Family Law* 9 (1): 171–79.

Brickey, S., and E. Comack (1987) "The Role of Law in Social Transformation: Is a Jurisprudence of Insurgency Possible?" *Canadian Journal of Law and Society* 2: 97–119.

Comack, E. (1988) "Justice for Battered Women? The Courts and the 'Battered Wife Syndrome.'" *Canadian Dimension* 22 (3): 8–11.

Davis, N., and C. Stasz (1990) *Social Control of Deviance: A Critical Perspective*. New York: McGraw-Hill.

Fine, B. (1984) *Democracy and the Rule of Law: Liberal Ideals and Marxist Critiques*. London: Pluto Press.

Galanter, M. (1983) "Mega-Law and Mega-Lawyering in the Contemporary United States." In *The Sociology of the Professions: Lawyers, Doctors and Others*, edited by R. Dingwall and P. Lewis, 152–76. London: Macmillan.

Goldberg-Ambrose, C. (1989) "Theory, Practice, and Perception in Rape Law Reform." *Law and Society Review* 23 (5): 949–55.

Hagan, J. (1986) "The New Legal Scholarship: Problems and Prospects." *Canadian Journal of Law and Society* 1: 35–56.

Kelman, M. (1987) *A Guide to Critical Legal Studies*. Cambridge: Harvard University Press.

McDaniel, S. (1991) "Feminist Scholarship in Sociology: Transformation from Within?" *Canadian Journal of Sociology* 16 (3): 303–12.

McKercher, W. (1989) *Freedom and Authority*. Montreal: Black Rose Books.

MacKinnon, C. (1979) *Sexual Harassment of Working Women*. New Haven: Yale University Press.

Mandel, M. (1989) "The Rule of Law and the Legalization of Politics in Canada." In *Law and Society: A Critical Perspective*, edited by T. Caputo, M. Kennedy, C. Reasons, A. Brannigan, 305–15. Toronto: Harcourt Brace Jovanovich.

Milovanovic, D. (1988) *A Primer in the Sociology of Law*. New York: Harrow and Heston.

Moorehead, A. (1974) *The Fatal Impact: An Account of the Invasion of the South Pacific, 1767–1840*. Harmondsworth: Penguin.

Russell, J. (1989) *Liberties*. Vancouver: New Star Books.

Simon, R., and J. Lynch (1989) "The Sociology of Law: Where We Have Been and Where We Might Be Going." *Law and Society Review* 23 (5): 825–47.

Stanko, E. (1990) *Everyday Violence: How Women and Men Experience Sexual and Physical Danger*. London: Pandora Books.

Taylor, I. (1981) *Law and Order: Arguments for Socialism*. London: Macmillan.

——— (1983) *Crime, Capitalism, and Community*. Toronto: Butterworths.

Thompson, E.P. (1977) *Whigs and Hunters: The Origin of the Black Act*. Harmondsworth: Penguin.

Tomm, W., and G. Hamilton, eds. (1988) *Gender Bias in Scholarship: The Pervasive Prejudice*. Waterloo, Ontario: Wilfrid Laurier University Press.

York, G. (1990) *The Dispossessed: Life and Death in Native Canada*. London: Vintage.

Young, I. (1990) *Justice and the Politics of Difference*. Princeton: Princeton University Press.

INDEX

Institute for Scientific Information, 34
Instrumental Marxism, 35
    attempts to go beyond, 40
    criticism of, 38, 200
International Confederation of
    Midwives, 168
International law, focus on
    individual rights, 118
International Woodworkers of
    America (IWA), 60
IWA, *see* International
    Woodworkers of America

J'Accuse, 108
Jackson, M., 153
Japanese Canadians, internment
    of, 112
Jefferson, Thomas, 109
Jim Crow laws, 114, 121n
Jimenez, M., 175
John Porter Award, 156n
Johnson, Albert, 152
Jordan, B., 162
Jordan, W., 64
Judges' Rules, 112
Judicial activism, 126
Judiciary, the
    abstract decision-making and, 128
    appointments to, 127
    autonomy of, 126
    class bias in, 127
    corporate advantage and, 128
    historical specificity and, 126
    as male preserve, 127
    as nonpartisan, 125
    relation to economic elites, 124–5
    role of small claims courts, 128
    as social policy setter, 126
Juridic subject, 37
Jurisprudence, in Milovanovic, 4–5,
        see also Feminist jurisprudence
Justice, 49
*Justice Denied: The Law versus
    Donald Marshall*, 92

Kadi-based justice, 30
Kamenka, E., 32, 33
Karenga, M.R., 40
Käsler, D., 28, 31
Kaufman, K., 172
Keegstra, Jim, 119
Kelman, M., 10, 198
Kennedy, M., 61, 62, 109
Khmer Rouge, 40
Kidder, R., 129, 130, 135
Kinsey, R., 113
Kitzinger, Sheila, 79, 161, 163, 193n
Knuttila, M., 38
Kronman, A., 28, 29

Labelling, 93–94
Labour law
    in B.C., 59
    business unionism and, 57
    ICA Act and, 60
    repressive character of, 57
    stabilization objective in, 59
    strikes and, 58–59
    weakening of unions and, 60
Lachmann, L., 31
Lakeman, L., 71
Langbien, J., 50, 51, 65n
Lang, Raven, 178
LaPrairie, C., 104, 140
Lavallée, Angélique, 81
Law, *see also* Criminal law;
        Labour law
    as agent of reform, 150–51
    capitalism and, 28, 33–42
    class nature of capitalist, 41
    commodity exchange school of, 37
    in communism, 39
    conservative critique of, 3
    definitions of, 5–6
    dynamic quality of, 61
    facilitative function of, 7, 8
    as force behind capitalism, 27–28
    formal and rational dimensions
        of, 30

To the Owner of this Book:

We are interested in your reaction to *The Sociology of Law* by Brian Burtch. With your comments, we can improve this book in future editions. Please help us by completing this questionnaire.

1. What was your reason for using this book?
    _____ university course
    _____ college course
    _____ continuing education course
    _____ other (specify)

2. If you used this text for a program, what was the name of that program?

3. Which school do you attend?

4. Approximately how much of the book did you use?
    _____ all _____ 3/4 _____ 1/2 _____ 1/4

5. Which chapters or sections were omitted from your course?

6. Which is the best aspect of this book?

7. Is there anything that should be added?

8. Please add any comments or suggestions.

Fold here

POSTAGE WILL BE PAID BY

Heather McWhinney
Editorial Director
College Division
Harcourt Brace Jovanovich Canada Inc.
55 Horner Avenue
Toronto, Ontario
M8Z 9Z9

Tape shut